£10.00

A DIFFICULT DEATH

A Difficult Death

The Life and Work
of Jens Peter Jacobsen

MORTEN HØI JENSEN

Foreword by James Wood

Yale
UNIVERSITY PRESS
New Haven and London

Published with assistance from the Danish Arts Foundation.

DANISH ARTS FOUNDATION

Published with assistance from the foundation established in memory of Calvin Chapin of the Class of 1788, Yale College.

Yale University Press books may be purchased in quantity for educational, business, or promotional use. For information, please e-mail sales.press@yale.edu (U.S. office) or sales@yaleup.co.uk (U.K. office).

Set in Janson type by IDS Infotech Ltd., Chandigarh, India.
Printed in the United States of America.

Library of Congress Control Number: 2017934991
ISBN 978-0-300-21893-0 (hardcover : alk. paper)

A catalogue record for this book is available from the British Library.

This paper meets the requirements of ANSI/NISO Z39.48–1992 (Permanence of Paper).

10 9 8 7 6 5 4 3 2 1

All illustrations are courtesy of the J. P. Jacobsen Society and Thisted Museum.

For my family

In loving memory of my grandmothers,
Else Sørensen (1937–1999)
Birte Høi Jensen (1940–1999)

I have no other comfort to offer you except the solemn fact that death is the eternal peace, the great silence, where no suffering exists, and no sorrows, no worries, no disappointments—nothing at all.

JENS PETER JACOBSEN, from a letter to his brother, William, September 9, 1881

Contents

CONTENTS

Foreword

The nineteenth century, prosperous in so many things, is also rich in eclipsed reputations. Nowadays, we only listen to a fraction of the music that Mendelssohn—one of the prodigies of the age—composed. Darwin displaced his brilliant competitor, the naturalist Alfred Russel Wallace. Sir Walter Scott, the most famous novelist in Europe at the time of his death, survives no longer as a popular possession but as a literary-historical fact. Byron and Tennyson, once in every pupil's pocket, now beseech us to take them down from the library shelves. As Morten Høi Jensen makes clear in this pioneering biography, few writers suffered as rapid a rise and fall as the great Danish novelist Jens Peter Jacobsen (1847–1885). His second novel, *Niels Lyhne*, was published in 1880, five years before his death. It was soon celebrated everywhere—admired by Thomas Mann, closely studied by Freud and Kafka (who mentions it in his letters), and revered by Rilke, whose quasi-novel *The Notebooks of Malte Laurids Brigge* is clearly indebted to it. Joyce thought highly of Jacobsen and seems to have drawn on *Niels Lyhne* for *A Portrait of the Artist as a Young Man*. Adorno claimed that Proust belonged to a literary tradition that began with Jacobsen.

Niels Lyhne is canonical in Danish (and more broadly, Scandinavian) literature and still has a presence in German writing and scholarship. And thanks to its close relation to *Madame Bovary* and *Sentimental Education*, it has not disappeared from French culture (it shares with Flaubert's novels a fierce interest in adultery, romantic illusion, and intellectual lassitude, among other themes). But by World War II, Jacobsen had largely dropped out of Anglophone literary discussion, despite his apparent kinship with novelists like Thomas Hardy and D. H. Lawrence and despite the influence his work had on the English critic and memoirist Edmund Gosse, the author of that classic work about loss of faith and the struggle between one generation and the next, *Father and Son*. (Gosse wrote an introduction for the first English translation of *Niels Lyhne*, in 1896, published under the slightly underwhelming title of *Siren Voices*.) Nowadays, even readers familiar with the works of Ibsen, Hamsun, or Strindberg (to choose the most famous Norwegian and Swedish writers of this period) may never have heard the name Jens Peter Jacobsen.

In this critical biography, the first in English, Morten Høi Jensen, a Danish-born critic and writer who now lives in New York, describes the contours of our lack, brilliantly restoring Jens Peter Jacobsen to a place in modern world fiction that should never have been vacated. In so doing, he brings alive a whole culture—that of Copenhagen in the 1870s and 1880s, "the Little Paris of the North," a city where European modernism was birthing itself (perhaps, as Jensen suggests, modernism's "first real battleground"). On one side, in aesthetics, French realism and naturalism were making their impact, and on the other, in intellectual thought, there was Darwinian evolution and radical atheism. Jens Peter Jacobsen, who had grown up in the small town of Thisted, on the Jutland coast, joined this world in 1867, when he began studying biology and zoology at the University of Copenhagen; his thesis on a particular family of green algae eventually won the university's Gold Medal. In Thisted, Jacobsen had had a conventionally religious upbringing, but by the time he reached the capital city (if not before), he was no longer a believer. In 1867, so we learn from this biography, Jacobsen was reading Kierkegaard, Feuerbach, and Heine. Ludwig Feuerbach, in his seminal book *The Essence of Christianity* (first published in German in 1841 and translated into English in 1854 by a young George Eliot), had argued, essentially, that God is inside us: we create God for our own purposes, and every central element of formal religion corresponds to a particular human desire or need. Jacobsen, clearly caught by this strain of thinking and perhaps also by the biblical criticism of David Friedrich Strauss, wrote in his diary, around this time, that he viewed Christianity "as a mythology no different than the Greek and the Norse." In Copenhagen, his roommates were like-minded young radicals: "Within a few years," writes Jensen, "the Danish translators of Feuerbach, Taine, and Darwin would all be sitting within shouting range of each other." That Danish translator of Darwin was none other than Jens Peter Jacobsen, whose versions of *On the Origin of Species* and *The Descent of Man* appeared in 1872 and 1875 respectively. As Jensen comments,

Jacobsen "was far better placed to grasp Darwin's achievement than any of his literary contemporaries."

But Jacobsen moved between scientific passion and artistic precision (to use Nabokov's phrase) and eventually brought
a naturalist's eye to realist prose fiction. He began to pursue
literature single-mindedly in the early 1870s; he told Edvard
Brandes (the younger brother of the critic Georg Brandes,
who became Jacobsen's somewhat tyrannical encourager) that
he had "always" known he was a poet. In 1873, at the age of
twenty-six, he was diagnosed with tuberculosis. The last decade of his short life—he died in 1885—was spent, like Chekhov's, under the sentence of consumption. He wrote slowly,
with Flaubertian sluggishness and agony, sometimes, only a
few sentences a day. (Jensen, in a sparklingly prosaic correc-
tion, reminds us that Jacobsen was also lazy, a fault the novelist himself conceded.)

Jacobsen's oeuvre, then, is very small—some poems, a few
short stories, and two novels. One of the short stories, enti-
tled "The Plague in Bergamo," strikingly anticipates Camus's
La Peste (it is about the collapse of Christian faith that occurs
when the plague arrives at, and seals, the town), though there
is no evidence that Camus ever read it. His first novel, *Marie
Grubbe: Seventeenth Century Interiors* (1876), is one of those
books that simultaneously founds and dissolves a genre. It is a
historical novel (about a late seventeenth-century noblewoman's moral and social fall) that also inaugurates modern
Danish realism; the novel's historical context, says Jensen, is
often little more than "a backdrop." Yet even as realism,
Marie Grubbe is a curious, original work, "essentially a series
of carefully constructed scenes or episodes that sometimes

exist almost independently of each other." Arresting and sus-
pending conventional narrative storytelling, Jacobsen turns
his first novel into an anthology of moments; the reader isn't
surprised to learn, from this biography, that Christopher
Isherwood, himself something of a master of frozen scene-
painting, admired *Marie Grubbe*.

Marie Grubbe's connection to *Niels Lyhne* lies in the author's overwhelming interest in religious faith and the com-
plications of heresy. One of Marie's lovers, the heroic soldier
Christian Gyldenløve, falls ill. On his deathbed, he refuses to
have anything to do with conventional religious belief: "I'll
have none of your Hell or Paradise. I just want to die, just to
die, nothing more." But he is terrified into theological submission by a priest who describes the torments of hell in gar-
ish detail (in *A Portrait of the Artist*, Joyce would parody this
kind of hellish sadism in Father Arnall's bullying sermon). He
ends his life, in Jensen's words, a "pathetic, hysterical man
whimpering before the God he once rejected and cursing the
woman he once desired."

And Marie Grubbe's own relation to religious belief
somewhat resembles Stephen Dedalus's: Jacobsen's novel
closes with Marie's affirmation, in reply to Master Holberg's
catechistic style of questioning, that she does not believe in
"the resurrection of the flesh." To Holberg, she offers the
shrewd objection that since she is not one single self but many
selves, she cannot possibly know which self would be raised to
eternal life: "And how shall I be raised? As the young innocent child I was when I first came out in the world, knowing
nothing and nobody, or as I was when I was admired and
envied, the king's favourite, a rich jewel in the court's crown

or as the poor, old and hopeless Marie the ferrywoman? And shall I have to answer for the sins they committed, the child, the woman in her prime, or is one of them going to answer for me? Can you tell me that, Master Holberg?" Holberg piously reminds her that she only has one soul. But Marie asks her interlocutor what he considers more likely—that someone who spent her entire life sinning against God but who at the last minute has a sudden conversion and repents and turns to God is more pleasing to Him than "someone who has also been hard towards Him, full of sin and contempt, but who then, for many a year in her life, has strived to do her duty and born every burden without a murmur, but has never repented her previous life to God or man? Do you think that she who has lived as she believed it was right to live, without any hope of reward hereafter, and never praying for that, do you believe that God will thrust her from Him and cast her away because she never entreated Him, not with a single word of prayer?"

It's a magnificent speech, alive with that oddly lyrical, proudly earnest belligerence that characterizes Jacobsen's relation to his inherited Christianity. But *Niels Lyhne*, whose proposed title was simply *The Atheist*, systematically dramatizes what is only intermittently emphasized in *Marie Grubbe*. For Jacobsen's second novel is not merely one of the indispensable modern novels, not merely a lushly written and moving portrait of romantic disillusionment and marital failure; it is one of the greatest atheistic novels ever written and almost certainly the most intense.

Niels, Jacobsen's dreamy, spoiled, sensitive hero, is a kind of male Emma Bovary—Jacobsen's novel testifies, like so many late nineteenth-century novels and stories of adultery, to the massive and quickening example of *Madame Bovary*. Yet adultery comes so late in the novel that it seems just one among a series of minor failures rather than a single, canonical errancy. At the age of twelve, Niels witnesses the untimely death of his glamorous cousin Edele and consequently suffers a profound crisis of faith. He begs God to intervene, but his prayers are met with silence.

> But if God had turned away from him, then *he* could also turn away from God. If God had no ears, then Niels would have no voice; if God had no mercy, then Niels would have no adoration, and he defied God and turned Him out of his heart. . . . He took sides, as completely as he could, against God, but like a vassal who takes up arms against his rightful master, because he still believed and could not banish his faith.

So Niels grows up a bitter atheist—the sort who childishly stamps his foot in the earth every time the pastor mentions the Lord's name at Edele's funeral. In Copenhagen, he dabbles in writing and moves in a circle of young, free-thinking modernist artists. He falls in love with an older woman, but the relationship is not much more than a young man's heated fantasy. (In time, she abandons him.) His father dies, and then his mother sickens. Mother and son go abroad for her health. She dies in Switzerland, certain at the end that she will see God on the other side of the grave.

Eventually, Niels falls in love again, with another of his cousins, a woman named Fennimore, and once more he is unlucky in love—Fennimore marries Niels's old friend Erik Refstrup, a dissolute and aimless artist. Two years later, Niels is summoned by Erik to the Refstrup house in the country: the marriage is in trouble; Erik is not painting but spending all his time with a boorish crowd of rustic drinkers and gamblers. Niels stays for a long time with Erik, and while his friend is away drinking and gambling, he and Fennimore begin an adulterous relationship. Yet just as it occurs late in the novel, so also is it fleeting. One day, news comes that Erik has been thrown from his horse and killed. Fennimore, alone at the time, feels that God has judged her and punished her and falls to her knees, wildly repenting of her adultery. When Niels arrives, she turns on him in a paroxysm of hatred and throws him out of the house: "I hate you, Niels Lyhne!"

For two years, Niels travels abroad and finally returns to his old childhood home, where he enjoys the unreflective labor of farming. Here at last, he finds happiness in love: he marries Gerda, a seventeen-year-old neighbor, and they have a son. He feels protective of this young soul and in particular doesn't want to rob her of the consolation of her Christian faith. But she is eager to share everything with him, eager to be instructed, so he explains to her, in good Feuerbachian fashion, that all gods are human inventions and that belief in a personal God is an escape, "a flight from harsh reality."

Harsh reality intervenes: in the spring, Gerda falls mortally ill. The deathbed scene is intensely moving, as the young woman, barely out of her teens, cries to Niels, "If you were going along—but alone . . . I'm afraid." Her fear provokes a recanting. She begs Niels to get the pastor. "It's impossible, Niels, for everything to be over at death. You can't feel it, you who are healthy." The pastor arrives, and—in a scene reminiscent of Christian's deathbed conversion in *Marie Grubbe*— Gerda reverts to her childhood faith, "the deep submission before the almighty, judging God . . . and the humble, bold

yearning for the new pact of bread and wine with the inscrutable God."

She dies, but worse is to come. A few months later, Niels
comes home from the fields to find his little boy very ill. This
final fateful punishment breaks his resolve. At first he raises
his clenched fist threateningly to heaven, but then he prays
greedily for God to save his son. His grief at the death of his
child is compounded by dreadful remorse at his own weakness. A test had been presented to him, and he failed it and
made supplication to a God in whom he did not believe. "He
had been tempted and he had fallen," writes Jacobsen, in a
knowing inversion.

As Morten Høi Jensen shrewdly makes clear, Jacobsen's
book is more "misotheistic" than atheistic—"misotheism" being the term usefully revived by Bernard Schweizer in his
book *Hating God* (2010) to describe several modern writers
who might be called God-haters rather than outright God-
deniers. (Schweizer doesn't mention Jacobsen.) In Jacobsen's
world, God does not answer prayers and is thus invisible or
nonexistent—but God does not cease being invoked to answer prayers. Jacobsen captures the structural contradiction
of militant God-hatred: constant address is made to a God
who is supposedly not believed in. Of course, the paradox is
familiar enough—from Dostoevsky, for one. But Jacobsen is
perhaps more acute, and more explicit, than any other novelist I have read about the difficulty of annulling God, about the
impossibility of expelling God, from the grammar of thought.
(Here, Nietzsche is Jacobsen's philosophical kin.) Whenever
Niels tries to cancel God, his cancellation takes the form of a
banishment rather than an extinction; he is always conceding

God's presence; his imagination runs away into the abyss of God's presence. Niels ends in a kind of angry paralysis, imprisoned in the contradiction of Beckett's celebrated line from *Endgame:* "The bastard! He doesn't exist."

Jens Peter Jacobsen's great novel captures a particular moment of nineteenth-century militant atheism, but his book has the ever-renewed relevance of the classic work and speaks directly to us today. For Morten Høi Jensen's superb biography has rediscovered Jacobsen's work at a time of recrudescent religious fundamentalism and in a time when our own contemporary atheism (the so-called New Atheism) often strikingly resembles the militant atheism of the late nineteenth century. Contemporary atheism, which owes its own recrudescence to its desire to fight rising Islamic fundamentalism and evangelical Christianity, sometimes appears to define religion *only* as Islamic fundamentalism and evangelical Christianity—and is thus locked, as Jacobsen would wisely point out, into an essentially mimetic relationship to the very belief it is supposed to negate: the candle snuffer and the candle belong together. Among many other qualities and beauties, Jacobsen's timely, timeless work provides profound and bitter counsel about how, while we go about trying to banish God, in a world very different but sometimes eerily similar to Jacobsen's nineteenth-century Danish milieu, we merely prove how difficult it is to banish talking about God.

James Wood

Acknowledgments

I wish to express my deepest gratitude to Yale University Press for its willingness to publish a book about a largely forgotten Danish writer written by an entirely unknown Danish writer. In particular, I would like to thank my brilliant and perceptive editor Jennifer Banks and her assistant editor Heather Gold for their close reading, their support, and their patience. I also greatly appreciate the dedication of my copy editor, Bojana Ristich.

The Jens Peter Jacobsen Society in Thisted welcomed me with open arms on my two visits to Thisted and willingly answered questions throughout the writing process. I am especially grateful to Svend Sørensen, Jytte K. Nielsen, and Else Bisgaard.

I have benefited from the existing literature on Jacobsen, most of it in Danish, and gratefully acknowledge my debt to the work of Anna Linck, Niels Lyhne Jensen, Frederik Nielsen, Brita Tigerschiöld, Aage Knudsen, and Kristian

Himmelstrup. A special thanks to Jacobsen's formidable English translator, Tiina Nunnally, from whose editions of *Niels Lyhne* and *Mogens and Other Stories* I am delighted to quote throughout this book.

I would not have undertaken to write this book were it not for the encouragement of James Wood, who has remained an unshakeable pillar of support throughout the years. I am profoundly grateful for his help and his magnificent foreword and for the continued inspiration of his literary criticism. His writing has moved me in more ways than I can do justice to here.

I would like to thank my family, especially my parents, my siblings, and my grandfathers, for their love and support. A special thanks to the select few who read and offered invaluable comments on individual chapters: my father, my grandfather, my younger brother, and Bronwen Durocher. Thanks also to Alyssa Reeder, Ben Clague, Chad Felix, Nevada Ryan, Brandon Ward, and Matthew Dreiling for their support and friendship throughout the writing process.

Prologue

In 1902 Rainer Maria Rilke fled his wife, Clara, and newborn daughter for Paris to undertake a commission for a monograph on Auguste Rodin. He rented a small, squalid room in the student quarter, on the rue Toullier, and made daily visits to see Rodin in his studio on rue de l'Université and in his home in the suburb of Meudon. He quickly came to admire the ageing sculptor's monastic devotion to his work; by comparison, the weeks and months that passed between Rilke's own creative bursts—he called them festivals of rare inspiration—were a source of constant frustration for the young poet. He explained to Rodin that "it was not only to do a study that I came to be with you,—it was to ask you: how must one live?"[1]

Yet it was not life that Rilke discovered in Paris but death. He warned his wife that the French capital was "very big and full to the brim of sadness,"[2] while to a friend he called it a "difficult, difficult, anxious" city—a star hurtling toward "some dreadful collision."[3] Years later he would begin his quasi-novel about a young Danish poet in Paris, *The Notebooks of Malte Laurids Brigge*, with the observation that it was a city in which people came to die rather than to live.

Rilke's initial revulsion with the French capital's teeming, squalid streets, compounded by his feelings of inadequacy about his work, filled his letters with self-pity and whimpering narcissism. No sooner did Clara arrive in the city than Rilke left it. In a letter to the Swedish writer Ellen Key he explained his "difficult" decision in early 1903 to leave for the Italian Riviera, only to find it crawling with German tourists. Thwarted, he journeyed further south, to Viareggio, a resort near Pisa, and took a room with a view of the sea at the Hotel Florence. There, Rilke stewed in a willed creative solitude, avoiding all contact with other hotel guests. He responded to a letter from a student at the military academy in Wiener-Neustadt, Franz Xaver Cappus (the "Young Poet" of *Letters to a Young Poet*). "I have been unwell," Rilke told him, "oppressed by an influenza-like lassitude that has made me incapable of anything." His letter goes on at some length about the dangers of irony before telling Cappus, possibly at the young poet's urging, about his favorite books:

> Of all my books just a few are indispensible to me, and two even are always among my things, wherever I am. They are about me here too: the Bible, and the books of the great Danish writer, Jens Peter Jacobsen. I wonder whether you know his works. You can easily get them, for some of them have come out in very good translation in Reclam's Universal Library. Get yourself the little volume of Six Stories of J. P. Jacobsen and his novel *Niels Lyhne*, and start on the first story, in the former, called "Mogens." A world will come over you, the happiness, abundance, the incomprehensible immensity of

a world. Live a while in these books, learn from them what seems to you worth learning, but above all love them. This love will be repaid you a thousand and a thousand times, and however your life may turn,—it will, I am certain of it, run through the fabric of your growth as one of the most important threads among all the threads of your experiences, disappointments and joys.[4]

Jacobsen was Rilke's only real companion in Viareggio (he had first read the Danish writer in Munich in 1897, at the urging of the novelist Jakob Wasserman). He carried his books with him on the beach and in the Pineta, and during a longed-for bout of creative energy even wrote a significant portion of *The Book of Hours* in his paperback edition of Jacobsen's stories. In a letter sent from Rome he referred to Jacobsen and Rodin as "the inexhaustible ones, the masters," while to the essayist and critic Arthur Holitscher he recalled how, years earlier, he had intended to go look up Jacobsen, much as he had looked up Rodin, only to discover that the Danish writer was long dead.[5]

Rilke looked on Jacobsen as a writer who could dwell with an almost scientific precision on the beauty of the natural world, who seemed to perform lyrical dissections of flowers and trees and at the same time fathomed the loneliest depths of humanity, its deepest disappointments and darkest doubts. In Rilke's letters, Jacobsen's name often appears alongside Rodin's. Like the sculptor, the Danish poet was an artist whose careful observation of the natural world allowed him to transform his experience of it into a perfectly formed art. There was a tangibility in their work, a physical presence that Rilke studied obsessively. "Both have made things, things with many sure boundaries and countless intersections and profiles," he wrote to Ellen Key.[6] It was this quality he felt his own poetry urgently needed, an opinion some of his friends shared; Rilke later explained that the novelist Jakob Wassermann had encouraged him to read Jacobsen in order to help him progress from the "lyrical vagueness" of his early poems.[7]

In early 1904, when Rilke and Clara were living in Rome, Arthur Holitscher wrote to the young poet encouraging him to write a book on Jacobsen. Rilke reacted warmly to this "beautiful" task and immediately set about obtaining a Danish grammar book and a German-Danish dictionary.[8] The timing wasn't bad either; Rome had lost its appeal, and the itinerant poet now looked toward Scandinavia as a possible place to live. He had only recently made the acquaintance of Ellen Key and resumed his correspondence with his former lover and confidant Lou Andreas-Salomé; in May 1904 he sent Andreas-Salomé an exhaustive letter (he himself referred to it as "that long letter"), outlining some of the projects he intended to pursue once he had put Rome behind him. Among them was the monograph "The Poet: Jens Peter Jacobsen," which Rilke said he would probably take up first. "You can't imagine how crucial he has become for me," he wrote, and he continued:

> I have approached him on ever new paths, sometimes alone, sometimes with my wife (who reads him so well and with such empathy); indeed, no matter where one wanders amid things of real importance one can be sure of coming out in a place where he also is (if one walks far enough); and how strange it is to find his and Rodin's words often agreeing so exactly: one has that crystal-clear feeling one gets in mathematical proofs at the moment when two distant lines converge, as from eternity, at a single point; or when two large complicated numbers which

bear no resemblance to one another simultaneously withdraw in acknowledgment of a single simple integer at the heart of all.—Strangely inviolate joy issues from such experiences. . . . I have begun learning Danish, chiefly so that I can read Jacobsen and some of Kierkegaard in the original.[9]

Rilke soon resolved to spend the summer and fall by himself in Denmark and Sweden, with the assurance that "as soon as I have arrived there and begun to settle in, I will go straight to my interrupted work and immerse myself in it for as long as possible."[10]

He arrived in Denmark on the morning of June 9, 1904, after a cold, wet, and windy crossing by steamboat from Kiel. He spent just two days in Copenhagen—taking in the sights, among them Rodin's Burghers of Calais, in front of the Ny Carlsberg Glyptotek—before crossing Øresund for Malmö, Sweden, where he had accepted an invitation from the artist Ernst Norlind and his fiancée Hanna Larsson to stay at their estate, Borgeby-gård, the remains of a castle built in the middle of the sixteenth century.

In a room with a large window looking out on the idyllic countryside, Rilke was as far from the seedy underworld of Paris and the "bad museum" that was Rome as he could be. He spent a few hours every day working on his Danish, as well as translating Søren Kierkegaard's letters to Regine Olsen, before walking barefoot in the surrounding fields and pastures, amid cattle and elderberry bushes, talking to the various guests who routinely visited Borgeby-gård. Among them was a young student of zoology who, as Rilke excitedly wrote home to Clara, walked about with a copy of Jacobsen's novel *Niels Lyhne* in his pocket.

But when a few restful months in the country failed to yield much in the way of poetic inspiration, Rilke again grew sullen and restless. He was alone among the Swedes and struggled to follow his vegetarian diet. "I have not accomplished much," he wrote to Lou Andreas-Salomé in August.[11] When she replied from Hotel Bellevue in Copenhagen, Rilke mistook it for an invitation and got on a train the following morning only to find that she had already left the city.

Rilke initially warmed to Copenhagen: "a city like no other, strangely inexpressible, completely dissolving in nuances. . . . One feels Jacobsen, Kierkegaard, hears the language like an interpretation of all this."[12] He stayed there for some time and was eventually joined by Clara. They met his publisher, Axel Juncker, the painter Vilhelm Hammershøi, and not least the celebrated and deeply influential critic Georg Brandes—"dear and good," as Rilke described him, "but in the end more an amusement park than a human being."[13] (Brandes, apparently, was more interested in Clara than in her husband.) Rilke had also written to Juncker to try and arrange a meeting with the novelist and journalist Herman Bang, but it is unlikely that the two ever met—despite Rilke's public admiration for Bang's novels. (If they did cross paths, Jacobsen would undoubtedly have been the main topic of conversation; as a young man, Bang had been under the irresistible sway of Jacobsen's style and in 1879 wrote one of the earliest and most insightful essays on Jacobsen for the newspaper *Nationaltidende*.)

For Rilke, all of Copenhagen seemed imbued with the spirit of Jacobsen. "Yes, Copenhagen is Jacobsen's city," he wrote. "I view [it] through Jacobsen and out of love for him."[14]

The Danish language, on the other hand, was more challenging to master than Rilke had at first expected. If his translations of Jacobsen's poems are anything to go by, it seems he never acquired more than a rudimentary grasp of Danish and probably acted wisely by later turning down an offer to translate a new edition of Jacobsen's poems.

While linguistic difficulties may have persuaded Rilke to abandon his intention of studying the Jacobsen archives at the University of Copenhagen, poor health and habitual restlessness didn't make matters any easier. He and Clara struggled to find an adequate room in Copenhagen and felt they were becoming "more and more homeless."[15] In the fall, Rilke felt ill enough to check into a sanitarium in the coastal town of Skodsborg, though with the exception of a weak heart valve the doctor could find little with which to indulge the hypochondriac poet. Rilke thus spent a final, gloomy month in Scandinavia making little progress on his work. In the years to come he continued to assure Arthur Holitscher that he hadn't abandoned "my Jacobsen book," but as his biographer Ralph Freedman has written, it "permanently remained an unfulfilled project."[16] Rilke set sail from Copenhagen on December 14, 1904, never to return.

Rilke was introduced to Jacobsen at a time when the Danish writer was at the peak of his posthumous fame. German literary culture was then greatly inspired by the new movements in Scandinavian letters, and in particular by the work of Jacobsen, Henrik Ibsen, August Strindberg, Herman Bang, and Knut Hamsun. An article in the inaugural issue of *Freie Bühne für modernes Leben* (later the *Neue Rundschau*) went so

far as to describe Scandinavia as "the promised land of literature,"[17] while some of the most influential publishers at the
time, like Samuel Fischer and Albert Langen, rose to promi-
nence in part because of their heavily Nordic catalogs. Even
Thomas Mann, who in *A Sketch of My Life* (1930) claimed that
he had "devoured" Scandinavian literature as a young man,[18]
once told an interviewer, "I am quite Nordically-inclined, and
perhaps it is J. P. Jacobsen who has had the greatest influence
on my style so far."[19]

Within a generation, from about 1890 onward, Jacobsen
became a cult literary figure in Europe's German-speaking
countries. His work was eagerly translated and discussed in
artistic circles from Vienna to Berlin and his poems were set
to music by the likes of Arnold Schoenberg and Alexander
von Zemlinksy. Reclam's edition of *Niels Lyhne*, published in
1889, sold roughly ten thousand copies in six years, while the
handsome edition of Eugen Diederich Verlag's *Collected Works*
of Jacobsen had sold almost twice that (eighteen thousand
copies) by 1909.[20] Stefan Zweig called *Niels Lyhne* the *Werther*
of his generation, while the critic and translator Marie Herzfeld claimed that it had become "a kind of prayer book for
the young painters and poets."[21] Freud was bowled over by it,
Robert Musil nearly copied a scene from it word for word,
and Gottfried Benn carried it with him everywhere. So conspicuous was the Jacobsen vogue in Germany that an entire
meeting of the literary-historical society in Bonn in 1907 was
devoted to the issue.

By then Jacobsen's influence already extended beyond
continental Europe. In Britain he was eagerly read by George
Gissing, T. E. Lawrence, and Henry Handel Richardson and

considered by James Joyce to be among Flaubert's successors. Boris Pasternak's son recalled that *Niels Lyhne* had a permanent place on his father's desk during the years he spent writing *Doctor Zhivago*. Jacobsen's influence extends even to the Harlem Renaissance writers Nella Larsen and Zora Neale Hurston; they both read Hanna Astrup Larsen's translation of Jacobsen's first novel, *Marie Grubbe*, which was reviewed in *The Nation* in 1918 with the claim that "Jacobsen was one of the greatest writers of prose of the nineteenth century."[22]

Jacobsen's influence has been immense—astonishingly immense, in fact, given how little he wrote and how young he was when he died. Born in 1847 in a small harbor town on the outskirts of the Danish peninsula, he wrote just two novels, a collection of poems, and a handful of stories before finally succumbing to tuberculosis in 1885, just a few weeks after his thirty-eighth birthday. His life was cruelly circumscribed; he never married, he had no children, and he spent much of his adulthood in the home of his parents, quietly wasting away and laboring patiently on his writing.

Though little read outside Denmark today, Jacobsen belonged to a bracing and prolific era of Scandinavian literature without which modern European letters would not be the same. He befriended and was encouraged by Georg Brandes— a man who "could, and did, make and break authors"[23]—and his brother Edvard, and in his own lifetime he came to be seen as the most original and unusual prose stylist in the Danish language. Strindberg and Ibsen both celebrated him; Knut Hamsun lectured on him during his trips to America in the 1880s; and artists like Edvard Munch, Ernst Josephson, and

the Skagen painters drew on his color-saturated style for inspiration.

Jacobsen's story is therefore also a story of innumerable
transformations in Scandinavian culture and politics. Though
not himself politically inclined, he rattled prevailing religious
pieties with his translations of Darwin's *Origin of Species* and
The Descent of Man. And as a friend and ally of Georg Brandes
in his crusade against the romantic idealism and pastoral
conservatism of Danish cultural life, Jacobsen was at the
forefront of a movement struggling to define the terms of
what it meant to be fully modern. *Niels Lyhne*, in particular, is
one of the great novels of the experience of modernity, a portrait of the disorientation and vertigo of modern life worthy
of the writings of Dostoevsky, Thomas Hardy, and Friedrich
Nietzsche.

Jacobsen's influence began to decline sometime between the
two world wars. In 1947 the *Times Literary Supplement* published an article on the centenary of his birth, going so far as
to claim that Jacobsen's virtues had been overshadowed by
Rilke. "That great shadow lies between ourselves and him,"
the anonymous author writes; "a real affinity has been pressed
so far that Jacobsen, the least assertive of men, remains half
engulfed by the varieties of tribute and imitation which Rilke
lavished upon his memory. And yet, if we can catch him for a
moment alone, an extraordinary and moving talent is there;
among the portentous invalids of the nineteenth century
Jacobsen has his own place."[24]

This book is an attempt to catch Jacobsen alone. It feels
disingenuous, even a little presumptuous, to call it a biography;

Jacobsen died so young and spent so many years in quiet, lonely suffering—what life is there to excavate? He kept a diary only briefly, was a dedicated but hardly prolific correspondent, and was regarded even by his friends as bordering on the unknowable. As his friend Alexander Kielland said, he was not exactly an open theme park.[25]

No, he certainly wasn't. At moments, I find it almost unbearable to contemplate what Jacobsen thought and felt, what preoccupied him and concerned him and filled his head during the many sleepless nights he had to endure as he lay dying in what he liked to call the "Siberia of Denmark." Of course, Jacobsen's fiction can only ever offer an oblique glimpse into those private thoughts, those many hours of loneliness and suffering, but for me his works stand out precisely because they face up to mortality without cynicism and without hope. Jacobsen rejects both the false comforts of religion and the notion, common today among certain New Atheists, that we should greet death without blinking an eye. As a scientist, Jacobsen knew that death marked simply the termination of our material existence, but he understood also that religion fulfilled a very basic human need: the desire to extend life beyond death and thereby lessen the awful prospect that on a day not of our own choosing, without regard for whatever hopes and dreams we may yet have, without care for the grief of the loved ones who will survive us, we will be wrenched from this life into cold oblivion. As perhaps only a great novelist can, Jacobsen examined these difficult, conflicting attitudes toward mortality, the ill-fitting fabric of our changing beliefs. In the pages that follow, I hope the reader will come to find his voice among the greatest, and most peculiar, in world literature.

Axel Helsted's deathbed portrait of Jens Peter
Jacobsen. Courtesy of Thisted Museum.

CHAPTER ONE

"Simply to Be Remembered"

Idyll! There are no idylls.
—J. P. Jacobsen, letter to Edvard Brandes, March 10, 1885

THISTED is built around a concave stretch of bay on the shoulder of the Danish peninsula, just ten miles east of Jutland's west coast. From there it climbs up the sloping moraine hills of Thy, surrounded by a variegated landscape of coastal plains, conifer woods, and sand dunes formed by centuries of sand drift and the depressions of the last Ice Age.

A little further south, in Silstrup, the landscape cuts abruptly into a wonder of cliffs and quarries whose unusual contours and geological layers expose a unique variety of plant life. Years earlier we might have spotted the young Jens Peter Jacobsen there—or Peter, as his parents simply called him—a tall, athletic boy with blond hair, digging in the dirt, inspecting plants, and collecting specimens for the pamphlet he wrote when he was just fourteen, "Silstrup's Strangest Plants," and which he affectionately dedicated to his classmates.

View of Thisted. The large building is Christen Jacobsen's home
and merchant house. Courtesy of Thisted Museum.

On the morning of his thirty-eighth birthday, however,
Jacobsen's days of botanical explorations were long gone. He
awoke in the apartment he shared with his younger brother,
William, on the first floor of his father's large home on the
harbor. Surrounding him were the scant possessions he'd
brought with him when he left Copenhagen the previous
summer: his papers and books, the painting of the Château de
Chillon from Switzerland, a red chaise longue he'd received
from anonymous female admirers. "My brother and I live
quite peacefully, like the old bachelors we are," he wrote to a
friend, "in lively contact with the old ones upstairs, but otherwise not connected to the outside world."[1]

That morning the previous day's edition of the newspaper
Politiken was brought to him as a special treat. Regrettably, no

one had seen the notice that Jacobsen immediately discovered upon opening the paper: "The poet J. P. Jacobsen, currently residing in Thisted, is at the moment fatally ill." This was hardly news to anyone, least of all Jacobsen, but neither was it something he enjoyed seeing broadcast everywhere. Whenever people asked him how he felt, he would usually shrug and say, "Thanks, I feel fine," while in letters to friends he spoke of his health only lightly and in passing. "There doesn't seem to be much of me left," he wrote to Edvard Brandes in December 1884, "and what little remains is best preserved in cotton."[2]

When Jacobsen left his beloved Copenhagen for good in July 1884, Edvard Brandes described his state as being downright frightening: "He's skinnier than he's ever been, his legs are dreadfully thin, and his posture is like an old man's."[3] Jacobsen's long struggle with tuberculosis, which had by now lasted over a decade, looked to everyone to be nearing its tragic denouement. He'd spent the last few years "living horizontally," to borrow a phrase from Thomas Mann, either in his sparsely furnished rooms in Copenhagen or near friends in the countryside. For a long time he had been like a character straight out of Mann: the artist-patient "sitting on the rocks," like the young radical Morten Schwarzkopf in *Buddenbrooks*. Mann, an admirer of Jacobsen, may well have been inspired by the image of the resigned Niels Lyhne, who, late in life, can be found sitting "on a fence or a boundary stone, and staring, in a strangely vegetative trance, out across the golden wheat or the top-heavy oats."[4]

When at the peak of his fame Jacobsen was asked by a friend to provide a little biographical information, the only

The Jacobsen family circa 1856. From left to right: William Jacobsen, Benthe Marie Jacobsen, Jens Peter Jacobsen, Ana Theodora Jacobsen, Christen Jacobsen, and Cecilie Marie Jacobsen. Courtesy of Thisted Museum.

thing he could think to share about his childhood was that he was "the older son of merchant Christen Jacobsen and Benthe Marie Hundahl. Born in Thisted April 7, 1847."[5]

Such reticence is characteristic. Jacobsen was modest and self-effacing almost to the point of unknowability. The few friends he had all complained of his unbreakable silence and coy reserve—conspicuous qualities in an age of literary loud-mouths and towering egos. Yet as a child, Jacobsen was anything but shy. A mediocre student whose eyes "sparkled with mischief," he was beloved by his peers for his boyish antics.[6]

He was a gifted mimic, an ardent explorer, and a recalcitrant trickster. For laughs, he would freeze food bowls onto the kitchen counter by mixing salt and snow (to his mother's grief) or leap like an acrobat among the pillars on the harbor (to the harbor master's grief). He led expeditions on the beach and in the forest, chasing snakes and catching snails. In the attic of his parents' house he built a makeshift laboratory, playing at being a scientist with his friend Nikolaj Nielsen. Later in life they would refer to one another as "my friend and fellow florist" and "amicus naturæ."[7]

Jacobsen was the oldest of four children. He had a brother and two sisters, the youngest of whom died at age four from scarlet fever. (Jacobsen's mother later gave birth to a stillborn son.) His parents were married in 1844 and lived in a small house on Skolestræde but moved a year after Jacobsen's birth into a large, two-story house on the harbor with a slate roof and an adjoining warehouse—a sign of the young family's good fortune and reputable standing in Thisted.

Christen Jacobsen was a frugal, hardworking man, and over the years he had accumulated a small but considerable fortune through various business dealings. He owned ships and property throughout Thisted, traded in livestock and timber, and in 1864 even invested in a foundry. As a young man he had traveled all over Thy buying butter, pork, eggs, and geese and selling them at a profit. He made enough money to buy a schooner and sometimes sailed as far as England. His travels opened the Jacobsen household to the wider world; the children sometimes gathered around the large oak table in the living room where their father and his friends played cards and told stories of life at sea. In the event that any of these stories assumed a mystical or superstitious character, Jacobsen resolutely declared them to be a load of nonsense.

Benthe Marie, the daughter of a parish clerk and a school-teacher, was a pious and sensitive woman, deeply devoted to her children, especially her oldest son. "You are first in my thoughts in the morning, and the last to go at night," she once told Jacobsen. "I always feel like you're closest to my heart."[8] The family adhesive, she was a formidable organizer, keeping tabs on three children and an industrious husband who often worked himself into affliction (a cold, a cough, general fatigue). But like her children, she probably preferred him to be off spreading manure in a field or assisting with the construction of a building somewhere; if poor health kept Christen at home, his restlessness curdled into irritability, as numerous letters to Jacobsen attest: "Father wasn't exactly in a good mood" (William); "Father sends his greetings. . . . His mood is up and down" (Cecilie Marie, Jacobsen's sister); "Father can't write as he is in a bad mood" (Benthe Marie).[9]

Remarkably, there are no records of religious conflict between Jacobsen and his parents. We shouldn't conclude from this that no such confrontation ever took place or that his parents were later thrilled by their son's well-known atheism, but it doesn't appear to have upset them the way Jacobsen's indolence or poor financial management did. Benthe Marie was unquestionably devout but perhaps not as fanatically religious as many other families were—especially in a town as remote as Thisted. Throughout the middle of the nineteenth century a number of fundamentalist communities sprang up across Denmark, among them the Church Association for the

Inner Mission, a German import, which was officially established in Stenlille in 1861. Hans Kirk's best-selling novel *The Fishermen* (1928), which takes place in a rural village not far from Thisted, offers a haunting portrayal of the influence of these puritanical movements, especially as they clashed with the progressive Christianity preached by the influential N. F. S. Grundtvig.

Christen Jacobsen, for his part, appears to have been the sort of man for whom religion was just another hang-up keeping him from his work. (He was unfazed by his wife's moral concerns over his decision to invest in a distillery in the early 1860s.) A childhood friend of Jacobsen's even wondered if Christen hadn't taken part in the low-grade smuggling common to remote areas of the country back then. It would not have been surprising to learn that this shrewd and self-made man, who had spent so much of his life at sea, who traded goods along the western coast of Denmark, and who like a real sailor sported two earrings even in his old age, also knew his way around customs officers and toll collectors.

At the time of Jacobsen's birth Thisted's population numbered roughly eighteen hundred. Twenty years later it had almost doubled, a sign of the small town's growth from minor village to industrious seaport. The building of the harbor in 1840 attracted businesses from across the region, kindling a growth in commerce and the expansion of new textile and shipbuilding industries. "Everything appears to be progressing in rapid strides in Thisted," a local newspaper reported in 1843; "the town now has a delightful harbor, one building is erected after another, and one newly arrived merchant after another announces his inventory."[10]

Still, its remote location kept Thisted isolated even as it prospered. It remained beyond the reach of the railways until 1882, and perhaps the town didn't quite keep pace with its growing population. "Back then we didn't know about sewers," a local contemporary of Jacobsen's recalled; "all the waste ran through open gutters in the streets and the farms, emanating a particularly terrible stench in the summer." In some homes the smell of waste had to compete with the smell of rotting corpses; Thisted did not have a mortuary until the late 1860s. Until then, bodies were either carried through the streets to the hospital or kept at home until the carpenter could build a casket.[11]

Perhaps all the dealings and goings on, mixed with the unsanitary surroundings, helped drive Jacobsen to his love of plant life. (Even as a boy, a childhood friend later recalled, Jacobsen could sit and stare for hours at flowers, spellbound by their beauty.) Growing up with all of Thy for a backyard certainly would have offered ample opportunity for escape and liberation. From its barren, sandy stretches of heath in the west to the fertile, rolling plains in the east, the land teems with an astonishing range and variety of plant species. The thin strip of land between Thisted and Aalborg is almost entirely flat, while the western coastline swells with sand dunes and gently swaying lyme grass. Additionally, there are thousands of burial mounds located throughout the land—a reminder of Thy's past as a densely populated Viking port. If Jacobsen and his friends were lucky, they might even have come across the odd tool or weapon from the Bronze Age.

The lack of incident, the white script of happiness, is secretly resented by the biographer and has in Jacobsen's case led many to rhapsodize over the innocence and splendor of his childhood—especially when contrasted to the pall of mortality that hung over his adult years. Rilke claimed that all the material for Jacobsen's work grew out of his childhood—"a great, immensely colorful childhood in which he found everything his soul needed to dress itself in imagined guises." A slightly inflated claim, to say the least. In *Malte Laurids Brigge*, the novel Rilke spent the first decade of the twentieth century writing, the narrative frequently revisits scenes from Malte's Danish childhood—scenes Rilke cobbled together from his reading of Jacobsen and Herman Bang and his own impressions of Denmark. The scholar Judith Ryan has shown how Rilke's own unhappy youth, combined with his reading of Ellen Key's *The Century of the Child* (1900), contributed to his belief in the centrality of childhood to an artist's development. In a letter to the painter Paula Modersohn-Becker, Rilke wrote of Jacobsen's portrayal of Niels Lyhne's youth and his consciousness of "the fact that there was a limit set to this happy time, and presently one day it would be no more. This consciousness roused in him a craving to enjoy his childhood to the full, to suck it up through every sense, not to spill a drop, not a single one."[12]

Was the eight- or nine- or ten-year-old Jacobsen, in the plume of health, conscious of the transient pleasures of youth? We can't know, of course. But the days would come when to look back on his years playing on the harbor or the beach, remote as they seemed, might have put a much needed smile on his lips. But that he should have idolized or grown sentimental over his past is probably a fiction of the dewy-eyed piety with which Jacobsen's contemporaries tended to recollect him. He himself was not so mawkish. The last line of his final letter to Edvard Brandes, dispatched on March 10, 1885, a little over a month before his death, was, "Idyll! There are no idylls."[13]

Jacobsen generally bore his illness without complaint, but the notice in the newspaper on his thirty-eighth birthday soured his mood. William had arranged for Jacobsen's close friends Vilhelm and Agnes Møller to travel to Thisted for the birthday celebrations, but Jacobsen, usually overjoyed at the prospect of a friend visiting, was now sunk in gloom. Nor did the fact that he knew he probably wouldn't see his friends again help matters. On the day the Møllers left, he passed the morning on his sofa in silence. Vilhelm Møller wrote to him a few days later to say how wonderful it had been simply to "sit with you and see you again and listen to you." Now, he added, "we'll have to make do by searching for you in our memories and our thoughts."[14] Eventually William had to write to Møller and instruct him to tell people to stop paying visits to Jacobsen. The toll of saying goodbye was too great.

Jacobsen had said his last farewell two years earlier. In the short story "Fru Fønss," which appeared for the first time in *Mogens and Other Stories* in 1882, he wrote what many considered at the time to be a thinly veiled farewell to readers and friends. The titular character, a woman whose children refuse to accept her decision to remarry, lays dying in Spain. Her final act is a magnanimous letter of farewell to those children, who for five years have refused to talk to her:

> The one who must die, dear children, is so bereft: I am so impoverished, because this entire lovely world, which for so

many years has been my rich, blessed home, is to be taken from me; my chair will stand empty, the door will close on me, and I shall never set foot here again. This is why I look on all the world with the prayer in my eyes that it will care for me; this is why I come and implore you to love me with all the love you once gave me; don't forget, to be remembered is the only part of the human world that will be mine from now on. Simply to be remembered, nothing more.[15]

Edvard Brandes later recalled that Jacobsen wrote the farewell letter in one sitting, with tears streaming down his face: "Jacobsen jokingly confessed that 'his own lovely words had made him sentimental.' 'But it really *is* touching,' he added. And his friends laughed obligingly, though they all knew that with these words Jacobsen had written his farewell to the world and was now urging those of us who were fond of him to remember him."[16]

When a few weeks later Jacobsen's name next appeared in the newspaper, it was in his obituary. On the afternoon of April 30 he passed away in the presence of his mother and William. "And then finally he died the death, the difficult death!" William wrote to Vilhelm Møller that night. "It's so unbearably sad to think that he with his enormous intelligence and kindness is gone, never to return."[17] Newspapers in Denmark already carried the news of his death the following day. Soon, writers across all of Scandinavia were in mourning. In Norway, it was not least the novelist Alexander Kielland who felt the passing of a great writer and friend. Jacobsen had spent many days with Kielland and his wife while they lived in Copenhagen in the early 1880s. "The greatest of them all is dead and gone," Kielland wrote. "He was one of the good old Danes: quiet and fine, noble and loyal."[18]

In Sweden, too, Jacobsen's death was the stuff of headlines. His obituary occupied the front page of *Ny Illustrerad Tidning* on May 23, 1885, while Carl Snoilsky's poem, "On J. P. Jacobsen's Death," appeared in both *Aftonbladet* and *Stockholms Dagblad*. "Jacobsen was loved by us all," Snoilsky wrote to Georg Brandes; "his death is like the passing of a dear friend."[19] August Strindberg, who was in Paris at the time, received a request from Edvard Brandes for his support for a memorial. "I didn't know Jacobsen had died!" the Swedish playwright exclaimed. "But of course I want to help honor his memory." (Henrik Ibsen refused to support the memorial when he learned that Strindberg's name was on the list. "The decrepit old Mountain King," Strindberg wrote, "has a mortal hatred of me.")[20]

On May 9, 1885, the sun shone brightly on the small chapel at Søndre Kirkegård, located on a hilltop in the western part of Thisted with a panoramic view of the Limfjord. Some three hundred people attended Jacobsen's funeral, most of them locals. Many were probably not familiar with Jacobsen's literary status and merely attended the funeral as a sign of respect to Jacobsen's well-known parents. Those who did know about Jacobsen's writings were probably deterred by the odor of atheism and freethinking that hung about them—or by the unusual and poetic style in which they were written. On May 2, an obituary in the local newspaper went so far as to write that Jacobsen was not a popular author—"for as a poet he belonged to literature's aristocracy. And to most people the flamboyance of form, the fine arrangement of language, is unfamiliar and unimportant."[21]

Only a few of Jacobsen's friends from Copenhagen made the long trip to Thisted: Vilhelm and Agnes Møller, the painter Axel Helsted, and the critic Erik Skram among them. Condolences arrived via telegram from Bjørnstjerne Bjørnson, Alexander Kielland, Holger Drachmann, and Jonas Lie. Georg and Edvard Brandes chose not to come. In a letter to Vilhelm Møller, Edvard explained his decision: "To hear a priest speak of him would be too onerous, I think."²²

As it turned out, the Jacobsens' decision to give their son a Christian burial was a controversial one. When the local pastor, Ludvig Birkedal Husum, came to discuss the funeral, Benthe Marie was anxious for him not to say anything inappropriate in his sermon—in other words, not to dwell on the fact that her son had been a well-known atheist. She showed Husum the book of Danish psalms that had belonged to Jacobsen, pointing out that he had made little notes in the margins next to the ones he liked best. Husum mistook this for a sign of religious longing, as he naively put it in his otherwise traditional sermon. "The deepest sorrow of this death," he concluded, "is that the disillusioned sigh of the departed's soul did not express itself in a prayer to the son of God and Man, our lord Jesus Christ."²³

Controversy ensued when, in the fall, Johannes Bertelsen, a childhood friend, claimed that Jacobsen had not really been an atheist and that he had privately regretted his loss of faith on several occasions, particularly in later years. Bertelsen even dared question the depth of Jacobsen's attachment to Georg and Edvard Brandes, insisting that he had never truly opened his heart to them. "How little, how very little, Brandes must have known him," he wrote in a memoir-essay published by Jacobsen's old school in Thisted.²⁴

These comments were gleefully taken up by conservative newspapers; the author of *Niels Lyhne*, the faithful acolyte of Georg Brandes, wasn't an atheist after all!—a maneuver transparently designed to provoke opponents on the left. Sadly, it worked. To the grief of Jacobsen's family, Edvard Brandes immediately sprung on the offensive. He launched a vehement tirade against Pastor Husum, Bertelsen, and the right, claiming that Jacobsen died as the fervent, impassioned atheist he had been throughout his entire adult life. "Grave robbers" he called them in an article in *Politiken*. He even went so far as to quote from William Jacobsen's account of his brother's death in a letter to Vilhelm Møller, which Møller had showed Brandes in confidence. As late as 1899, when his correspondence with Jacobsen was published, Edvard made sure in his foreword to damn the "priests and other fanatics" who had tried to claim Jacobsen for the church.[25]

Needless to say, the debate was a source of great embarrassment to Jacobsen's family. They had no stake in a symbolic dispute over the extent of their late son's atheism. Over the course of the last many months they had looked on as he quietly wasted away. No doubt it had been a grueling ordeal. And yet William insisted that not a single complaint had passed Jacobsen's lips, even as he lay in the throes of death. Hard to believe, but more than likely true; he only ever spoke of his tuberculosis in darkly comic terms. With morbid precision, he called his last months in Thisted his "living funeral."[26] Writing to friends, he complained occasionally of loneliness and isolation: "It's like walking around with an invisibility hat on your head," he wrote; "yes, a hat that makes you invisible even to yourself." But in spite of whatever farewells he'd said, implied or otherwise, he kept tinkering with his writing projects and thinking up new ones for as long as he was able. "The gods grant me a long life," he once wrote; "otherwise I'll never write as much as Wieland, and I really would like to."²⁷

CHAPTER TWO

A Sentimental Education

T HE journey from Thisted to Copenhagen in the second half of the nineteenth century was not an easy or comfortable one. It involved traveling roughly ninety miles along choppy roads in horse-drawn carriages to Frederikshavn, where a fishing boat ferried passengers to a ship that would sail them overnight to Korsør, a harbor town on the eastern coast of Zealand. The final leg of the journey was a four-hour trip by locomotive on the newly constructed railway to Copenhagen. For the sixteen-year-old Jens Peter Jacobsen, who first made this trip in the fall of 1863, traveling by rail must have been an unforgettable experience—much more exciting than sailing down through Kattegat in stormy weather and getting horribly seasick along the way. Unlike his seasoned father, Jacobsen wasn't exactly sailor material.

Jacobsen as a teenager, circa
1863. Courtesy of Thisted
Museum.

How incredible it must have been to arrive in the Danish capital for the first time—to see its horse-drawn trams and wide promenades, its gas lighting and Swiss-style cafés. The opening of the city's ramparts in 1856–1857 precipitated an enormous growth and expansion by erasing the old demarcation line and allowing new housing to be built in the so-called *brokvarterer,* or regional districts, in Østerbro, Nørrebro, Vesterbro, and Amagerbro. The opening of these old defenses and the construction of the railway—not to mention the decision to build a new underground sanitation system— meant that Copenhagen's population increased from just 180,000 in 1864 to 400,000 by the end of the century.[1] And aside from being quite ideally located en route to continental Europe, the city had all the requisite cultural institutions to make it the unofficial capital of Scandinavia: a university, an arts academy, a royal library, and a royal theater.

Jacobsen spent his first years in Copenhagen lodging in Frederiksberg in the home of a retired general named Brandt, whose wife had family in Thisted. It was a home away from home; Jacobsen spent his birthdays and even Christmas with the Brandts, who in turn treated him like family. One Christmas they very generously gifted him with a six-volume *Archiv für natur, kunst, wissenschaft und leben*, a massive German encyclopedia filled with illustrations from across the world. "The general and his wife send their regards," Jacobsen wrote to his parents in early 1864. "They are such kind and lovely people; as long as I live with them, I won't be led astray, and with God's help I never will."[2]

Jacobsen was enrolled in a cram school that would prepare him for his university entrance exams. Among his fellow students was Erik Skram, later an influential literary critic, who recalled Jacobsen as a "somewhat bashful, quiet, and loveable guy, tall and skinny, slouching and shuffling in his steps" and who didn't read a word of what he was assigned and seemed unlikely ever to amount to much.[3]

The lively young boy had become an introverted teenager. He neglected his studies in favor of publishing little journals and magazines, writing poems and sketches, and fishing for algae in Stadsgraven, the canal out by Christianshavn. He shambled his way through his subjects (composition, Latin, Greek, French, German, math, history, geography, and physics), occasionally perplexing his instructors and peers with his unusual points of view. In one of his essays Jacobsen suggested that Flagellants derived pleasure from the mortification of their flesh—a remark his confused teacher asked him to clarify. But Jacobsen had nothing more to add. The thought had simply occurred to him, he explained.

When he first sat for his entrance exams in 1866, Jacobsen failed to pass them. His parents received a letter from the head of the school regarding Jacobsen's performance. "Your son's abilities led us to expect a positive result from his exams, but in spite of repeated admonitions and reminders, despite urgent warnings against fiddling with an irrelevant subject (botany), we did not have the pleasure of seeing the diligence and perseverance that ought to accompany such abilities." The irrelevant subject was the obvious culprit: "Due to his love for botany he has neglected . . . the more immediate goal, his exams."[4] Jacobsen's mother was devastated: "In the past year we haven't heard a single cheerful or encouraging word about you; I'm so tired of shedding tears over your studies. . . . You're not a child any more, and it seems you'll never have enough discipline and resilience to amount to something great."[5]

It was recommended that Jacobsen entirely abandon his botanical research until his studies improved and he enrolled at the University of Copenhagen. "It is for the sake of your own future happiness that you must reach a position of independence in life," his mother wrote, warning her son not to fritter away his time on "useless" books.[6] In her letters she often conveyed stern reprimands from Jacobsen's father, who was reluctant to even send his son money enough for new clothes or school supplies. Evidently he was not thrilled with Jacobsen's choice of vocation. From an undated letter

Jacobsen wrote to him, it seems he'd asked his son to seriously consider finding an alternative career path. "If there was another line of work I was interested in or suited for, the choice would be easy," Jacobsen responded, "but nothing of the sort comes to mind, and to undertake such a change would just be a huge waste of time."[7]

Jacobsen's parents nevertheless continued to support their son, and Jacobsen in turn remained grateful, even if he occasionally had to remind them to send him money for food or clothing. Money, in fact, would remain a thorny subject for much of his life—Jacobsen never really earned enough to support himself, not even from his writing, and would be intermittently dependent on advances from his publisher, loans from friends, or the occasional (and often inadequate) literary grant. On the other hand, his sedentary, ascetic lifestyle, particularly in later years, meant that he was able to get by on very little—just enough to pay the rent, to afford the occasional purchase of books or clothes, and to pay for his travels.

Though he grew to love Copenhagen, Jacobsen dearly missed his childhood home, especially during the Christmas season. "It is now the fourth Christmas I'm celebrating here in the city, far from my home," he wrote to his parents in December 1867. "The bustle of Christmastime is so clear to me, the scent of baked goods in all the homes, the unusual traffic in the streets; it is not until adulthood that one truly begins to comprehend how wonderful childhood was and the immense influence it has on one's life."[8]

When the Second Schleswig-Holstein War broke out in the winter and spring of 1864 and Bismarck's Prussian troops dealt Denmark a number of humiliating blows, Jacobsen became anxious for his childhood home. "War—rumors of war—that's the word of the day," he wrote to his parents just a few days before the Danish general Christian Julius de Meza ordered his troops to retreat from the Dannevirke stronghold.[9] Following the decisive defeat at the Battle of Dybbøl in April and the ensuing Prussian occupation of Jutland, Jacobsen wrote to his parents with some alarm: "News of the seizure of the Dybbøl fortifications probably reached you immediately. I wonder now if the enemy will reach deep into Jutland. Thisted I hope will be exempt from his visit—but if he reaches Aalborg, how will I correspond with you?"[10]

Denmark's loss of Schleswig, Holstein, and Lauenborg—almost 40 percent of its territory—was a fateful blow. It meant that between 1814 and 1864, Denmark went from being a mid-sized European kingdom (encompassing Norway, Iceland, Greenland, and the Faroe Islands, as well as minor colonies in Africa and the West Indies) to being a small and vulnerable nation-state. A sense of national disillusionment swept the country. "Denmark's happy illusions were completely shattered," wrote the literary historian Elias Bredsdorff. "She woke up from her romantic dreams to bitter illusions."[11] These illusions were still discernible decades later, especially in the novels of Herman Bang, who as a young boy had witnessed the Danish Army's retreat on Als. "I think this lone image of flight and haste and disgrace has been enough to penetrate my entire life," he wrote in the preface to his novel *Tine* (1889). "I still feel those minutes of anxiety in my pen whenever I attempt to portray collapse, destruction, death, ruin."[12]

Jacobsen no doubt became privy to the realities of war through Erik Skram, who volunteered at age seventeen to join the Danish forces on Als and was severely wounded. "There I lay among the Prussians," Skram later wrote in his memoirs, "and only now did I see that blood was trickling onto my uniform through a hole in my chest and another in my hip. My left hand, penetrated by a bullet, was already rather contorted, my leg was bleeding heavily, and I must have hit my face as I fell because I was bleeding there too. All in all I must have been a pretty sorry sight."[13]

Even though he often longed for his childhood home, Jacobsen grew increasingly estranged from it. Living in Copenhagen was intoxicating. The death of King Frederik VII in 1863, whose funeral procession Jacobsen witnessed; the ongoing struggle between conservatives and liberals over the Danish constitution; and the war against Prussia—these were overwhelming developments for a provincial boy from the outskirts of Denmark to be in the thick of. "What a fateful year," he wrote to his parents in April 1864. "I've experienced more in the nine months I've lived over here than I have in my entire life."[14]

Jacobsen's biographers have tended to refer to his student years in Copenhagen as *kriseårene*, or the crisis years (1865–1867), a term that sounds a little too grandiose given that nothing outwardly dramatic or unusual happened. What Jacobsen experienced was a sentimental education, a restless process of self-discovery: anxiety, desire, self-consciousness, and feelings of inadequacy. The experience is memorably described in an astonishingly sensitive passage in *Niels Lyhne:*

There is a new feeling of power in seeing with his own eyes and choosing with his own heart like this, in participating in creating his own self; and so many things spring up in Niels's mind, so many unfathomed, scattered sides of his being gather so wondrously into a sensible whole. It is a thrilling time of discovery during which, little by little, with apprehension and uncertain jubilation, with disbelieving joy, he discovers himself. For the first time he sees that he is not like the others; a spiritual modesty stirs in him, making him shy and reticent and embarrassed. He is suspicious about all questions and finds references to his most secret thoughts in everything that is said. Because he has learned to read inside himself, he thinks that everyone else can also read what is written in him, and he withdraws from the adults and wanders around alone. All at once people have become strangely intrusive. He feels slightly hostile toward them, as if they were creatures of a different race, and in his loneliness he begins to take them to task and examine them, searching and judging.[15]

Jacobsen's delicate sensitivity to nuance and attention to detail, his powerful evocation of emotional atmosphere and the complex desires of his protagonists, has led to an extraordinary amount of guesswork and conjecture, much of it focused on his adolescence. His popularity in fin de siècle European culture meant that he was necessarily subjected to all the critical vogues of that time, particularly psychoanalysis. Additionally, the temptation to infer something of Jacobsen himself from the selves of Marie Grubbe or Niels Lyhne is made greater by the fact that so little is known about his private life. Worst of all from the point of view of the psychoanalyst, Jacobsen's sexual life is a complete mystery. It's doubtful that he even had one. In the years after his death he was often described as a slightly effete and even androgynous character; someone who stood above earthly temptation and animal desire; someone who, as one obituary put it, had a "fine and noble nature." Georg Brandes, never one to mince his words, put it more bluntly: "That he ever engaged in a love affair is something hardly anyone believes."[16]

The book that rears above all this, a book that any biographer must eventually resign himself to mention, is *J. P. Jacobsen: Digteren og mennesket*, an influential 1953 critical study by the literary scholar Frederik Nielsen. In this strange and divisive tome Nielsen claims that "the central element in [Jacobsen's] youthful crisis is the erotic." According to Nielsen, Jacobsen was prone to fantasies of a highly sexual nature—fantasies that, given his religious upbringing and the sexual puritanism of the time, were a source of both fear and shame to him. Nielsen believes Jacobsen prayed to God for relief from his impure and sinful fantasies and that God's silence is what eventually led to Jacobsen's atheism. He cites as evidence the youthful poetry cycle *Hervert Sperring*, which Jacobsen unsuccessfully submitted to Gyldendal for publication in 1868. In particular, the poem "Gud, frels mig dog!" ("Lord, please save me"), with its plea for God to "save me from the embrace of dreams," is pounced on like a smoking gun. In an earlier draft of the poem Jacobsen had written: "Oh save me from the embrace of dreams / Show me a woman / show me, send me a lovely maiden."[17] Nielsen rightly views this poem as a sign of Jacobsen's heightened sexual maturity, but he surely goes too far by suggesting that his fantasies were a source of almost physical discomfort. Nor does he seem to grasp that *Hervert Sperring* is a haphazardly composed collection, a book of lyrical exercises and pastiches, most of it written in a tone less somber than playful.

Alarmingly, Nielsen's dogmatic reading convinced him that Jacobsen was an algolagnic—a term introduced by the German physician Albert von Schrenck-Notzing in 1892 to describe sexual masochism.[18] Jacobsen's entire literary career, Nielsen argues, is a confession of masochistic desire—his pleasure at the thought of merciless submission, of being treated with contempt, of being insulted and downtrodden by someone in a position of power. Once again, however, Nielsen relies on a rather selective and didactic reading of Jacobsen's novels, mistaking the thoughts and feelings of his characters to be those of the author himself.

Inevitably, Jacobsen was also thought to be gay. In his 1908 book *De homoseksuelle* (The Homosexuals), his friend Emanuel Fraenkel, perhaps responding to rumor or maybe preempting it, felt compelled to remark that on the few occasions they had touched on the subject, Jacobsen hadn't seemed noticeably interested in homosexuality. And yet speculation persisted. In 1912 the German writer Hans Blüher (known also to Kafka and Thomas Mann) published an essay in the psychoanalytical journal *Imago* called *"Niels Lyhne* von J. P. Jacobsen und das Problem der Bisexualität" (*Niels Lyhne* by J. P. Jacobsen and the problem of bisexuality). Later still, the German psychiatrist Wilhelm Lange-Eichbaum "outed" Jacobsen as a latent homosexual in his 1928 *Genie. Irssin und Ruhm* (translated in 1931 as *The Problem of Genius*). The offending passage most often cited on this issue is a description of boyhood from *Niels Lyhne:*

> Of all the emotional relationships in life, is there any more delicate, more noble, and more intense than a boy's deep and yet so totally bashful love for another boy? The kind of love

that never speaks, never dares give way to a caress, a glance, or
a word, the kind of vigilant love that bitterly grieves over every
shortcoming or imperfection in the one who is loved, a love
which is longing and admiration and negation of self, and
which is pride and humility and calmly breathing happiness.[19]

Both *Niels Lyhne* and *Marie Grubbe* are filled with passages ripe for the enterprising psychoanalyst to deconstruct.
In both novels Jacobsen presents surprisingly nuanced and
complex portrayals of both male and female desire—proof,
surely, of Jacobsen's inclusive imagination and admirable
powers of sympathy. To be sure, the subconscious is a powerful current in all of his writing. Not surprisingly, Freud wrote
to Wilhelm Fleiss in 1895 that *Niels Lyhne* "has moved me
more profoundly than any other reading of the last ten years;
the last chapters I recognize as classic."[20] But as far as Jacobsen's own sexual desires go, we remain in the dark. As a recent
biographer sensibly points out, his "writing and his illness
probably inhibited his desire to pursue and fulfill whatever
relationships he nurtured in his fantasies."[21]

The most significant relationship of Jacobsen's "crisis years"
was his friendship with Anna Michelsen. Anna's home on
Storegade in Thisted was a place where local children often
came to play, encouraged by Anna's widowed mother, Jensine,
who enjoyed being surrounded by so much life and laughter.
(Anna's father died when Jensine was in her early thirties.)
The children put on plays or told stories, and no doubt Jacobsen endeared himself to Anna by showing off his literary tal-
ents. They sent each other playful poems and riddles, little
messages whose intimacy is betrayed by the almost private

language in which they were written. They plainly touched something in one another. "You and Anna are even bigger dreamers than I was," Jensine told Jacobsen. "You wrap yourself up with your books and your plants and she with her sewing and her thoughts."[22]

Yet even this relationship remains half-shrouded in mystery. After her death in 1924 Anna's surviving family burned Jacobsen's letters to her, and among Jacobsen's friends there was some uncertainty about what exactly had happened between the two. "Tell me everything you know and everything you can sniff out about this Ms. Anna Michelsen J. P. was in love with or who was in love with him," Vilhelm Møller writes to William Jacobsen in 1886, presumably while researching his abandoned biography of his late friend.[23]

All we really know is that Anna and Jacobsen slowly grew apart in the summer of 1865, even though Jacobsen often came to visit when the Michelsen family decamped to Copenhagen that fall, their apartment in Vesterbro becoming a kind of meeting place for the Thisted diaspora. Yet the two years Jacobsen had already spent in Copenhagen had distanced him from the safer, provincial world he'd left behind in Thisted—a world Anna, for better or worse, still very much represented from his perspective. Anna seems to have intuited this. "Peter is flaky and now we're boring him," she told her mother.[24] Though Jacobsen spent Christmas that year with the Michelsen family, the distance between him and Anna continued to grow. In October 1866 she sent him a letter saying she'd decided not to speak to him again, "for you have shown by your silence that you no longer care about me."[25] The letter breathlessly continues:

There was a time, Peter, when there wasn't a thought or a feeling I would've hidden from you; when did everything change, is it my fault or yours? It's as though I've suddenly gone from being a child to being old; I've become estranged from my childhood friend, I barely recognize myself anymore, where is my old home, where are the old familiar faces, I am a stranger among strangers. . . . I have now spoken to you from my innermost being; I know you better than yourself; I know how much good and noble there is in you; I have so many beautiful thoughts to thank you for; I know you will be victorious in your struggles, and I hope that when we meet again, God knows where, then we'll both realize that everything comes to us from a loving father's guiding hand that does not burden his children with more than they can bear.[26]

We can imagine Jacobsen's reaction to the letter's cloying religious sentiment. A few months later he confided to a short-lived diary: "I *am* not a Christian; I *have* been one," just as he'd responded to one of Anna's poems admonishing him not to "let God's light around you darken" by denouncing attempts to coerce his feelings about religion.[27]

Yet religious differences were not the only cause of the rift in their relationship. As she grew older, Anna suffered more and more frequently from nervous breakdowns. "Anna is a strange creature," her mother wrote to Jacobsen in 1864; "she lives in a world of her own; I don't know whether I should consider it a good thing or a bad thing."[28] Her grave demeanor and near-fanatical faith, routinely a matter of concern to her family, turned out to be symptoms of schizophrenia. In 1879 she was admitted to a psychiatric hospital for the first time. Her admission journal of May 17, 1879, reads, "The illness allegedly progressed as the result of an unhappy romance some years ago in that the patient, who is very religious, loved a freethinker who never proposed to her."[29] She was admitted again in 1882, this time to Sct. Hans Hospital in Roskilde, where she remained until her death in 1924. Once again her medical charts blamed her illness on "religious crises caused by her fear of committing herself to a childhood friend (the now deceased poet J. P. Jacobsen) because he was a freethinker, though she loved him."[30]

We don't know if Jacobsen ever truly considered Anna to be something more than a very intimate friend, even though his mother, probably responding to town gossip, warned him against an early marriage. Nor is it clear whether Anna was ever in love with him or if her feelings were colored by her illness. Jacobsen, at the time, was not aware of Anna's condition, thinking instead that his coldness was like that of a philosopher-seducer out of Kierkegaard. In a few marginal notes he made in a copy of an art history book by the Swedish critic Carl Gustav Estlander in 1867, this rather fictionalized interpretation of his relationship to Anna excited his imagination. Next to an image of "Cupid and Psyche," a 1798 painting by François Gérard, Jacobsen wrote, "If the exam wasn't so near I'd write a poem about this encounter, with myself like Kierkegaard and Regine. I am after all a Tyrant—god help me."[31] There's some dispute about the exact words—Jacobsen's handwriting in this instance was quite illegible—but the reference to Kierkegaard and Regine is clear. It is unlikely, however, that it's anything more than a youthful embellishment. On the contrary, Jacobsen remained affectionate toward Anna in later years, visiting her when he could and sending her copies of his books. When he later learned that she was not getting the treatment she needed because her mother refused to spend the money, he wrote an angry letter to the widow that resulted in a permanent break.

If these were crisis years, they were also years of restless intellectual discovery. "I am a man who wants to do too many things," Jacobsen wrote in his diary on December 18, 1867. "I'd like to study botany, aesthetics, art history, mythology, and probably much else besides."[32] He later told Vilhelm Møller that he'd already read most of the Danish classics by the time he arrived in Copenhagen in 1863 and that he began devouring Goethe, Schiller, and Wieland when he turned eighteen. At age twenty—in 1867, the denouement of the crisis—he read Kierkegaard, Feuerbach, and Heine. After them it was Shakespeare, Byron, and Tennyson in English, as well as the Eddas, the Icelandic sagas, Sainte-Beuve, and Taine.[33] From his notebooks and diaries we also know he discovered Edgar Allan Poe and Charles Algernon Swinburne around this time.

There's plenty in this catalog that would have excited a young man who'd already begun lifting the anchor of his childhood faith. The liberal reasoning of Feuerbach, Heine, and Taine, mixed with the dark obsessions of Swinburne, Poe, and Kierkegaard, was no doubt a toxic brew. Biblical criticism in particular was much discussed in Copenhagen's student circles. Among the city's intellectual elites the journalist Rudolph Varberg and the philosopher Hans Brøchner were influential proponents of both Feuerbach and David Friedrich Strauss. An 1867 diary entry betrays Jacobsen's familiarity with their ideas: "Christianity, as it exists in the Bible, seems to me too contrary to nature, too contradictory, for me to quietly accept it; I view it as a mythology no different from the Greek and the Norse, and in a thousand or maybe ten thousand years Christian mythology will be part of a general education, especially in the study of the literature of the past."[34]

Jacobsen's exposure to these ideas came as a result of his move, in August 1866, to a boarding house on Studiestræde 18 in Copenhagen's Latin Quarter, a cluster of narrow streets and colorful building fronts near the University of Copenhagen. He rented a room on the third floor of a building owned by an elderly woman, Marie Zoffman, with whom he would remain in touch for much of his life. Edvard Brandes later described Jacobsen's living conditions: "The two-ended room was furnished with a table and sofa on one side and a bed against the wall on the other. By the window was a desk. Around it, in considerable disorder, books, bottles with green algae . . . a box with white mice, and around Christmas time usually a basket of baked goods sent from home. This room knew nothing of splendor, or coziness, or comfort; it barely knew cleanliness."[35]

Despite these Spartan surroundings, Jacobsen was ensconced in a lush intellectual environment. His fellow lodgers included the Finnish sculptor Johannes Takanen (who like Jacobsen would die in 1885); Emanuel Fraenkel, a medical student; the theologian Poul Kierkegaard, translator of Ludwig Feuerbach, son of Peter Christian Kierkegaard, and nephew of the famous Søren Kierkegaard; and H. S. Vodskov, a literary critic and translator of Hippolyte Taine's *History of English Literature*. Within a few years, the Danish translators of Feuerbach, Taine, and Darwin would all be sitting within shouting range of each other, separated only by creaking floorboards or peeling drywall.

They called themselves "Studiestræde's circle of geniuses."[36] The most notable among them was undoubtedly Poul Kierkegaard. He was five years Jacobsen's senior and as eccentric and unstable as his heritage might lead one to suspect. "My uncle became Either-Or, my father became Both-And, and I remained Neither-Nor," he acidly remarked.[37] In rebellion against his pious family tradition and despite having obtained a degree in theology with high honors, Kierkegaard led a troubled, dissolute life in Copenhagen, drinking and running up debts wherever he went. Jacobsen once compared him to Hamlet, remarking that he possessed not just the Danish prince's existential doubts but his ferocity and indignation too. Kierkegaard, indeed, was often unstable emotionally. At a gathering of students he was described drinking "his usual morning potion: half a beer and two glasses of bad cognac. Then he walks up and down the room, the entire congregation in his thrall, quoting Goethe, Heine, Renan, Feuerbach, and Stiraer . . . a divided nature, an informed and highly intelligent man with a dangerous spiritual inheritance."[38]

In 1872, after having gone missing for twenty-four hours, Kierkegaard was admitted to a remote psychiatric hospital in Oringe, near Vordingborg, and diagnosed with schizophrenia. He never fully recovered. The majority of the next few decades of his life were spent in isolation in Aalborg, where he wrote little collections of satanic verses.[39] "He appears to me like a ghost," Fraenkel wrote after visiting Kierkegaard, "a kind, loveable ghost from my youth."[40] When Jacobsen visited him in Aalborg in 1877, he told Vodskov that he found him "tired, so very tired. I don't know, it seems to me that he's spinning the same old wheel, round and round, forever retracing his footsteps. I know we all do that to some extent, but at least the rest of us can peer out through the bars on occasion, to look at the sun, at all the darkness out there."[41]

In his calmer and more lucid moments, however, Poul Kierkegaard was a commanding intelligence, and he made a lasting intellectual contribution to Jacobsen's thought by introducing him to the work of Ludwig Feuerbach, whose *Essence of Christianity* (1842–1843) he was haphazardly translating during the Studiestræde years. Feuerbach's claim that God was merely a projection of human needs was absolutely central to Jacobsen's disillusionment with religion (as indeed it had been to George Eliot some years earlier), and the disillusionment is succinctly articulated by Niels Lyhne when he famously declares, "There is no God, and the human being is His prophet!"[42]

Of all his friends in Studiestræde, Jacobsen was closest to H. S. Vodskov. "No one taught him more, and no one had influenced his intellectual development more," Fraenkel told Anna Linck, an early biographer.[43] Yet like Kierkegaard, Vodskov had his demons. In Fraenkel's unsparing words, "His life was a tragedy. The tragic element lies in the disparity between his enormous gifts, his healthy genius, and his poor, sick body."[44]

Vodskov battled a severe depression his entire life and suffered a number of nervous breakdowns. He quit school at a young age to volunteer for the war in 1864, was often impoverished, and resided in Zoffman's boarding house until 1887. That same year, he turned down a prestigious offer as a university lecturer, gave up writing literary criticism, left Copenhagen, and spent the next twenty years studying ethnography and religious history while living alone on an island in Möckeln, a lake in southern Sweden. One might therefore be forgiven for assuming the Studiestræde years to have been among Vodskov's happiest. There, at least, he had Jacobsen; together they read English literature and acquainted themselves with the work of Charles Darwin; they wrote to one another in an endearing blend of French, English, and Danish. Vodskov wrote to thank Jacobsen for his friendship when, during a breakdown in 1871, he attempted to shoot himself. "I merely want to thank you in a few words, you whom I have to thank for elevating such a large part of my life with—no, the words won't even be my own—d'affection, de confiance, de douces et inoubliables causeries et de cette securité du coeur, le bien le plus precieux de l'intimité."[45]

But Vodskov was both thin-skinned and deeply self-conscious, and his need for reassurance from his friends, particularly Jacobsen, could be off-putting. Jacobsen in turn could be distant, fickle, and almost unreachably introverted, so perhaps it is not surprising that their friendship eventually reached an impasse. The more Jacobsen fell in with Georg and Edvard Brandes in the early 1870s, the more it infuriated Vodskov, who could not resign himself to the factional style of the Brandes brothers or to the political militancy of their criticism. He didn't believe literature needed to tow a party line. In fact, Vodskov may have understood better than Jacobsen that proselytizing for a literary-political cause was not something Jacobsen was temperamentally suited for. In the introduction to his book *Spredte Studier* (Scattered portraits, 1884), Vodskov assumed a defensive, even slightly aggrieved, tone:

> It was neither an easy nor a thankful task I set for myself when I wrote these essays. To combat our current breed of Free-thinkers while proclaiming the right to free thought; to unite the rightful appreciation of the scientist and critic Georg Brandes with a sufficiently firm protest against the polemicist; to reproach our reading public's injuriousness toward so many of the best writers of the left and simultaneously guard oneself against that same left as an entity and party; above all, to call irrelevant our entire accursed mishmash of literature and politics, whether under the guise of "right" or "left"—all of this is terribly difficult, and the value bestowed upon it by party followers is rather predictable.[46]

Vodskov broke with Jacobsen in 1872. He sent him a wounded letter, accusing Jacobsen of a tendency to discard his friends once he'd gotten what he needed from them. "You can no more continue to associate with them than you would keep a lamp that doesn't light up," he wrote. They kept in touch but never regained the intimacy of the Studiestræde years. After Jacobsen's death, Vodskov wrote, "I cannot help but feel that it would have been better for both of us if we hadn't parted ways. But it couldn't have been otherwise. We'd been too close to each other to settle for only half a friendship."[47]

Though Jacobsen pursued both literary and scientific interests, he never felt that they were in any way incompatible. On the contrary, he saw it as his special "calling" to find some way of uniting the two:

> There are moments in my life when I think that the study of Nature is my life's calling; but at other times it seems as if

poetry should be my vocation, and this occurs precisely when some fine poem has aroused my enthusiasm or when I have been reading Nordic mythology. If I could transfer Nature's eternal laws, its delights, mysteries, and miracles into the world of poetry, then I feel that my work would become more than commonplace.[48]

Everything changed in the fall of 1867 when Jacobsen enrolled at the School of Natural Sciences at the University of Copenhagen. At long last he could dedicate himself entirely to botany, the pined-for mistress his parents and teachers had kept him from with all their instructions and prohibitions. In his first year as a university student he studied chemistry and zoology and embarked on a research trip to Bornholm, an island in the Baltic Sea twenty-three miles south of Sweden. Oddly enough it was his mother who sent Jacobsen the money for the trip, a generosity he did not let pass unnoticed. "I thank you as sincerely as I can," he wrote to her, cautiously adding, "My only regret is that [the money] has to come out of your own pocket, as this trip is by no means for leisure but for my studies."[49]

Set him loose in a flowerbed or drop him into a bog somewhere and Jacobsen was in his element. Bornholm, an isolated and sparsely populated island, teemed with undisturbed flora. In a letter to his mother he said the local botanical society in Svaneke had invited him along on a trip with an assortment of "counselors, commanders, doctors, adjuncts, and professors," none of whom managed to find anything noteworthy. Jacobsen couldn't resist mocking them. "When I set foot here on the first day, I'd already found three plants that were new to Bornholm," he bragged.[50]

Not without reason. Jacobsen was undoubtedly a passionate and highly skilled botanist. Though he always portrayed himself as idle and lackadaisical, especially as he withdrew into his "living funeral" in later years, he was incorrigibly focused and detail-oriented. He *loved* flowers, colors, the play of light on a surface. His every work is a testament to this love. In a single passage in *Niels Lyhne* we see snowdrops, crocus blossoms, yellow primroses, blue violets, daisies, gentians, anemones, dandelions, and "hundreds of other flowers." In the same novel we see the "gentle periwinkle, Rousseau's favorite flower, sky-blue the way no sky is ever blue."[51]

Jacobsen could be lush and overindulgent in his descriptions, thickly caking his prose in layers of luxurious color, but he possessed a remarkable double vision: the ability to look at a flower or plant from the perspective of an artist and scientist simultaneously. At his finest, he perfectly imbricated his botanical knowledge with his metaphorical talent. In an early chapter in *Marie Grubbe* we see southern wormwood that had "slung itself in bands of white here and there, around thirsty busy lizzies, Japanese lanterns, wallflowers and carnations, which were standing, their heads together, like sheep in an open field."[52] Notice how Jacobsen, like a botanist, begins by carefully cataloging the flowers and then how the sentence breaks suddenly into metaphor, as if the artist had stepped in to quell the scientist. It's an unusually perceptive person who can see something about which he knows everything—a plant or flower, say—as something *other* than what it is.

Perhaps because they sensed a change in their son's work ethic, Jacobsen's parents objected less and less to his scientific interests. Certainly they now had every reason to be proud. In the summer of 1870 Jacobsen traveled on behalf of the Danish Botanical Society to Anholt and Læsø, two remote islands in Kattegat midway between Jutland and Sweden, and he produced an exhaustive catalog of the plants he found there—a catalog researchers would refer to for years to come. He returned home to Copenhagen with dozens of new plant specimens preserved in a herbarium that doubled in size every few months. In scientific circles within the university, Jacobsen was beginning to make quite a name for himself.

In 1870 the university announced a gold medal competition for the study of a family of green algae known as *Desmidiaceae*, results to be submitted by December 1872. Jacobsen felt that it had been designed with him in mind. He immediately wrote to his father and asked him for money to buy the microscope necessary to carry out his research. "Since I am the only Danish botanist currently occupied with the topic in question, I consider it my duty to respond," he wrote, adding for good measure, "In botanical circles here in the city it is rumored that the study has been conceived out of consideration for me."[53]

To hear their son speak of his "duty" to the university must have been a first for Jacobsen's parents. Had he finally pulled himself together and started taking responsibility for his own life? Did Jacobsen's letter sway them both, or did his mother give the performance of a lifetime to convince her husband of *his* duty toward their son? Whatever the case, it took no more than ten days for the money to reach Jacobsen. He must have been flabbergasted. He sent his father a brief note of gratitude, followed by a lengthy letter to the entire family a few days later on December 23, 1870:

Of all the wonderful things a person can have in this world, few are as significant as a happy childhood; if the road ahead seems long and burdensome, if wind and rain oppress you, then at least the memories of childhood are light and bright and always a comfort to turn to. Thank you, precious parents, for giving me so kind a refuge from gloomy thoughts: the memory of a happy childhood.

I must also convey my gratitude for the generous Christmas present I received the other day. It gives an incredible confidence to one's ability and hard work to know that one has the same resources as others. Rest assured I've already been busy; I bought a little desk for the microscope and test tubes to stand on [the desk]; to the right of them is a large stack of all the necessary materials, and to the left the chemical-biological reagents gleam in their glamorous bottles.[54]

Jacobsen's research for the study, which would occupy so much of the next two years of his life, took him across the entire country. He spent a summer rummaging around Thy and traveled from Vejle to Varde, from Silkeborg to Viborg. The *Desmidiaceae* algae are especially prevalent in bogs and wetlands, so Jacobsen could often be spotted in shallow water out in Lyngby or Ordrup, up to his elbows in moss and dirt. It was half-jokingly said that there was not a lake or a bog in all of Denmark that Jacobsen hadn't waded in.

His diligence proved worthwhile. In the spring of 1873 he was awarded the university's gold medal for his study, titled "Aperçu systématique et critique sur les desmidiasées du Danemark." In a moving gesture he sent the gold medal itself to his parents. "It is really you who ought to receive the medal," he wrote, "because ultimately it is owing to the excellent schooling and education you have provided me with that I was able to win it."[55] According to the Danish botanist Thyge

Christensen (1918–1996), Jacobsen's study remains the only overview of this particular family of algae ever carried out in Denmark.[56]

When he wasn't knee-deep in a bog somewhere or bent over his microscope in Studiestræde, Jacobsen had become a regular fixture at the Student Union in Krystalgade. He and Vodskov often dined there. The food was bad but the conversation engrossing; all the most controversial topics of the day were hotly debated amid velvety clouds of tobacco smoke: new French literature, socialist politics, aesthetics, atheism, and the latest advances in the natural sciences. Jacobsen quickly earned a reputation for his reticent but authoritative intellect. When he deigned to peer out of his shell and speak, people listened. "You're so conservative, you still walk around lamenting the abolition of Negro slavery!" he once rebuked a fellow speaker.[57]

It was also here that Jacobsen met Vilhelm Møller, who would remain a lifelong, and indeed his closest, friend. Møller, a former law student, was a restless literary entrepreneur and later a translator of Ivan Turgenev and Charles Dickens. In 1870 he launched *Nyt dansk maanedsskrift* (New Danish monthly), a literary journal modeled on the *Revue des deux mondes* that would take up the most topical social, religious, and political questions for debate. The inaugural issue, published in October 1870, included a short story by Hans Christian Andersen; translations of stories by Turgenev; and an article "On Evolution in the World of Plants," by J. P. Jacobsen.

Jacobsen's brief article was a prelude to a series of much longer essays about the work of Charles Darwin that Vilhelm

Møller commissioned from him between 1871 and 1873. When exactly Jacobsen first stumbled onto Darwin's work isn't known, though presumably he'd come across his name at the University of Copenhagen or at the Student Union or possibly during his own scientific research. In any case it was a fateful and formative encounter.

It is difficult now to fathom the outrage, dissension, and horror that greeted the publication of Charles Darwin's writings in the second half of the nineteenth century. *On the Origin of Species* (1859) and *The Descent of Man* (1871) were like bombs under the traditional Christian understanding of humanity and its place in the natural world. Just as the scientific revolution of the sixteenth and seventeenth centuries had deposed the earth from the center of the universe, so Darwin's ideas displaced mankind as the center of creation. The conclusions to be drawn from these theories—conclusions Darwin shied away from—were disconcerting to many. The timing of *The Descent of Man*, in particular, was alarming; it was published "at a moment when the sky of Paris was red with the incendiary flames of the Commune."[58]

Thus mild-mannered Darwin became "the most dangerous man in England."[59] He was "the pin-up for thinking atheists everywhere"—despite the subtleties and nuances of his own wounded agnosticism.[60] Wrenched from their context, his theories were like Nietzsche's hammer, smashing the foundations of religious and political orthodoxy. "Not only is a death blow dealt here for the first time to 'Teleology' in the natural sciences," Karl Marx noted with glee, "but their rational meaning is empirically explained."[61] Darwin, no doubt alarmed at the reckless application of his theories, would later decline an offer to have the English edition of *Das Kapital* dedicated to him.[62]

Although Darwin's ideas were not entirely new to Denmark, they had yet to reach a broad audience. Jacobsen, beginning with his Darwin essays, thus emerged as the foremost Danish champion of Darwin, a position that would endear him to the radical literary circles of Georg and Edvard Brandes, to whom the theory of evolution was yet another tool in the arsenal of their political and literary assault on Danish society.

For Jacobsen, however, the discovery of Darwin was first and foremost the discovery of an intellectual kinship. What appealed to him above all was the scientific imagination, the attention to detail, the sensitivity to plants and animals everywhere apparent in Darwin's works. The sheer scope and vision of *On the Origin of Species* must have astonished Jacobsen, who after all knew something about scientific research and empirical observation. He was far better placed to grasp Darwin's achievement than any of his literary contemporaries. (Years later, in Rome, he would hopelessly try to explain the theory of evolution to an uncomprehending Henrik Ibsen.)

Nor were Jacobsen's articles primarily polemical. Instead, he rightly saw himself uniquely positioned to explain and advance Darwin's theories to a general readership. The fact that he did so in a lavish lyrical style only distinguished him further. The oft-quoted opening paragraph of "Darwin's Theory," published in *Nyt dansk maanedsskrift* in January 1872, is typical:

> Nature is like a wonderfully great palace with thousands of large halls and small rooms, with shadowy secret passages that lead out into the light of day, and with open galleries that lead

back into gloom and darkness. There are entrance halls with open colonnades where one can walk right in and rooms that are accessible when one pulls firmly at the doors; but there are also many, many doors that it would take decades of effort and care to open, and there are doors where all our ingenuity and exertion would be in vain. For a long time the palace was deserted; many stood afar off and gazed upon its beauty and majesty; a few were occupied in the courtyards, and fewer yet took hold of the closed doors. But now it is bustling; door after door is being forced open, and one person after another comes out of the palace and tells tales of all the wonderful things he has seen there. About a half dozen years ago an old man came out of the palace. He had wandered around for about twenty, maybe thirty, years among the many small rooms, through many winding passages, until he came to a great hall with a marvelous vaulted dome, with great depths and large, wide vistas. And he told of what he had seen in the rooms and the halls. And some thought that he had reached the heart of the palace, but others insisted that he had been dreaming in the courtyard.

The man was Charles Darwin, and what he explained was that every living thing on earth was like a huge garment weaving itself, in which any single thread's form and color determined the other and that, as time passed, became richer and lovelier.

Now we will follow him on his wanderings and learn what he discovered—first in the small rooms, then in the great hall.[63]

Readers who mistook this passage for the opening of a story by Hans Christian Andersen might have been forgiven. Certainly it is stylistically closer to Andersen than to Darwin. Yet the sense of wonder, the imaginative scope, the direct appeal to the reader—all these things betray Jacobsen's passionate sympathy with Darwin's famous closing words: "There is grandeur in this view of life, with its several powers, having been originally breathed into a few forms or into one; and that, whilst this planet has gone cycling on according to the fixed law of gravity, from so simple a beginning endless forms most beautiful and most wonderful have been, and are being, evolved."[64]

In addition to being highly literary, Jacobsen's essays patiently and pedagogically communicated Darwin's theories and discoveries. He displayed his understanding of these theories by contributing his own examples and analogies—a kind of scientific homage, if you will. And though aware of the subversive nature of Darwin's ideas, he was both excited and convinced by what he, like many others, thought of as a massive testament to human progress and enlightenment. In his essay on *The Descent of Man*, he anticipated objections to Darwin's application of the theory of evolution to human beings: "And even if this view, too, should at first glance seem like crass materialism, like a wanton affront to the majesty of humanity—does it not, after careful consideration, turn out to be healthier and nobler than the obscure dreams of Adam and Eve in the elusive garden of Eden, just as it is fundamentally more ideal, in that it points toward perfection with the promise of a steady growth in human intelligence!"[65]

Jacobsen found in Darwinism a rational, scientific narrative that could supplant the religious narrative of his childhood. He allowed that the existence of God was a question that would remain unanswered, but it was equally a question that had lost its meaning. God was mythology; evolution, reality. "Whence knowest thou that the belief in a God at all is not a limitation of man's mode of conception?" Feuerbach asked in *The Essence of Christianity*.[66] Darwin exploded humanity's mode of conception, opening the door to entirely new possibilities of human discovery. Jacobsen was exhilarated.

Jacobsen's essays on Darwin, despite being written for a small literary monthly, did not go unnoticed. In December 1871 they provoked a letter from the formidable bishop and politician D. G. Monrad, the father of the Danish constitution of 1849 and the disgraced head of state during the Second Schleswig-Holstein War. Monrad, who had read Darwin while living in New Zealand for several years, disparaged the so-called "ape theory," dismissing it as quasi-scientific speculation, and mockingly suggested that in order for the theory to be proved, an Ape Academy ought to be established to convert monkeys into people. Jacobsen, undeterred by his opponent's eminence, rose to Monrad's challenge. In his ironizing response he wrote that the proposed academy was quite unnecessary: "From the dawn of the earliest organisms right down to the rise of the first primates, the entire earth has been one big ape academy."[67]

Encouraged by Vilhelm Møller, Jacobsen sought to interest the venerable Frederik V. Hegel, publisher of Gyldendalske Boghandel (or Gyldendal, as it is known today), in a Danish translation of *On the Origin of Species*. Hegel not only agreed to the proposal, but he also suggested Jacobsen translate *The Descent of Man*.

It was an astonishingly bold move by a man not known for courting controversy. And yet the genteel, conservative Hegel is probably the single most influential publisher in Scandinavian literary history. Beginning with Bjørnstjerne Bjørnson in the late 1850s, virtually every Norwegian writer of note in the second half of the nineteenth century longed to be published by him. He was, Bjørnson said, "my fatherly patron." When Gyldendalske published Ibsen's *Brand* in 1866, one of the strongest literary relationships of the time was forged. "When I came into contact with you as a publisher, it was a turning point in my writing life as well as in my circumstances," Ibsen later told Hegel.[68] All in all, some sixty Norwegian authors were published in Denmark rather than Norway between 1860 and 1890.[69]

Jacobsen had originally offered to abridge his translation and supplement it with his own notes and commentary (and thereby lessen the risk of causing offense), but Hegel wisely encouraged him to translate *On the Origin of Species* in its entirety. The book was thus published serially from 1871 onward and subsequently in its entirety a year later. (Jacobsen's translation of *The Descent of Man* appeared three years later, in 1875.) It marked the first occasion of what would be a short-lived but fruitful relationship between author and publisher—a relationship characterized by mutual respect and affection. For fourteen years, Hegel was an unshakeable pillar of support for the ailing Jacobsen, sending him money when he was abroad and going out of his way to ensure that applications for government funding were delivered to the right people. There was little he felt he could refuse Jacobsen, even as he patiently waited (sometimes in vain) for promised novels or loan repayments.

Jacobsen, for his part, was eternally grateful. "My most heartfelt thanks for your patience on this occasion as on many others," he wrote Hegel in late October 1880, "and for the kindness with which you have so readily helped me in difficult times."[70]

CHAPTER THREE

The Modern Breakthrough

It was difficult to account for the repulsion and even terror of
Georg Brandes which I heard expressed around me whenever
his name came up in the course of general conversation.
—Edmund Gosse, *Two Visits to Denmark* (1911)

AT 6 p.m. on November 3, 1871, a large crowd gathered
in Auditorium 7 at the University of Copenhagen's main
building on Vor Frue Plads. Among them were some of Copenhagen's most influential cultural and intellectual elites,
including the future politician and newspaper editor Viggo
Hørup, the poets Holger Drachmann and Sophus Schandorph, and the conservative bishops D. G. Monrad and H. L.
Martensen. Also present were Vilhelm Møller and the twenty-
three-year-old Jens Peter Jacobsen, not to mention a congregation of buzzing newspapermen and journalists. The occasion for their presence was a widely publicized lecture with a
title both vague and grandiose: "Main Currents in Nineteenth-
Century Literature."

Georg Brandes and Jens Peter
Jacobsen (right) in a caricature from
the satirical magazine *Punch* in 1881.
Courtesy of Thisted Museum.

The man standing at the pulpit—his thick, coiffed hair parted dramatically in the middle—was the literary critic Georg Brandes, not yet thirty and already an auspicious presence in Copenhagen's intellectual circles. He was the translator of John Stuart Mill's essay on *The Subjection of Women*, the author of a dissertation on Hippolyte Taine and French aesthetics, and—more forbiddingly—a freethinking Jew in a conservative Christian country. Worse still, he was hell-bent on persuading his fellow Copenhageners that they were living in the provincial backwaters of Europe, sheltered from the momentous social and political storms raging south of the border.

"I consider it a duty and an honor to pay tribute to those principles in which I believe," the young critic opened, "my faith in the right of free inquiry and in the ultimate victory of free thought."[1] Brandes's lectures were designed to awaken Danes—and, by extension, all Scandinavians—from their historical and political slumber. He inaugurated the Modern Breakthrough, a thrillingly productive period of Scandinavian literature that saw the emergence of generations of emboldened new writers who would all, in their own way, attempt to subvert the ossified religious, political, and sexual institutions of Scandinavian society. Brandes was an unapologetic, indeed often courageous cosmopolitan—a "Good European," as Nietzsche later called him[2]—and in his opening lecture he scolded Denmark for its insularity and isolationism. "It has been the misfortune of our small and remote country," he complained, "that it has not produced any great European movement of the spirit."[3]

Brandes was well placed to make such accusations: he had just returned from a year-long journey through England, Germany, France, and Italy, travels in which he had met and befriended Taine, Ernest Renan, and John Stuart Mill, among others. He had read voraciously and kept a watchful eye on current events (the Franco-Prussian War, the Paris Commune, the Capture of Rome) and had grown more and more impatient with the parochial state of affairs back home. A rebellion was brewing. "What one is not inclined to say aloud," he had written in Italy, "I will here admit to: the most lively hatred of Christianity; by my entire heart I shall always take up Voltaire's *Écrasons l'infâme*. I hate Christianity down to the marrow of my bones."[4]

49

While abroad, Brandes had maintained a lively correspondence with Henrik Ibsen, then living in self-imposed exile in Dresden. Ibsen sympathized with the young critic and
detected in his writings a kindred spirit. When Brandes fell ill
in Rome, he received an inspirational letter from the Norwegian playwright: "What matters is the revolt of the human
spirit," Ibsen intoned, "and *you* will have to be among those
who lead the way."[5] Brandes enthusiastically accepted this
role. On his way back to Denmark he paid Ibsen a visit in
Dresden. As they parted, Ibsen called out to Brandes: "You
shake up the Danes, I'll shake up the Norwegians!"[6]

Main Currents of Nineteenth-Century Literature, Brandes's
lecture-turned-book that over the course of two decades
swelled into a six-volume epic, adopted a panoptic view of
European literature and history, portraying figures such as
Chateaubriand, Lord Byron, and George Sand in an attempt
to trace the evolution of free thought and progress in European letters between the French Revolution and the uprisings
of 1848. Brandes was partly inspired by the example of Taine
and Renan and like them viewed all literature as inseparable
from the spiritual atmosphere of its time. Their emphasis
on the psychology of an author precipitated Brandes's
rejection of the Hegelian aesthetics of his philosophical
studies at the University of Copenhagen. "My university
education," he later wrote, "had been an abstract metaphysical one." He complained of the university professors'
solemn preference for German philosophy: "The existence
of English empiricism and of French positivism was not
recognized."[7]

Yet Brandes was not a philosopher, and his appetite for Taine's positivism was never particularly strong. "Taine looked upon criticism as applied science," he wrote later in life. "But no methodical research can give us the key to a composite human spirit."[8] Perhaps the most obvious influence on *Main Currents* was Sainte-Beuve's psychological and biographical portraiture: Brandes organized his book as a series of comparative studies of the most important writers of the period in a way that recalled the great Frenchman's famous essays. What he added to Sainte-Beuve's formula was an impassioned antipathy to Christianity and an insistence that all good literature was politically oriented toward a reformation of society in the interests of liberty and progress.

Though it would later come to be regarded as a central text of nineteenth-century criticism—Thomas Mann called it the "bible for young intellectuals"[9]—the immediate reception of *Main Currents* was entirely hostile. News of the unrest in Paris in the spring of 1871 was still fresh in the skittish minds of Copenhagen's conservative and national-liberal elites, and though Georg Brandes was no socialist, he was vocally anti-establishment. He wrote in favor of women's rights and the separation of church and state, but he did so with a dogged intent to unsettle and provoke. Accordingly, influential conservative newspapers caricatured him as a licentious, atheist Jew tearing apart the moral fabric of Danish society. D. G. Monrad even wrote a small pamphlet, *Free Thought and Dr. Georg Brandes's Lectures*, in which he lamented that Brandes, once a promising young critic, had proved to be little more than a fiery ideologue.

The reaction to *Main Currents* proved costly. When Carsten Hauch, professor of aesthetics at the University of

Copenhagen, died in 1872, everyone expected Brandes to replace him, but by then his freethinking provocations had gone too far, and his application went unanswered—despite the fact that Hauch had explicitly singled out Brandes as his natural heir. The university's negligence weighed heavily on the young critic. "They say that everyone in the philosophical faculty is against you," Henrik Ibsen wrote to him. "But, dear Brandes, would you want it any other way? Is it not the faculty's very philosophy you wish to take aim at? A war such as yours shouldn't be waged by a royally appointed civil servant. If they weren't slamming the doors in your face it would be because they weren't afraid of you."[10] As a final insult and since the university couldn't find a more qualified candidate— indeed, since there *wasn't* a more qualified candidate—the position remained vacant for almost twenty years.

Brandes continued his lectures into the New Year even as opposition to him in magazines and newspapers swelled. In February 1872 Gyldendal published the first volume of *Main Currents*, titled *The Emigrant Literature*, with an initial print run of 1,200 copies. Stymied by negative reviews, however, sales were discouragingly low; it would take six years for the first edition to sell out. Marginalized, Brandes grew more and more despondent. "Everything looks black," he wrote in his diary. "All roads are closed."[11]

Fortunately his lectures did not fall on deaf ears: the young freethinkers associated with *Nyt dansk maanedsskrift* supported him and invited him to contribute to their journal. Aside from Brandes's essay on Ernest Renan, the first issue of 1872 also featured an article on poverty by Vilhelm Møller, a poem by Holger Drachmann on English socialists, and an essay on Darwin by J. P. Jacobsen.

Brandes had plans for a journal of his own, but lacking the necessary capital and having been declared a persona non grata by Copenhagen's cultural elites limited his options. Through *Nyt dansk maanedsskrift* he managed to secure enough support to establish Litteratursamfundet (the Literary Society, which became known colloquially as the Freethinkers' Society), a more or less unofficial mouthpiece for his ideas. In March 1872 the inaugural meeting took place in the old Restaurant Vincent on Kongens Nytorv 21—the most celebrated banquet hall in Copenhagen, owned by the famous Alexander Vincent and right next door to the Hotel d'Angleterre. Aside from the Brandes brothers, Jacobsen, Vilhelm Møller, Holger Drachmann, and Sophus Schandorph were all present, along with the philosopher Harald Høffding, Poul Kierkegaard, the distinguished poet and literary historian Kristian Arentzen, and a handful of like-minded young writers.

Since many of them had never met before, the meeting got off to an awkward start, but as soon as the food and wine were served, the atmosphere quickly loosened up—perhaps to a fault. Following a speech by Georg Brandes, in which the young agitator outlined the society's goals and advocated for the abolition of the state church, a boozy Sophus Schandorph (fresh from a previous social engagement) stood up and semi-coherently warned that perhaps it would be better to stay with Christianity for a little while yet. By the time sherry was served, the banquet hall looked and sounded more like a public tavern; Schandorph spent the majority of the evening picking himself up off the floor, while Poul Kierkegaard was goaded into reciting the Sermon on the Mount due to his "physiognomic resemblance to Christ."[12] Drachmann's young wife showed up and enjoyed herself immensely, and a few more half-intelligible speeches resounded into the night. Not until the early hours of the morning did the party finally break up. It was agreed by all that future meetings ought to be more scrupulously organized.

If ever Copenhagen deserved its inflated epithet—"the Little Paris of the North"—it was during the 1870s and 1880s. Never before had so many artists, writers, philosophers, and critics clogged the city's cobblestone streets. Strolling down Strøget, Copenhagen's main walking street, passersby could have wandered into Café Bernina, on the corner of Vimmels-kaftet and Badstuestræde, and found Knut Hamsun binge-drinking with the Norwegian painter Christian Krohg or the Brandes brothers presiding over their acolytes during a noisy gathering of local freethinkers. Wealthier patrons may have preferred the d'Angleterre on Kongens Nytorv, just across from the Royal Theater, a stone's throw from the bench where August Strindberg had sat making his first acquaintance with the works of Friedrich Nietzsche. In one of the city's many bookstores they might have picked up an issue of the literary journal *For ide og virkelighed* and read the first Danish translation of a Walt Whitman poem or flipped through a copy of *Ny jord*, containing a fragment of Hamsun's novel *Hunger*, the publication of which turned the starving eccentric into an overnight literary sensation.

Jacobsen, for his part, relished Copenhagen's French-style cafés, which had first appeared in the city in the 1840s.

From early morning to late night agitated young men quarreled amid a clutter of plush sofa cushions and mahogany tables, drinking coffee and bad Hungarian wine and eating Danish pastries or meat stew. "Our literary society more or less lives constantly at the café," Herman Bang wrote in 1882, "and with a certain *laissez-aller* litters its café habits wherever it goes."[13]

Jacobsen was especially fond of Café Peter à Porta, on the corner of Gammel Torv and Nygade, in which the respected and charismatic old actor F. L. Høedt was known to entertain his admirers with stories of the theatrical world. From there Jacobsen would wander over to Café Ginderup or Café Pleisch and drink a so-called "mixus" (a combination of coffee and cocoa) and finally drop by the less appealing Café Mokka Meyer before calling it a night around three or four in the morning—unless he could convince a few friends to join him in Studiestræde for a final salvo of passionate conversation. He was, Edvard Brandes said, an "incorrigible night owl."[14]

Jacobsen had first met Georg Brandes in 1869, when he paid him a visit in his apartment on Krystalgade in order to interest the swashbuckling critic in his poems. Nothing came of this meeting—Brandes politely dismissed the poems without reading them—and their paths wouldn't cross again until a few years later, when they likely met in the Student Union or at Peter à Porta. Jacobsen was already known to the Brandes brothers for his articles on Darwin and for his impassioned and principled reply to D. G. Monrad in *Nyt dansk maanedsskrift*, distinguishing him as an attractive recruit in the cause of *free thought*.

Despite Brandes's advocacy of Jacobsen's talent, however, they were never particularly close. "Your brother Georg and I walked around last night after the lecture and spoke about Danish poetry," Jacobsen wrote to Edvard Brandes in 1873. "God help us, how little we agree."[15] This was hardly surprising. No two people could have been more different than Jacobsen and Georg Brandes—one a skinny, long-haired botanist, the other a combative, cutthroat rhetorician. Jacobsen was silence itself, whereas Brandes, for all his literary activity, was probably more invigorated by conversation and debate than he ever was by reading. (His mother joked that half of the people who attended his lectures were mesmerized young women.)

Georg's younger brother Edvard, on the other hand, was quick to recognize the shy and introverted Jacobsen's need of a friend and companion, someone who both understood and respected his guarded independence. Edvard, too, found social situations uncomfortable, often preferring his own company to a room full of strangers. He helped Jacobsen find his footing in Copenhagen's new literary circles, while the young botanist in turn helped Edvard become more independent of his brother. The biographer Kristian Hvidt even claims Edvard became a better writer as a result of his affinity with Jacobsen and calls his introduction to their published correspondence one of the best things he ever wrote. That might be going too far, but there's certainly no doubting his deep and lasting affection for Jacobsen: "No one was as attentive a listener as he, no one a more caring adviser," Brandes wrote.[16]

Rumors of the circles Jacobsen traveled in raised a few eyebrows back home in Thisted. Fortunately William, who visited Jacobsen in Copenhagen early in the summer of 1872, was kind enough to send their parents a reassuring letter claiming their elder son had not, as they feared, become a socialist: "As for the socialist cause, you can go ahead and relax, it's obviously just nonsense. Peter was very angered to hear that you considered him a socialist and thought him capable of associating with such scoundrels, as he put it."[17]

Nothing could have been further from their son's nature than to mount the barricades on behalf of an abstract political cause—or any other cause, for that matter. Years later he would write to Edvard Brandes: "I am too aesthetic in a good and bad sense to be able to join in such direct procurator-speech-types of works, in which problems are supposedly debated but actually are just postulated as solved"—an almost direct rejoinder to Georg Brandes's exhortation that contemporary literature ought to take social and political problems up for debate.[18]

Jacobsen's antipathy to politics and ideology would always make him a slightly peripheral figure in the Brandes circle. So too would his aloof and reticent demeanor. Edvard described him as "a tall and lanky fellow who didn't know where to put his arms or legs" and to whom it was an ordeal to enter into a crowded room. "He blushed and paled, tripped over his long legs and rescued himself by retreating into a corner as quickly as possible, where he observed everything going on around him."[19] At a Literary Society meeting in March 1872 he was asked to lecture on the works of Charles Darwin. According to his early biographer, Anna Linck, it was "a complete fiasco":

> Dense, unintelligible, [speaking] in a clumsy style he stood there, the glowing and enthusiastic Darwinist, and delivered his lecture without being able to articulate a single word of

what he thought and felt so deeply. He would have been a helpless laughing stock of the entire gathering had he not recently presented a work that had won him the unqualified admiration and esteem of this circle and many others beyond it. He had written "Mogens," and one could forgive the author of "Mogens" an awkward, incoherent lecture.[20]

Jacobsen's novella had appeared out of the blue as far as his friends were concerned. To them he was the modest young botanist, the gangly Darwinist, not the most promising prose writer of the new generation. Yet on a winter's night in early February 1872, when Edvard Brandes and Jacobsen had been lying around in the dreary room in Studiestræde drinking Hungarian wine and eating dry cake, Jacobsen suddenly mentioned that he had been writing poetry since childhood. Brandes, sleepily supine on a sofa liable at any moment to collapse, half-jokingly dared Jacobsen to read some aloud. Retrieving a crumpled-up piece of paper from a drawer somewhere, Jacobsen obliged his friend with mock solemnity:

> Have you lost your way in dark forests?
> Do you know Pan?
> I have felt him.
> Not in the dark forests
> while all silence spoke.
> No, that Pan I've never known.
> But love's Pan I have felt,
> when all that spoke fell silent.

Brandes sat up straight. "Why, you're a poet!" he exclaimed. "Yes, I know," Jacobsen said quietly; "I've always known that."[21]

Edvard Brandes was astounded. "It was quite impossible for anyone else to gauge his thoughts. Nothing in Jacobsen's speech or demeanor had revealed until then that he harbored dreams of being a poet," he later recalled. "His behavior was as modest as his lifestyle was common."[22] Erik Skram, Jacobsen's friend from his student years, was likewise surprised that Jacobsen of all people should have ended up writing "Mogens," effectively inaugurating a new era in Danish literature. "It didn't occur to me in those days that Jacobsen read any fiction," Skram later wrote. "He never made any remark that suggested he had literary inclinations."[23]

Compared to the strong-willed agitators and inflated egos surrounding him, Jacobsen was a lovable eccentric. Everyone respected and liked him, but his social awkwardness made it difficult for him to ever assert himself. Eventually he earned the nickname "His Excellency" due the remote and semi-aristocratic aura that surrounded this kind but quiet being perennially seated in a far corner of the room, his long legs crossed and a habitual cigar burning away slowly between the tips of his fingers.

Jacobsen, of course, was painfully conscious of everything that separated him from literary men of action like Georg Brandes or Holger Drachmann or even his close friend Vilhelm Møller, who in addition to running a literary monthly and translating Ivan Turgenev was now busy raising a family. Jacobsen complained of the innate laziness of his being in a letter to Edvard Brandes:

> And I, the lonely one—I am an ass—I am Darwin's translator; that and my Desmidiaceae are the only useful things I'll ever do. I am the famous sloth or aye-aye, who takes two years to crawl to the top of a tree and, having finally reached the top, simply falls back down again. I am the patient sculptor with a modeling stand, modeling tools, a sculptor's blouse and paper hat and wet

cloths to cover the clay—but no clay, nothing to sculpt from whatsoever. And when you don't have that, when you have neither useful indignation nor passion nor personality, then you might as well sleep away your days and sit up all night at a café and discuss the new d'Angleterre, the new theater, and the old actors or else take your hat and walk straight out of existence, if you have the courage for it. If only said ass could fall in love— wildly, madly, oh God, like an animal!—but no appetite, not at all, no desire for pleasure, lust, no courage or zest for life.²⁴

Jacobsen's comparison of himself to the aye-aye (a type of lemur native to Madagascar) is like a comical predecessor to Camus's *Myth of Sisyphus* (which Jacobsen later foreshadowed in *Niels Lyhne*) and a telling admission of both anxiety and self-irony, two qualities that are never far apart in Jacobsen's letters. Even when he had every right to, Jacobsen never made a fuss of his curtailed existence, always ensuring that any complaint of physical discomfort was at once subdued by a joke at his own expense. It isn't stoicism exactly but rather a quiet acceptance of life *as it is*, of the fact that in most cases we can do absolutely nothing to change it, and that in the end our most cherished ideas and beliefs and convictions are like handfuls of dust thrown against the solid rock of an indifferent existence.

The passage also illustrates a central motif in Jacobsen's life and work: the estrangement of the self from life. Even before he was quite literally prevented from living out his life to the fullest, Jacobsen had become aware of an abyss separating the individual from the world around him—a condition Kierkegaard had written about so perceptively and one that would swell many decades later into a literary and philosophical fashion in the cafés and salons of Paris. The Italian writer Claudio Magris, in his great essay on Jacobsen, calls it a *nos-*

talgia for life: "not for a particular kind of life, the absence of which is lamented, or for some specific object, whose loss makes the writing painful and unhappy, but a nostalgia for life itself, as though it had always been absent."[25]

Jacobsen, like many other writers at the end of the nineteenth century, was responding to a radical shift in humanity's place in the universe. The decline of religious authority, the rise of revolutionary politics, and the advent of evolutionary science represent a paradigm shift in humanity's understanding of itself. It meant that traditional social structures were arbitrary and malleable, that mankind was in control of its own destiny, and that the stern God of theodicy had slackened to atavistic mythology. This is the moment when, as the philosopher Charles Taylor puts it, the limited, static conception of the universe was swept away: "Our sense of the universe now is precisely defined by the vast and the unfathomable: vastness in space, and above all in time; unfathomability in the long chain of changes out of which present forms evolve."[26]

For some, the disenchantment of the universe marked a release from the shackles of tradition and oppression, empowering mankind. For others, the disenchantment was internalized. Jacobsen, like Nietzsche and Dostoevsky, would come to recognize that the unmooring of the self from its traditional place in the cosmos was an ambivalent, and deeply disorienting, experience. "Mogens" was his first attempt to show the lived experience of this disorientation on the small scale of a single human life.

"Mogens" is the story of "a tall, powerfully built man in his early twenties" with a passion for nature who falls in love with, and is eventually engaged to, Kamilla, a local councilor's daughter.[27] Mysterious and enigmatic, Mogens carries no social or cultural baggage; he claims not to read books unless they have Indians in them and admits to taking no interest in politics. When Kamilla asks him if he is a student, he says he is simply "nothing."[28] Later he disparages Kamilla's social circle: "How alike they are, those people! They all know the same things and talk the same way, they all have the same words and the same opinions." When Kamilla challenges him, Mogens remarks, "They annoy me, those fellows. When you look them in the eye, it seems you're almost guaranteed that from now on nothing extraordinary will ever happen in the world."[29] Jealous of the attentions one of Kamilla's male friends shows toward his new fiancée, Mogens stresses, "You *aren't* his, not at all. You are *mine*, you have pledged yourself to *me*, like Doctor Faust did to the Devil, you are mine in body and soul, every inch of you, totally and for all eternity."[30]

One evening a fire breaks out near the councilor's house. Mogens races to the scene and climbs a ladder to try and save Kamilla but is pinned beneath a joist while frantically searching the flame-engulfed building. Unable to move, he watches helplessly as Kamilla plunges to her death:

> Then he heard a groan from the other side of the pit, and he saw something white moving on the floor of Kamilla's room. It was her. She was on her knees, holding one hand to either side of her head as she swayed back and forth at the hips. She stood up slowly and approached the edge of the abyss. She stood rigidly erect, her arms hanging limply at her sides, her head seeming to wobble on her neck; slowly, very slowly, she bent forward at the waist; her lovely long hair swept the

floor—a sudden, brilliant flash, and it was gone; in the next instant she pitched headlong into the flames.[31]

Mogens cannot accept his loss. He succumbs to self-destructive despair and spends the next few years drinking and carousing, driven only by desire and lust. Lying on Bredbjerg Grønhøj one evening, he realizes that "despair had taught him to see everything was unjust and deceitful, the whole world was one great tumbling lie; loyalty, friendship, mercy—all lies, every bit a lie." Love, meanwhile, is merely desire—"burning desire, smoldering desire, steaming desire." Looking down on the town below him, he becomes aware of the gulf separating him from his childhood faith. "And what if they were right, those other people? What if the world were full of beating hearts and the heavens full of a loving God? But why don't I know that? Why do I know something different? And I do know something different, so scathing, bitter, and true."[32]

Eventually, however, Mogens falls in love again, this time with Thora, whose cousin he befriends by chance. Though he struggles briefly with the dark fantasies of his past life of debauchery, Mogens's faith in love is given a chance of renewal. He and Thora marry and are last seen walking happily across a green field toward an embankment with yellowing rye, into which they disappear from view.

What distinguished "Mogens" in the eyes of its contemporary readers was the carefully honed and unconventional style in which it was written. The opening sentence is particularly famous: "Summer it was, in the middle of the day, at a corner of the preserve." There is an immediate lightness, even joyfulness, of effect in those words. Herman Bang would later say that Jacobsen was already a fully formed writer at the time of his debut. "If one knows even the slightest thing about artistic production," Bang wrote, "then one would know that an art such as the one displayed in "Mogens" couldn't have been developed in a single day."[33] There were faint stylistic echoes of H. C. Andersen, but Jacobsen's lavish attention to physical detail had no real precedent in Danish prose. Clearly, his botanical excursions across the country had been literary as much as scientific: "Mogens" was his earliest attempt to fulfill his stated ambition to "transfer Nature's eternal laws, its delights, mysteries, and miracles into the world of poetry."[34] In the opening scene, in which Mogens dozes beneath an old oak tree, for instance, the beginning of a rain shower is vividly, rhythmically described:

> Suddenly a little round dark spot appeared on the light gray soil, then another, a third, fourth, more and still more; the entire mound had turned gray. The air was all long dark streaks, the leaves nodded and swayed, and there was a rushing sound that turned to seething; water poured down.
> Everything glinted, sparkled, spluttered. Leaves, branches, trunks, everything glistened with wetness; each little drop that fell on the ground, on the grass, on the stile, on anything at all, split and scattered in thousands of tiny beads. Here and there little drops hung on and became larger drops, dripped down, joined with other drops, turned into small streams, vanished into narrow furrows, rushed into big holes and out of small ones, sailed away with dust, with splinters and fragments of leaves, depositing them on land, setting them afloat, spinning them around, and putting them ashore once more.[35]

Edvard Brandes later identified this passage as the first instance of naturalistic prose in Danish literature—an orthodox opinion that survives to this day. Generations of critics have drawn parallels between Jacobsen's Darwinism and the literary style of "Mogens." The critic Vilhelm Andersen, for instance, read it as a story of "mate selection," while Aage Knudsen read it in the imposing shadow cast by Émile Zola, who was then beginning to make his mark on Scandinavian literature. In a study of Jacobsen published in 1950, Knudsen writes that "Mogens" is an almost literal illustration of Zola's claim that "art is a corner of nature seen through a temperament."[36] Similarly, the scholar Alrik Gustafson claimed "the central idea in 'Mogens' is that nature *in itself* is sufficient unto the spiritual wants of man, that no romantic 'additions' to it are necessary or desirable. Jacobsen here rigidly rejects, as intellectually dishonest and spiritually superfluous, the supernatural existences with which Romantic poets had invested their nature."[37]

Though Jacobsen wrote "Mogens" while working on his translations of Darwin, the eagerness of critics to interpret it as a literary endorsement of the Darwinian worldview is misguided. If Jacobsen "rigidly rejects" anything in "Mogens," it is surely the entire notion of "a central idea." Far from being an affirmation of an objective view of nature, the story shows us the very difficulty of affirming such a view. In what will be a familiar trajectory throughout his major work, cherished ideas and worldviews are shown to be inadequate to the incongruous, vacillating nature of human existence. Mogens, in any case, has no ties to Copenhagen's intellectual circles, no knowledge of a naturalist worldview—he is an intellectual *tabula rasa.* The man who *does* hold strict views on nature, Kamilla's father, is subtly mocked by Jacobsen: "The Councilor protected nature, he defended it against the artificial; gardens were nothing more than corrupted nature, but gardens with style were nature gone mad. There was no style in nature; our Lord had assuredly made nature natural, nothing but natural."[38] Later, the councilor is seen cutting flowers in his garden.

Mogens, on the other hand, is awakened by Kamilla's death from an untroubled, vegetative existence into an inherently meaningless world of animal desire. By the time he meets Thora, he has begun to control those desires, but he has yet to affirm the indifferent universe surrounding him. Thora admits to believing in trolls and elves while Mogens tries to articulate what it is about nature he feels drawn to:

"I can't explain it, but it's something in the color, in the movement and in the form a thing has, and in the life within it, the juices that rise up in trees and flowers, the sun and the rain that make them grow, and the sand that drifts together into hills, and the rain showers that furrow and cleave the slopes. Oh, it doesn't make any sense at all when I try to explain it."

"And is that enough for you?"

"Oh sometimes it's too much! Far too much! Since there are shapes and colors and movements so delicate and lovely, and beyond all this there's also a mysterious world that lives and rejoices and sighs and yearns, and which can speak and sing about all of it, then you feel so forsaken when you can't get any closer to that world, and life becomes so dull and so oppressive."[39]

At the end of the story, as they walk together into the garden room, Thora compares it to Hansel and Gretel's gingerbread house, then to a Turkish palace, before she is impatiently interrupted by Mogens: "Why can't it just be what it is?" Thora replies that it can—"but that's not enough."⁴⁰

The struggle to endure life as it is foreshadows both Jacobsen's later work, especially *Niels Lyhne*, and his own soon-to-be circumscribed existence. Despite his Darwinism and his place in the company of Copenhagen's freethinkers, he was much more sensitive to this struggle than most of his critics have allowed. The scholar Jørn Eslev Andersen has rightly pointed out that all of Jacobsen's central characters are in fact bad Darwinists—"they differ from any given norm or standard." One of the central themes of Jacobsen's work, Andersen argues, is "the clash between monstrous human nature and biological indifference."⁴¹

Nor was Jacobsen ever really taken with Zola. Heredity and the social environment of his characters were of little concern to him, and despite his remark about transferring "nature's eternal laws" into poetry, he did not think fictional characters were reducible to the scientific method. In any case, we are told next to nothing about the characters in "Mogens." Perhaps this is why Herman Bang said Mogens "stands outside of time." It is, he wrote, "a psychological study in loosely connected images"—impressionistic rather than naturalistic. The Austrian novelist Robert Musil went further. Remarking on the story's "epic breadth," he claimed that it was "really just a circumscribed novel."⁴²

It's possible, as other critics have suggested, that Jacobsen envisioned Mogens as a composite of the European "types" that Georg Brandes called attention to in *The Emigrant Literature:* Rousseau's Julie, Goethe's Werther, and Chateaubriand's René. Similar to Turgenev's notion of "superfluous men," they are individuals who, as Brandes put it, find that a world of possibilities has opened up before them but that their own powers have not quite kept pace. They are thus "thrown back upon themselves, and their self-communings increase their self-centeredness and thereby augment their capacity for suffering."[43] If Musil felt that "Mogens" was too broad to be confined within a short story, then maybe it is because Jacobsen was feeling his way toward the kind of subject matter he would elaborate on in *Marie Grubbe* and *Niels Lyhne*.

Finally, it is worth noting that the emphasis placed by critics on the allegedly naturalistic detail of "Mogens" also fails to account for Jacobsen's transformation of that detail. In the famous scene of the fire, for instance, there are images that recall Charles Baudelaire and point forward to T. S. Eliot. (When Jacobsen writes that "yellow flames licked up along loose moldings and picture frames," it is hard not to think of Eliot's "yellow smoke that rubs its muzzle on the window-panes,/Licked its tongue into the corners of the evening.") What's more, Jacobsen indulges a kind of Shklovskian estrangement, slowing down the process of the reader's perception: "He stopped at the window: one side of the sky was so bright that the snow-covered rooftops melted into it; in the other direction several long clouds were sailing by, and beneath them the air had an oddly reddish tinge, an unsteady rippling glow, a smoldering red haze; he flung open the window; there was a fire over near the councilor's house."[44]

Jacobsen already knew, as he was writing "Mogens," that it was not enough to simply *observe* physical detail, as he did when carrying out his botanical field trips. It had to be molded, shaped, imagined. Facts were for botany; fiction was about images and metaphors. This was a subtle insight for a twenty-five-year-old debut author intoxicated by science to make, yet it was an insight he felt strongly about. Zola, he complained, was monotonous; "constantly he applies his colors with a brush, but then what is a spatula for?"[45]

"Mogens" appeared in *Nyt dansk maandesskrift* in two parts in the February–March 1872 issues. What did Georg Brandes make of his young comrade's first foray into fiction? Though he publicly confirmed the story's reception as a kind of fictional mouthpiece for his literary-critical program, he panned it privately. "Considered as a short story, 'Mogens' is total nonsense to me," he wrote in a letter to the Norwegian novelist Alexander Kielland.[46] Jacobsen's serial indulgence of adjectives and his curiously mannered prose, Brandes felt, were tiresome and eccentric. It wasn't the last time he would make these complaints.

"Mogens" was nevertheless a breakthrough—literary as well as personal. Jacobsen was now a published writer of fiction; the cherished dream of his teenage years had been fulfilled. His mind was already brimming with ideas for more stories. From Varde, a little town on the southwestern coast of Denmark, Jacobsen wrote to Vilhelm Møller that he was already working on two new stories. "I'm a little unsure about which one to begin with, one called 'Lorentz' or one called 'Sodom and Its Glory,'" he wrote, adding, "In the event that anyone says something good or bad about my friend Mogens, maybe you could write me a few words about it."[47]

In the summer of 1873 the now twenty-six-year-old Jacobsen embarked on his first trip abroad. In late June he set out by way of Lübeck and Berlin to Dresden, where he had arranged to meet Edvard Brandes and his new wife, Harriett. From Dresden he wrote to Georg Brandes complaining about the German food, particularly something called remoulade: "It's a nightmare of condensed milk, sugar, salt, and vinegar that swells in fat waves across all kinds of seafood. . . . I wish it would be decreed in Danish churches that upon entering one received a spoonful of remoulade, then I'd show you a land of freethinkers; God help me there wouldn't be a soul left in the state church."[48]

From Dresden the three friends traveled onward to Prague—"a delightful old city," as Jacobsen wrote to his parents. "I can feel I am getting closer to the South; there are fruit sellers on every street corner with ripe apples, peaches, and apricots. . . . It is beyond beautiful here in Prague."[49] After the Bohemian capital they reached Vienna in time for the Weltausstellung, or World Exhibition, a hugely anticipated fair at the Prater that was marred by bad weather, a cholera epidemic, and the financial crash of May 9. It's possible Jacobsen ran into Henrik Ibsen there; the Norwegian playwright was serving as an arts juror and spent most of the summer in the Austrian capital. Despite the crisis and the threat of disease, Ibsen was impressed by what he saw. In particular, he felt the exhibition would help correct the mistaken notion that "the Slavic race is taking little or no part in the great common work of civilization. . . . I maintain that Russia has a school of painting equal to that of Germany, France, or any other country." Such an assessment would have been news to Fyodor Dostoevsky, who grumbled in his diary about the exhibition, convinced that Europeans would fail to understand the Russian arts. Our Russian national landscapes, he said, "will create no great effect in Vienna."[50]

Jacobsen was more interested in the Hofburgtheater (now the Burgtheater), where the celebrated actors Adolph Sonnenthal, Josef Lewinsky, and Charlotte Wolter were then in their prime. This was the theater Stefan Zweig called "the microcosm that mirrored the macrocosm, the brightly colored reflection in which the city saw itself," and whose barber the young Zweig would frequent in the hopes of hearing a little gossip about Sonnenthal or Wolter. "To have one's play given at the Burgtheater was the greatest dream of every Viennese writer," he wrote.[51]

A little more than a kilometer southeast of the Hofburgtheater was the newly erected Musikverein, home of the Vienna Philharmonic Orchestra, a building designed by Theophilus Hansen, a Danish architect known to the Brandes brothers. Four decades later the Musikverein's ornate Great Hall would be the setting for the premiere of Arnold Schoenberg's "Gurrelieder," the famous cantata based on Jacobsen's early poems. It would be Schoenberg's biggest success yet.

From Vienna Jacobsen, Edvard, and Harriett traveled west to Munich, stopping along the way to hike at Berchtesgaten, and then continued through Innsbruck to Riva, where they stayed at the Hotel Sole d'Oro, in whose "magnificent hotel garden" Jacobsen's Niels Lyhne later overhears the enchanting Madam Odéro singing:

> The fresh scent out there, the curving swells which, smooth and clear as glass, rose and fell beneath the garden wall, and the whole exuberance of colors on all sides—blue lake and sunburned mountains, and white sails that fled across the lake,

and red flowers arching above her head—all this and then a dream she could not forget that was still cradled against her heart. . . . She could not remain silent; she had to take part in all this life.[52]

Edvard Brandes later claimed that although Jacobsen did not actually encounter a Madam Odéro at the hotel, there was an Italian hostess whose generous attentions did not go entirely unnoticed by Jacobsen.

"To travel—that is life and happiness," Jacobsen wrote.[53] According to his companions, he was "from morning to evening youthfully and enthusiastically eager to see everything worth seeing."[54] He absorbed scores of galleries and museums and took careful note of works by Rubens, Michelangelo, and Correggio. In Innsbruck he saw a passion play performed by three hundred peasants that lasted more than five hours. To his family back home he sent excited letters eagerly documenting the many new sights he encountered, letters that sometimes touchingly revealed his provincial origins: "The vines hang full of grapes," he wrote from Riva, "and they are as common here as potatoes in Thy."[55]

The variety of trees and flowers he encountered completely absorbed him: "Laurel trees and cypress trees, between them apricot trees and olive trees, fig trees along the road that aren't ripe yet. Oleanders in the open air grow to be three times as tall as I am and are quite red with flowers. . . . I have stood at my window a moment and looked up toward the mountains and along the lake; the sun has retreated; it's four o'clock; it is once again possible to venture outside."[56]

But by the time the travelers reached Italy, something was amiss. While on his way to see the Santi Giovanni e Paolo

Church in Venice, Jacobsen was suddenly overwhelmed by abdominal pains and diarrhea. He was raced back to the hotel, where he was told to rest for a few days—the thought being that summer heat and an unfamiliar diet were to blame for his illness. A few weeks later, in Florence, Edvard and Harriett went to Jacobsen's room at their hotel to find their enthusiastic companion sunk in a chair, looking unusually pale and anxious. "What's wrong with you, are you sick?" Edvard asked. "No," Jacobsen replied, "I'm not sick, but I spat out blood."[57]

While brushing his teeth that morning, Jacobsen suddenly discovered his mouth was filled with blood—not, as he initially thought, from cutting his gums with his brush but from suffering a minor hemoptysis; he was coughing up hemorrhaged blood, a telltale sign of active pulmonary tuberculosis. It was not an uncommon infection in Jacobsen's family, so chances are he recognized the symptoms. Though he didn't mention it in his letters to his parents, he made it clear that he'd exhausted his appetite for travel and would be returning home shortly. "If only you knew how I long for pan-fried fish and a Danish aquavit!"[58]

Two months after Jacobsen returned home, a friend in Copenhagen wrote to the municipal hospital in Thisted where Jacobsen was being treated to inquire about his condition. The doctor explained that on his return from his travels, Jacobsen's condition had been "highly alarming." He had lost a considerable amount of weight and suffered from both coughing fits and night sweats. Further examination of the patient confirmed tuberculosis of the right lung. A prolonged sojourn in Egypt would be ideal, the doctor opined, but also admitted that so far recuperating in the home of his parents in Thisted had done the young patient a world of good. "Whether he will be able to reach his previous work rate," the doctor concluded, "is difficult to say."[59]

Because tuberculosis has an "undefined incubation period,"[60] there's no way of determining exactly when Jacobsen was exposed to *Mycobacterium tuberculosis* (the bacterium that causes most cases of tuberculosis). Some of his early biographers suspected that exposure to cold weather and a damp environment—wading around barefoot in a bog, for instance—were to blame, while others have written vaguely of Jacobsen's having a "weak chest" in his youth. It is more likely, however, that he was exposed to the bacteria in Copenhagen; tuberculosis flourished in areas of overcrowding, malnourishment, and poor living conditions. In the nineteenth century it was regarded as "the great killer of industrialization and rapid urbanization."[61] In Denmark it was the cause of 14 percent of all deaths between 1890 and 1899 alone.[62]

Little was known about tuberculosis at the time, despite its epidemic sweep through the industrializing capitals of Europe in the eighteenth and nineteenth centuries. It was not even identified as a single disease until the 1820s. In the 1860s the Frenchman Jean Antoine Villemin eventually proved its contagiousness, though it was not until 1882 that the German bacteriologist Robert Koch identified the tubercle bacillus (a discovery for which Koch was later awarded the Nobel Prize in physiology or medicine). Until then, however, tuberculosis— or consumption, as it was commonly known—was widely regarded as a condition that disproportionally affected sensitive young men. As Susan Sontag put it in her seminal essay "Illness as Metaphor," "The person dying (young) of TB really was perceived as a romantic personality." Consumption was synonymous with resignation, with being unfit for earthly life. It was invariably a kind of exile from life, a "retiring from the world without having to take responsibility for the decision."[63] It was a culturally visible disease precisely because it had an air of glamor about it: it was the fashionable disease of John Keats and Emily Brönte, of Puccini's *La bohème* and Verdi's *La traviata*. "Opera as tuberculosis reached an apogee in the nineteenth century," as Helen Bynum caustically puts it.[64]

The myth of tuberculosis as an edifying disease was probably scant comfort to Jacobsen. He was given a rather grim sentence of a few of years at best; at the age of twenty-six such a diagnosis must have been a demoralizing blow. If he despaired, however, he left no trace of it; outwardly he assumed an armor of understatement: "As far as my health is concerned," he wrote to his landlady in Copenhagen, "my chest isn't exactly as it should be, and there's something slightly the matter with one of my lungs."[65]

Jacobsen spent a year in Thisted recovering and fattening up in the care of his family. He enjoyed their longed-for company, but he was also anxious to resume his literary life in Copenhagen. In the ten years since he had first left Thisted he'd become an incurable metropolitan, a denizen of cafés, restaurants, and literary salons. Now he would have to experience it all vicariously, mailman permitting.

He complained to Edvard Brandes that in Thisted "there is no one to talk to, no one who thinks of ideas or has ideas or has even heard of ideas." He was not in any great pain, he reassured his friend, but he had no time to read or write because every moment of every day was spent eating, walking, and taking medication. "I'm only allowed to smoke one pipe of tobacco a day and no cigars whatsoever."[66] To Agnes Møller, Vilhelm Møller's wife, he explained that his days consisted of "(1) going for walks; I know nothing more boring; (2) reading physiology and bad novels; (3) playing scherwenzel and whist; (4) being cranky. Beyond that I live in happy ignorance of anything new—domestic and foreign—literature and everything else."[67]

Despite the light-heartedness of his correspondence with friends, it must be assumed that Jacobsen suffered greatly—physically as well as emotionally. He would spend the remaining eleven years of his life as an intermittently bedridden invalid, with death constantly at his heels—"too weak to live, and not sick enough to die," as Martin Heidegger contemptuously described him.[68] He lost weight, coughed constantly, and had little energy for sustained work. Such is the paradox of the tuberculosis myth: whatever glamor was associated with it, the disease itself was a slow, painful descent into certain death. A friend of the tubercular George Orwell once wrote that spending any length of time in a room with Orwell became increasingly uncomfortable as the disease wasted him away: "It was the rotting lungs that you could smell, not at once, but increasingly, as the evening wore on, in a confined room: a sweetish smell of decay."[69]

CHAPTER FOUR

A Woman without Qualities

Just before the commencement of the last third of the
century which has now closed, the whole reading world of
Denmark was startled by the appearance of a book so new in
its methods, so profound in its analysis of character, so
marvelous in its descriptions of Nature, that it immediately
took rank amid the classics of the country and its author
leaped at once into immortality. The book was the great
historical romance, *Marie Grubbe*, the writer a young man
stricken with a mortal disease—Jens Peter Jacobsen.
—Margaret Thomsen, *Denmark, Past and Present* (1902)

Had I read any of the books she'd lent me?
I hadn't, but said: Yes, I'd read Jacobsen's *Frau Marie Grubbe*.
And what did I think of it?
"It's very good," I said, peevish because guilty.
—Christopher Isherwood, *Goodbye to Berlin* (1939)

Marie Grubbe was a revelation.
—August Strindberg, letter to Edvard Brandes

IN May 1874, the English writer Edmund Gosse embarked on
his second trip to Denmark and made the acquaintance of

Jens Peter Jacobsen photographed
in Montreux, Switzerland, on
April 24, 1878. Courtesy of
Thisted Museum.

Georg Brandes, who at the time was living in Møntergade in
the center of Copenhagen. "In the course of our conversa-
tions," Gosse wrote, "Brandes frequently expatiated on the
theme that a revival in Danish prose was really more impera-
tively needed than one in verse."[1] There was nothing in
Danish prose that could be compared to Walter Pater or
Stevenson, Brandes complained. Gosse reminded him of a
young man whose name he'd mentioned in a letter and of
whose prose writing he'd claimed to have high hopes. "Ah!"
Brandes said, "that must have been been J. P. Jacobsen. Well,

he is the solitary man who shows anything like first-rate promise." He continued: "He is a botanist and a Darwinian, but he has begun an historical romance, of which I have read the early chapters. The style in them is amazing; there has been nothing like it in Danish before. . . . He is the only one, and now—*han dör*, he is dying. He lies hopelessly ill, with consumption, at a little town in the north of Jutland, called Thisted; he will probably die without having produced anything finished enough for publication."[2]

Thankfully, Jacobsen's death was not quite so imminent. In the spring of 1874 he still had eleven years of "broken life" before him, as Gosse put it,[3] and despite his recent sentence of tuberculosis he was determined to continue writing. But the road to recovery was an uphill battle, and much of 1874 was spent simply adjusting to the horizontal life. "Plans?" he wrote to Edvard Brandes in March. "No plans, no travels, no works, nothing. Recover, raw egg yolks, double beer, Swedish bingo."[4]

Because so much of life would now be denied him, Jacobsen developed the touching habit of living vicariously through his friends. He corresponded with their wives, sent them cards on their birthdays, and became a somewhat avuncular figure to their children. He often stayed with Vilhelm and Agnes Møller, either in Copenhagen or out in Humlebæk, enjoying nothing more than a seat in a rocking chair with a cigar in one hand and a hot toddy in the other. Such pleasures, of course, concealed deeper sorrows: Jacobsen occasionally lamented his permanent bachelordom, especially when he received word that someone had gotten married or engaged. "Fraenkel writes that he's gotten married," Jacobsen remarked to Vilhelm Møller in 1876. "Everyone is getting married, while I must walk my darkly path alone."[5]

Jacobsen had begun *Marie Grubbe* in the months before his trip through continental Europe. "Just think," he wrote to Edvard Brandes in March 1873; "I get up every day at eleven and go to the Royal Library, where I read old documents and letters and lies and descriptions of murder, adultery, corn rates, whoremongery, market prices, gardening, the siege of Copenhagen, divorce proceedings, baptisms, estate registries, genealogies and funeral sermons. All this is to become a wonderful novel called *Marie Grubbe: Seventeenth Century Interiors*. You know, she's the one Holberg writes about in his epistles, and Andersen in 'Chicken-Grethe,' and who was married first to U. F. Gyldenløve and later to a ferryman."[6]

The historical Marie Grubbe, born in 1643, was the daughter of the nobleman Erik Grubbe, who owned an estate called Tjele near Viborg in central Jutland. Admired for her beauty, Marie was married in 1660 to Ulrik Frederik Gyldenløve, the viceroy of Norway and the illegitimate son of King Frederik III. Their turbulent marriage was annulled on the king's orders in 1670 after prolonged estrangement and marital infidelity. Following a tour of Europe, Marie was married to the nobleman Palle Dyre from 1673 to 1690, when her open affair with Søren Sørensen Møller, a stable boy half her age, caused a public scandal. Marie was subsequently denounced by her father. She married Møller, and the couple embarked on an impoverished, vagabond existence before finally settling on Falster, an island south of Sjælland, where they ran a small ferry transport. Marie died there in 1718.

Marie's scandalously tragic life inspired several literary works before Jacobsen's novel, most notably Steen Steensen Blicher's novella *The Diary of a Parish Clerk* (1824) and Hans Christian Andersen's story "Chicken-Grethe," as well as the aforementioned epistle by Ludvig Holberg. Holberg had in fact met Marie in the spring of 1711, when an outbreak of the plague forced the young playwright to flee Copenhagen. He traveled as far as Falster and lodged in Marie and Møller's house. Nearly forty years later he described their encounter in his epistle on unusual marriages:

> An example from the history of our time is a noblewoman whose loathing of her first husband, though he was considered by all commoners to be the finest and most gallant of gentlemen in the kingdom, was insurmountable; their marriage culminated in a divorce, and after a second marriage, which likewise had an unhappy ending, she embarked on her third marriage to a common sailor with whom, though he abused her daily, she claimed to be living a much happier life than she had in her first marriage. I heard this from her own mouth when I stayed at her house, which was located by a ferry crossing in Falster, while her husband was under arrest for misconduct. So it seems that what might be abhorrent to others set alight love and pleasure in her.[7]

Jacobsen's decision to write his first novel about an infamous noblewoman's self-imposed fall from grace must have raised a few quizzical eyebrows among his friends. What use was historical fiction in the Brandes-led crusade against the conservative literary establishment? What was its contribution to the social and political issues of the time? What on earth was the appeal of this historical trifle to the talented young author of "Mogens"?

To begin with, for an author with "a deficit in his psychological realm of experience," as Jacobsen touchingly put it in a letter to Vilhelm Møller,[8] there was the explosive nature of the material right there for the taking: love, war, adultery, murder, scandal, royalty, disgrace, and so on. Additionally, the trajectory of Marie's fate was something Jacobsen may have recognized from all the so-called *guvernante romaner* (governess novels) he'd consumed while recuperating in Thisted. It was a genre that focused on the domestic lives of young heroines poised to overcome social barriers on their path to self-realization—or, more often than not, a convenient marriage. Jacobsen had read a shelf's worth of books by Countess Dash, Henriette von Palzow, Baroness Jemima von Tautphoeus, Catherine Gore, and Lady Georgina Fullerton—sometimes, admittedly, because he couldn't get his hands on anything else, the local libraries in Thisted tending not to carry the latest by Flaubert or Zola.

But much more significant is the fact that Jacobsen was fascinated by the counterintuitive nature of Marie Grubbe's fall from grace. The entire seed of the novel lies buried in Holberg's observation that Marie "claimed to be living a much happier life than she had in her first marriage." A noblewoman married into wealth and royalty who ends up living in poverty with a drunk, abusive sailor—and then has the audacity to claim she prefers her new life to the old! Surely this contradiction spoke volumes about human nature. What's more, Georg Brandes had remarked in an essay on Hans Christian Andersen in 1869 that Marie Grubbe was "too much of a character for it to be possible for a fairy-tale writer to explain her nature."[9] Perhaps Jacobsen had read this and saw an opportunity to take up the mantle of one of his favorite writers.

Though he made a habit of jotting down old-fashioned words and could spend hours a day staring at the changing light on historical buildings in the streets of Copenhagen, Jacobsen did not intend for *Marie Grubbe* to simply be a historical romance or a drama of the court nobility. He was intrigued by the transgressive and macabre works of writers like Edgar Allan Poe and Charles Algernon Swinburne and clearly fascinated by the enigma of self-destructive and even masochistic behavior. This is the real locus of the novel. The historical frame, particularly the 1659 assault on Copenhagen by the Swedish Army, which figures prominently in the early chapters, is little more than a backdrop: "On the ramparts the guards were walking slowly back and forth, staring out over a land of darkness where all was quiet, despite thousands of enemy soldiers being encamped out there."[10]

Of course, the real giveaway is the novel's subtitle: "Seventeenth Century Interiors." Frederik V. Hegel, Jacobsen's publisher at Gyldendal, cautiously advised against the presence of any foreign words in the novel's title, but Jacobsen was adamant that "interiors" remain. The book could not be called a story or a portrait, he explained.[11] To Edvard Brandes, who helped publish the book's early chapters in his and Georg's new monthly journal, the auspiciously titled *Det nittende aarhundrede* (The nineteenth century), Jacobsen similarly demanded: "*Interiors* must remain."[12]

Jacobsen's insistence says a lot about his conception of the novel and about the careful thought that went into its architecture. *Marie Grubbe* is essentially a series of carefully constructed scenes or episodes that sometimes exist almost independently of each other. Mikka Haugaard, in the introduction to her 2015 translation of the novel, writes: "We witness a series of moments that curl themselves around the plot of *Marie Grubbe*, but there is no 'and then': this is a modern novel and at its heart lies not so much a story as a vivid sense of the moment, the conjurer's magic with words and place."[13]

The reader's first encounter with Marie is certainly vivid. Adrift in the garden at Tjele, the fourteen-year-old emerges from a Rousseauian thicket of colors and adjectives:

> The air below those crowns of lime trees had swayed across brown heath and thirsty fields; it had been baked by the sun and filled with the dust of the road, but just now the thick, hanging screen of green had made it clear, the cool lime leaves had chilled it, and the scent of yellow lime flowers had made it wet and given it weight. Now it lay there shimmering, quiet and content, in that vault of pale green, caressed by gently trembling leaves and the quick beat of the wings of white and yellow butterflies.
>
> Those lips that breathed the air were full and fresh. The breasts it swelled were small and young. Her feet were tiny, her waist slender and her figure slim. A kind of lean strength lay in her whole body.[14]

It is an enchanting opening—six pages of sensuous, caressing prose in which Marie gathers flowers and fantasizes suggestively of a young woman's brutal imprisonment: "Her body bent forward, she follows him, and the big man puts the palm of his sweaty hands on her naked back and he pushes her ahead. Ahead to the black, snorting stallion. Then they sling her into the grey dust of the road and fasten the long tail of the horse round her ankles."[15]

No sooner do we encounter the young Marie than she is whisked off to live with her aunt Regitze in Copenhagen—a decision Marie's negligent father is pressured into by his housekeeper-cum-mistress, Ane Jensdatter, who resents the well-bred Marie: "Ah'm going to tell ye there's more stubborn in Marie than do her good in th' world," she prophetically (and drunkenly) tells the unsympathetic Erik Grubbe—a man wonderfully described as being "always so much himself that he could never be anything else for anyone. He wouldn't become fourteen years old when he chatted to a fourteen year old, he wouldn't become a woman because he was talking to a little girl. He was always more than fifty, and always Erik Grubbe."[16]

In Copenhagen Marie is as lonely and isolated as she was in Tjele. In stark contrast to the Dano-Swedish War stirring beyond the city's fortifications, her life is a blank book of days upon days of ennui: "What was to become of her? One day was so like another, with nothing to look forward to. Could this go one and on?"[17]

She is awakened from her lonely existence by the heroic exploits of Christian Gyldenløve, the illegitimate son of King Christian IV and commander of the Danish armies: "Suddenly life appeared very different, there was more to the world than the sum of the everyday; that beauty and grandeur, that rich world which was the subject of history books and poems was something one could encounter."[18] During a visit to Madame Regitze's, Christian Gyldenløve and Marie share a furtive kiss, and Marie's imagination is set aflame with romantic longing and erotic desire: "She had a vague sense of being enslaved, of having lost her freedom. It was as if someone had his foot pressing on her neck, as if she had been crushed into the dust and could not rise again."[19]

Marie revels in her secret world of fantasies and dreams until Christian suddenly falls fatally ill—from syphilis, it is implied. His death is one of the novel's most famous and celebrated scenes. As he lies dying, he is attended by a priest whom he scornfully rebuffs: "I want nothing. I'll have none of your Hell or your Paradise. I want to die, just to die, nothing more."[20] But gradually the priest wears down his tough exterior and wins him over with a fearful and graphic vision of hell: "Then go to a place of torment for the eternally damned, where an ungodly host are tossed on the boiling waves of an endless sulphur sea, their limbs torn in sick suffering, their hot mouths gasping for breath among the blazing flames on the surface."[21] When Marie secretly visits Christian in his bedchamber for the last time, she finds not the hero of her dreams but a pathetic, hysterical man whimpering before the God he once rejected and cursing the woman he once desired.

Marie is disillusioned by his death. She decides for herself that "there was no shining figure one could long for, love and worship, no sun to stare oneself blind at till all became one mass of glowing rays and colour. The world was dull, grey and empty, and utterly trivial, insipid and commonplace, every bit of it." Eventually she becomes "pale and wasted."[22]

One is reminded here of Flaubert's Emma Bovary, who is similarly despondent following the ball at Vaubyessard in the early years of her marriage to the hapless Charles. When several months pass without an invitation, Emma finds that the days have become identical: "They would keep following one another, always the same, immoveable, and bringing nothing new." She grows pale and suffers from heart palpitations and longs for "adventure, masked balls, for shameless pleasures that were bound, she thought, to initiate her into ecstasies she had not yet experienced."²³

Likewise, Marie is almost physically pained by the slow monotony of everyday life. Being a woman, hers is an existence spent constantly waiting and being shut up inside, forced to behave according to straitlaced etiquette and suffocating morality. Indeed *Marie Grubbe*, along with *Madame Bovary*, is one of the great depictions of the poverty and tedium of women's lives before the social and political advancements of the twentieth century. It is a tedium not even marriage can undo; Marie finds her life virtually unchanged following her marriage to the decidedly unheroic Ulrik Frederik Gyldenløve (also, a little confusingly, an illegitimate son of the king). She feels like "a prisoner who sees life gliding past, season by season, barren and fruitless. And she felt as if the sum of time was being counted out in her presence, penny hour by penny hour, each and every one of them to fall at her feet with a stray sound as the clock struck before becoming dust; and then a painful longing for life would come over her, and she wanted to wring her hands and scream as if she were being tortured."²⁴

Whatever psychological deficits he thought he had, Jacobsen's portrait of Marie, particularly during her tumultuous marriage to Ulrik Frederik, is uncannily persuasive. His sympathy with a noblewoman's oppressed and inhibited existence is an impressive imaginative achievement. When the boorish Ulrik Frederik, convinced that marital life means simply wasting away with all the other court nobility, embarks on a year-long journey to fight and win glory in Spain, Marie lives in almost total isolation, etiquette demanding that she remain at home. She spends entire days in bed and becomes prone to irrational whims and flights of madness. At one point, she traces a knife along "the course of blue and pale-purple capillaries running beneath her white skin."[25] She even tries biting into her flesh.

In one of the novel's most striking passages, Marie impulsively tries to stab Ulrik Frederik on his return from Spain. Drunk on wine, beer, and his continental exploits, he tries to force himself on his wife. The next morning, as he half-heartedly apologizes for his behavior, Marie lunges at him:

> While she was playing with the knife, she had suddenly noticed Ulrik Frederik's lace shirt was open, and at that moment a sudden, irrational desire had risen within her to strike that white breast with that cold, shiny steel, and she did it, not because she wanted to kill or even to hurt him, but perhaps just because the knife was cold and his chest warm, or because her hand was frail and feeble, his chest tough and tenacious, but mainly because she could not stop herself. Her will had no power over her mind, or her mind power over her will.[26]

Marie's marriage to Ulrik Frederik descends into a decade-long torment, during which he is openly unfaithful and by turns afraid of and in love with his estranged wife. Jacobsen's portrayal of their disintegrating marriage is a brilliant inversion of traditional gender roles. When Marie at one point kisses her husband, she does so "in a moment of serene benevolence, like a king giving a loyal servant a ring as a sign of his royal favour and mercy."[27] Later, when his pathetic and hopeless confession of love is rebuffed, Ulrik Frederik "sank down on the floor and began to crawl about on his knees, snarling like a wild beast and drumming his clenched fists on the floor till the knuckles bled." He then throws himself on his bed and weeps, shouting for Marie "with gentle words of love."[28] Shortly after, Marie dismisses him as a whore—"a cursed and corroded whore, not a man."[29]

Marie, meanwhile, is intrigued by the melancholic Sti Høeg, her thirty-something brother-in-law, a kind of Kierkegaardian aesthete who speaks to Marie of "the companions of melancholy," a secret society of "those who by birth have been given a different nature and temperament from others, who have larger hearts, quicker blood, more ardent longings and passions. They desire more strongly, and their yearnings are wilder, more burning than those of the common crowd of the nobility."[30]

But Marie, in contrast to Sti Høeg's lofty resignation, explains her own suffering as the kind of "grief you feel for a well-concealed defect of nature, some intrinsic damage to the soul, one that makes you completely different from other people." She expresses an insatiable hunger for life yet worries that she has led herself astray. Something within her is broken and cannot be healed. "I don't know, but it seemed to me that the origin of my bitter pain might be that I had plucked a string that must not sound," she says, "and by its tone something within me had been torn so that time couldn't heal it, and I would never find my vigour again to force open the door of life—no, I would have to stand outside, listening to the music at the party, unasked and unwanted, like a crippled maid."[31]

Yet Marie, who longs for warm, full-blooded life, eventually rejects the simpering, sickly melancholy of Sti

Høeg—who looks, Jacobsen wittily writes, "like someone following his own hearse with measured steps."[32] Even the uncharacteristic, manly ferocity he displays during a brawl at an inn cannot efface the weak and nervous impression he otherwise makes on Marie, who dismisses him as a "creeping maggot that can be crushed and has no sting."[33]

When they eventually part ways in Paris, Marie is deflated. She has lost all confidence in herself and in life: "A quiet corner where she could lay her weary head to rest, never to lift it again, that was the total sum of her desires."[34] She drifts about through Europe and arouses the flattering attentions of a younger man in Nürnberg. His affections are not lost on Marie, who feels her old confidence returning—until, with almost comical haste, the young man falls from the saddle of his horse and is dragged to his death. Marie is crushed and sinks into grief. By the time she returns to Denmark, she is thirty years old—divorced, destitute, and deprived of hope. She returns to Tjele and in 1673 resignedly marries the stolid Palle Dyre, a privy councilor.

The Hungarian Marxist critic Georg Lukács wrote that Marie Grubbe's problem was "a typical modern problem" and its historical backdrop almost entirely arbitrary. "As a *typical* destiny Marie Grubbe's story has its place in Jacobsen's own time, the second half of the nineteenth century," he claimed.[35] He, too, saw points of comparison with Flaubert's novels, particularly in the disillusionment of Jacobsen's heroine. Marie, like Emma Bovary, yearns for a kind of "hero" figure, and her disappointment in this quest brings her to a state of almost total ruin. In both cases the disillusionment is not merely romantic or sexual but also metaphysical: both women are repeatedly disappointed in their search for purpose and meaning in life. In his study *The Horror of Life*, the historian Roger L. Williams defines Flaubert's pessimism, or *le bovarysme*, as follows: "At the root of that pessimism was Flaubert's conviction that we are all determined to see ourselves other than as we really are; and, consequently, to aspire to that which is not only unattainable, but which will bring us to ruin. The term implies a hatred for reality, which we seek to escape through the exercise of romantic imagination, the quest ending inevitably in grief."[36] But rather than submit his heroine to a grim and protracted death, Jacobsen does something more subtly provocative: he gives her a kind of happy ending. After sixteen years of uneventful marriage to Palle Dyre (so uneventful, in fact, that Jacobsen dispenses with those years in a single sentence), middle-aged Marie, now "pale and plump,"[37] recklessly engages in an affair with Søren Sørensen Møller, the overseer of the Tjele estate. When the affair is made public, Marie and Palle Dyre are divorced, and Marie is denounced by her father. She leaves Tjele and embarks on a peripatetic existence with Søren Møller. "On the whole," Jacobsen tells us, "they lived together very happily. Marie continued to love her husband more than anyone in the world, and if he was drunk and beat her from time to time, then it did not matter much."[38]

The novel's final tableau is the visit of Ludvig Holberg. He arrives to find Marie Grubbe alone; Søren Møller is awaiting trial for the death of a ship's captain killed under murky, alcohol-fueled circumstances. Holberg lodges at the house for several months and gradually befriends Marie. They spend balmy summer evenings together, talking and staring

out to sea. Holberg cannot fathom Marie's grief at the arrest
of her husband or her preference of Møller over Ulrik Frederik, "who is praised by all as a master of etiquette and fine manners." Marie calmly explains that her preference comes down
to "an irresistible attraction." Holberg is incensed. "We might
as well pack all the morality of the world in a chest and send
it to Hell and live as our hearts desire," he objects. "Don't you
believe in God, my good woman . . . and in the eternal life?"
Marie dodges the question: "I believe that everyone lives their
own life and dies their own death, that's what I believe." Holberg is not convinced: "Do you believe in the resurrection of
the flesh?" Their final exchange is worth quoting in full:

> "And how shall I be raised? As the young innocent child I was
> when I first came out in the world, knowing nothing and no-
> body, or as I was when I was admired and envied, the king's
> favourite, a rich jewel in the court's crown or as the poor, old
> and hopeless Marie the ferrywoman? And shall I have to an-
> swer for the sins they committed, the child, the woman in her
> prime, or is one of them going to answer for me? Can you tell
> me that, Master Holberg?"
> "But you have one soul, my dear."
> "Do I now?" asked Marie, becoming lost in her thoughts.
> "Let me speak to you candidly," she continued, "and tell me
> honestly what you think: do you believe that someone who all
> his life has sinned gravely against his God and Maker, but who
> in his last hour, lying on his death bed, confesses his sin and
> repents with a sincere heart, submitting to God's mercy with-
> out doubt or hesitation, do you believe that he is more pleasing
> to God than someone who has always been hard towards Him,
> full of sin and contempt, but who then, for many a year of her
> life, has strived to do her duty and born every burden without
> a murmur, but has never repented her previous life to God or
> man? Do you think that she who has lived as she believed it
> was right to live, without any hope of reward hereafter, and

never praying for that, do you believe that God will thrust her from him and cast her away because she never entreated Him, not with a single word of prayer?"[39]

Jacobsen ends the novel a page or so later; for all intents and purposes, Marie and Holberg's theological debate is its provocative conclusion. What to make of it? A contemporary Danish priest and literary critic, Søren Matthiesen, argues in his book *Rygtet om Guds død* (The rumor of the death of God) that the exchange represents a clash of two worldviews: on the one hand Marie's earthly individualism, her calm willingness to pursue her desires as she sees fit, without hope of eternity or heavenly reward, and on the other hand Holberg's belief that such a view amounts to little more than complete relativism, even nihilism. In Matthiesen's slightly polemical reading, Marie admits to God's existence precisely by rejecting Him. "The Marie who asks for God's forgiveness and eternal life is not someone for whom God is dead," he argues. "On the contrary, the notion of God's death is meaningless when confronted by the question of the eternal God and the eternal life."[40]

To be sure, Marie and Holberg's exchange reveals the difficulty of rejecting God entirely. It touches on a paradox of atheism that Jacobsen will dramatize more fully in *Niels Lyhne*. But Matthiesen's reading is too narrow, too literal. Is it not possible that Marie is merely entertaining the idea of God for the sake of argument? For the majority of the novel her attitude toward religion is largely one of indifference. She neither invokes nor rejects Him; she merely lives "without any hope of reward hereafter."

Matthiesen's reading also overlooks a more important issue at stake in Marie's comments: her rejection of Holberg's suggestion that she has only one soul. By listing her various incarnations—the innocent child, the king's favorite, the old ferrywoman—she is picketing the idea that the self is whole, rigid with fixed coherence. "Being . . . is nothing but the delirium of many," as Robert Musil puts it in *The Man without Qualities*.[41]

The focus of the novel is on Marie Grubbe, yet in almost every chapter she has undergone some new transformation. These range from the sudden and disruptive to the gradual and imperceptible. She is always Marie Grubbe, but Marie Grubbe is never the same; she repeatedly wriggles out of her own character. The consequences to be drawn from these transformations are significant, especially at the time of writing. Jacobsen shows us that the self is not stable; it is always in the process of gathering and unraveling itself, like a formation of clouds. This is Marie's challenge to Holberg. She is essentially saying, "What's this one soul nonsense? I am large; I contain multitudes!" Thus the novel's title asks not only who is Marie Grubbe, but also what is a literary character—and, by extension, what is a self?

Read with these questions in mind, *Marie Grubbe* becomes a challenge to the novelistic representation of coherence. It is interesting that August Strindberg and Knut Hamsun, the two major Scandinavian writers most often celebrated for unraveling perceived ideas of literary character, were both admirers of *Marie Grubbe* and Jacobsen's writing.

In the early 1880s August Strindberg toyed repeatedly with the idea of adapting Jacobsen's novel for the stage. "Salute Jacobsen from his great friend and admirer," he wrote to Edvard Brandes in July 1881. "Ask [him] if he has anything against my adapting *Marie Grubbe* for the stage—I believe I can do it; I've planned the five acts, but I merge some events, omit others, turn two characters into one and so on, concentrating the action and, above all, creating a tight argument."[42] Though he only ever got around to dividing up his copy of the novel into acts and scenes, *Marie Grubbe*'s influence can be felt in Strindberg's plays of the 1880s, particularly *Miss Julie* (1888).

In his long preface to that play, Strindberg railed against the "middle-class notion about the immobility of the soul"— the idea that character was synonymous with fixed and constant natures. "Because they are modern characters, living in a period of transition more hysterically hurried than its immediate predecessor at least, I have made my figures vacillating, out of joint, torn between the old and the new," Strindberg wrote. "My souls (or characters) are conglomerates, made up of past and present stages of civilisation, scraps of humanity, torn-off pieces of Sunday clothing turned into rags—all patched together as is the human soul itself."[43]

Strindberg may well have been inspired in this insight by *Marie Grubbe.* Certainly it is an insight that Jacobsen had already anticipated. Faced with complaints about the novel's incoherence—its character's contradictory nature, the disjointed and shapeless narrative—Jacobsen later argued in a letter to Edvard Brandes that fictional characters were often *too* coherent. "In reality," he argued, "there are so many facets of human nature that don't add up; why should something as complex as the spiritual aspect of human nature, culled from so many places, formed and influenced by so many things, make up an organic whole?" He conceded that a novel had to cohere as a whole, "but unless books should become encyclopedias of human knowledge, one has to make certain demands of the reader's intelligence and not anxiously and thoroughly draw a red thread through all phases and stages of a given character."[44]

This radical vision of literary character is strikingly similar to Knut Hamsun's. Hamsun lectured passionately on both Strindberg and Jacobsen during his time in America and was said by a friend to have been "moved by the color-saturated aspect" of Jacobsen's prose, which otherwise resembles his own very little.[45] And as with Strindberg it is difficult not to turn one's thoughts to *Marie Grubbe* when reading the following passage from Hamsun's famous manifesto, "From the Unconscious Life of the Soul" (1890):

> What if literature as a whole began to concern itself a little more with interior states than with betrothals and balls and trips to the country and that sort of thing? One would have to give up writing about "types"—who have all been written about before—and "characters"—whom one meets every day at the fish market. And possibly one might even end up losing that part of the audience that reads only to find out if the hero and the heroine end up together. But on the other hand there would be more individual cases in literature and of these something more akin to the interior life that mature people experience nowadays. We would learn something of the secret stirrings occurring unnoticed in remote areas of the soul, the unpredictable chaos of perception, the delicate life of the imagination held under the microscope; the meanderings of these thoughts and feelings in the blue, trackless, traceless journeys of the heart and mind, curious workings of the psyche, the whisperings of the blood, prayers of the bone, the entire unconscious life of the soul.[46]

"I dream of a literature with characters in which their very lack of consistency is their basic characteristic," Hamsun said elsewhere.[47] Marie Grubbe's idle puncturing of her skin with her teeth, not to mention her sudden lunge at her husband with a knife, is the sort of irrational impulse that might have struck Hamsun when he read the novel. In *Hunger*, the unnamed narrator likewise attempts to take a bite out of his own flesh: "Something began stirring in my brain, some thought in there scrabbling to get out, a stark-raving mad idea: what if I gave a bite? And without a moment's hesitation I squeezed my eyes shut and clenched my teeth together."[48]

It's a shame Jacobsen didn't live long enough to encounter *Hunger*. His and Hamsun's paths would inevitably have crossed; the manic Norwegian was a cult figure in Copenhagen in the 1890s, particularly following *Hunger*'s publication by P. G. Philipsens Forlag—a publication Edvard Brandes had helped to bring about after the poor and destitute Hamsun came to see him and forced the manuscript into his hands. Brandes reluctantly agreed to read it when he saw the desperation in the author's eyes. "It hooked me right away," he wrote to a friend. "And the more I read, the more hooked I became. It was not simply talented the way many other things are. There was something in it that shook me. There was something of Dostoevsky in it."[49] (By comparison, Georg Brandes reportedly dismissed the novel without even finishing it. "Brandes may have raised the banner against God, the priesthood and politicians," Hamsun's biographer, Ingar Sletten Kollen notes, "but never against reason itself.")[50]

Jacobsen wrote *Marie Grubbe* in fits and starts, most of it between 1875 and 1876. He worked at a Flaubertian pace, sometimes writing just a couple of pages in as many months. "I wish I'd never created that woman," he quipped to Edvard Brandes in early 1876. "We walk around staring and eyeing each other angrily—day in and day out. It's like an unhappy marriage."[51] To Emilie Brandes, Edvard's and Georg's mother, he wrote, "[Marie Grubbe] is the slowest and most intractable woman capable of walking in a pair of shoes with rosettes on them."[52]

Jacobsen finally dispatched the last pages of his novel at the post office in Thisted on December 4, 1876, during a ferocious blizzard. *Marie Grubbe: Seventeenth Century Interiors* thus appeared in Copenhagen's bookstores on December 15, 1876. On December 24, just nine days later, the first printing —1,250 copies—had already sold out. Jacobsen couldn't believe it. "Of all the things I've ever dreamt of," he wrote to Edvard Brandes, "a second printing was certainly not among them."[53] To Vilhelm Møller he said he was in a state of "quiet astonishment—like a man who quite unexpectedly finds himself ascending in a hot air balloon."[54]

Marie Grubbe was an instant success. Buried in snow almost three hundred miles away, its author anxiously awaited news of its critical reception in Copenhagen. "Not a single newspaper, letter, or package has reached town today," he wrote to Vilhelm Møller on December 20. "And to know that in *Dagbladet* and *Telegrafen* is a review of my first novel!" Three days later nothing had changed: "Still no mail, the fjord freezes over before one's eyes and the snowdrifts peer in through the windows on the second floor," he reported. "My windows are frozen thick; for half an hour now I've amused myself by carving a large square peephole that immediately freezes back over again. I give up."[55]

The general verdict, when it finally did arrive, was almost unanimously, though not unreservedly, positive: "One has to place *Marie Grubbe* in a class of its own along with the most significant achievements in our literature," Edvard Brandes wrote in an unsigned review in *Morgenbladet*.[56] The editor Carl Carstensen agreed: "It has no real equal," he wrote in *Dagens nyheder*.[57] Others likewise affirmed *Marie Grubbe*'s status as a milestone in Scandinavian letters, even if they were a little unsure of what to make of its peculiar style and disjointed composition. An unsigned review in *Dagbladet*, for instance, wondered if Jacobsen had in fact abandoned his original plan for the novel halfway through; the final chapters, the reviewer claimed, were not the measured "interiors" of the early sections but rather a summary of Marie's eventual fate. "This has an adverse affect on Marie Grubbe," the reviewer opines; "she has become . . . a shattered statue, a heap of fragments, superb on their own terms but not in such a way that one is able to piece them together."[58] Even Edvard Brandes agreed that the novel was more perfectly executed in its first half; his review singled out the later chapters for being "somewhat vague and loosely sketched."[59]

Another more predictable criticism leveled at Jacobsen's novel was the matter of its style. The prose was seen as too indulgently obstructive. Most critics granted its originality, but the luxurious detail, the sumptuous colors, and the intangible mosaics were simply exasperating to get through. *Dagbladet*'s anonymous reviewer thought readers would be put off by the "meticulous, almost anxious observation and reproduction of all these small characteristics and details."[60] Case in point:

The light danced in gold and silver threads, was reflected in polished silver and steel, gliding in golden streaks down silk gowns and silk trains. Soft as reddish dew, its breath fell on dark velvet, and in white sparks it descended like stars on diamonds and rubies. Shades of red competed with yellow, while those of clear sky blue enclosed brown. Sea green colours cut bold streaks of light through white and blue violet; coral red disappeared between shades of black and lilac, and yellow-brown, pink and steel grey whirled together. Light and dark, one hue and another, all merged into a happy wave of colours.[61]

It's hard to keep track of what is going on here, but Jacobsen's attempt to isolate nuances and light disintegrates into a kitsch orgy of color. He is a fanatic with a palette. Presumably it's the sort of passage that led later generations of writers, including Martin Andersen Nexø and the Nobel Prize–winning Johannes V. Jensen, to dismiss Jacobsen as a mere stylist. "To concern oneself with language directly is the same as looking at a window instead of through it," Jensen remonstrated.[62]

Jacobsen might have countered that looking through a window is to look *at* a piece of glass and *through* it at the same time. In any case it is an unfortunate reader who does not pause repeatedly to consider the beauty and originality of Jacobsen's writing. In *Marie Grubbe* we hear the "fall of dust-light raindrops" like "an imperceptible whisper, always dying and beginning afresh." We see a beach in winter, "thick with wrecks: ice covered hulls, splintered masts, broken boats, dead ships"; yew trees "like the dark columns of a temple whose roof has collapsed"; and the branch of a yellowing apple tree "blushing with fruit."[63]

Georg Brandes—eager, no doubt, to fashion Jacobsen after his own image—wrote a long review in *Det nittende aarhundrede* in January 1877 that tried to place Jacobsen's style within the larger framework of recent European literature. Toward the end of his long essay he writes the following:

> In the lucid and reticent style there is something that betrays the influence of certain masters of modern French literature, like Prosper Mérimée and Gautier; in the tendency to draw interiors there is something that reminds one of Balzac, and the pointedness and accuracy of the analysis have a coincidental parallel in Flaubert, not to mention the most recent heir to the great movements in the French novel; there is something in the portrait's warm, sensual splendor akin to the very best of Zola. And there is on the other side of the lyrical boundaries a certain powerful sweetness and sound that exists only in Keats.[64]

Swaddled in so many illustrious names, Jacobsen all but disappears from view. He later explained to Brandes that he hadn't read Zola until after *Marie Grubbe* was published and that he felt he'd learned "more from Beyle and Shakespeare than Mérimée, more from Sainte-Beuve than Taine."[65]

Still, Brandes's public verdict was important. His was the literary opinion that mattered—enough for the celebrated Bjørnstjerne Bjørnson, then in his mid-forties, to write to Brandes and object to his appreciation for *Marie Grubbe*. "I don't share your admiration," he protested, claiming that Jacobsen "sees nothing first-hand" and accusing his style of being an imitation of French decorative painting. Brandes immediately sprang on the charm offensive: "Imagine a quiet, timid farmer's son from Jutland . . . so bound to Denmark that he was half in despair when he first crossed the border and completely in despair in Italy—and you think *he* was influenced by French paintings? No, if he was influenced by anyone, it was by two poets who cannot be said to be particularly French: Andersen and B. Bjørnson, particularly the latter, as he has often said himself."[66]

Jacobsen, though he thanked Brandes for jumping to his defense, did not seem particularly bothered by Bjørnson's comments. "My style is much closer to Hans Christian Andersen's fairytales than to Bjørnson's," he calmly remarked.[67]

CHAPTER FIVE

"Poor Freethinkers"

OPENHAGEN was the first real battleground of European Modernism. In the years following Georg Brandes's first series of lectures on "Main Currents in Nineteenth-Century Literature," the notion of the "modern" had grown to become a programmatic slogan for writers to rally around. And though Brandes's vision of modern literature was explicitly sociopolitical and realist, his influence proved more expansive and cosmopolitan: he traveled and lectured widely, lived in self-imposed exile in Berlin between 1873 and 1880, and later became the first vocal champion of the works of Friedrich Nietzsche. In lecture halls across the continent, he championed the "Men of the Modern Breakthrough," as he later called them: the Scandinavian writers whose careers he had helped to inspire or reinvent, including Bjørnson, Ibsen, Jacobsen, Drachmann, and

Jens Peter Jacobsen circa 1881. Courtesy
of Thisted Museum.

Schandorph. He was, as Stefan Zweig would later describe
him, the "international master of the history of literature"
and the most influential critic in Europe at the time.[1]

The very liberal literary culture that flourished around
Brandes in Copenhagen attracted writers from all over Scandinavia and turned the city into a crossroads of restless literary production and social transformation. Ibsen's *A Doll's
House* and Strindberg's *Miss Julie* both premiered in the Danish capital, heaping scorn on the institution of marriage and
the role of the sexes. Hamsun's *Hunger* and Herman Bang's
Haabløse Slægter (Hopeless generations) were instant literary
sensations and, in Bang's case, the object of a scandal. Other
writers, including Alexander Kielland, Holger Drachmann,

Henrik Pontoppidan, and Johannes V. Jensen, all came to seek their literary fortune in the city. So too did a number of important painters: the Norwegians Christian Krogh and Edvard Munch and the Danish Skagen painters, most notably P. S. Krøyer and Michael and Anna Ancher.

But the first major work of the Modern Breakthrough was *Marie Grubbe*. It turned Jacobsen into a household name virtually overnight. It was quickly translated into both Swedish and German and became the subject of intense debate in Norway, where the women's rights activist Camilla Collett and the young writer Amalie Skram (from 1884 on the wife of Erik Skram) both championed what they saw as a literary rallying cause for women's emancipation. Skram, whose 1885 novel *Constance Ring* so scandalized Frederik V. Hegel that Gyldendal went back on its agreement to publish it, praised *Marie Grubbe*'s "brilliant prose," heralding it as "a new beginning" for Danish literature.[2] Collett was more overtly polemical: "Marie Grubbe is the woman of the future," she wrote; "[Jacobsen] has given us an illustration of the position of woman in our modern Christian century."[3]

Despite being increasingly associated with incendiary ideas like Darwinism, realism, atheism, and now feminism, Jacobsen maintained his habit of shying away from public debate. He likely felt it was not the job of the artist to engage in polemics, but then he barely had the time or stamina to be an artist, let alone a socially engaged one. Publicly he maintained an aloof and reticent persona, mercilessly caricatured by Henrik Pontoppidan in his great novel *Lykke-Per* (Lucky Per, 1904), in which the "lonely melancholic" poet Enevoldsen is reported to have died "during the composition of a sentence."[4]

If Jacobsen were alive today, he might have earned the ambivalent sobriquet "a writer's writer." Known and admired by all, he was nevertheless relegated to the sidelines while the likes of Hamsun, Strindberg, Bang, Brandes, and Drachmann, each of them embroiled in various public scandals and open conflicts, published tome after tome. "If the gods granted me but a single wish," Jacobsen wrote to Edvard Brandes, "I'd ask not for gold or health, but simply: energy."[5]

Alas, while everyone else appeared to be converging on the Danish capital, Jacobsen once again returned to Thisted, where he sat playing cards with his brother or tended to the vegetables in his parents' garden. He longed desperately for "large, broad, crowded streets, gas-lit storefronts, and rattling carriages," and for the company of his friends.[6] In letters he commented eagerly on the few books of his contemporaries he was able to get his hands on, as well as the foreign literature people were kind enough to send him. "I've put aside Zola's new book *L'Assommoir*, half in admiration, half in terror," he wrote to Georg Brandes; "the process of reading it is akin to the sensation of descending into a salt or coal mine. I won't lie; I felt a grateful little smile on my lips when I escaped and once again saw the blue sky above me."[7]

Encouraged by his doctor to spend the winter in Egypt, Jacobsen in September 1877 settled for Montreux in Switzerland, where he remained until May 1878. He reached the town by way of Hamburg, Heidelberg, and Basel and settled in a comfortable room at the Pension Bellevue, located on a hilltop above the train station with a gorgeous view of Lake Geneva and the Savoy Alps on one side and the Château de Chillon and the Dents du Midi on the other. "There is no other room in town with a view like mine," he wrote to Georg Brandes. "I'm beginning to get a sense of what a mountain truly is."[8] So enchanting was the view that he bought a painting of the Château de Chillon and later hung it on the wall of his room in Thisted.

Montreux was a popular resort destination among Russians and Europeans. Consumptive patients like Jacobsen were shielded in winter from the cold northern winds; in the spring and summer, the town glistened in the sunlight reflecting off of the lake, yielding an abundance of fig trees, pomegranate shrubs, and vineyards across scattered points of elevation. Many came for the fabled grape cure, lasting from September to October, which prescribed that patients eat almost nothing but grapes for up to four weeks.[9]

Not far from the pension was a small library to which Jacobsen made frequent pilgrimages, reading almost exclusively French literature: Gautier, Balzac, Stendhal, Cherbuliez, Zola, and, most important, Flaubert, whose *Three Tales* had just been published. Jacobsen liked "A Simple Heart" and considered "Saint Julian" a masterpiece ("It really is an old church window, a pearl of a window") but didn't care for "Herodias." It was boring, he said, and only served to remind him of *Salammbo*, which he couldn't stand.[10]

Jacobsen's fellow guests at the pension were a cosmopolitan bunch. They included a Cuban family, a middle-aged Dutch woman, two elderly English ladies, and three Poles. To his parents Jacobsen reported speaking in his excellent German, in passable French, and occasionally in poor English. "I increasingly spend a lot of time here at the pension, as the other guests are very pleasant," he wrote.[11] No doubt he stood out with his lanky height, his dramatically forked mustache, and the cherished *pince-nez* perched on the bridge of his nose. Two guests in particular warmed to him: the thirty-eight-year-old Baron Buchholtz and his younger sister, Anna Buchholtz, often touted as the inspiration for Madame Odero in *Niels Lyhne*. Jacobsen frequently dined with the siblings and on one occasion even embroiled them in a pillow fight.[12] It was Anna and Jacobsen who were closest. Anna's beautiful singing voice and literary aspirations (including an interest in the novels of Benjamin Disraeli) made her an attractive companion during afternoon walks in the garden of the pension. She even managed to tease out details of Jacobsen's novel-in-progress from the usually tight-lipped author, who in turn acted as a confidant to the quick-witted baroness. Was there a glimmer of romance? Not if *Niels Lyhne* is any clue:

> There was no question of them being in love with one another, or at any rate not very much; it was one of those vague, comfortable relationships that can arise between men and women who are past the first youth with its flaring up and striving for some unknown happiness. It was a kind of fleeting summer in which you stroll primly side by side and shower yourself with bouquets, pat yourself with the other person's hand, admire yourself with the other person's eyes. All the beautiful secrets, all the lovely, irrelevant things you keep hidden, all the knick-knacks of the soul are brought forth and passed from hand to hand and held up appraisingly in an artistic search for the best lighting while you compare and explain.[13]

Jacobsen and Anna continued to correspond even after they parted; there was briefly talk of Jacobsen's coming to visit the Buchholtz estate in Russia, but plans never materialized. When he left Montreux in May 1878, the sight of his empty chair in the dining room so depressed Anna that she forced her brother to take her to Zurich instead. "The seven wonderful months we spent together are gone forever," she wrote to Jacobsen.[14]

When he wasn't socializing or exploring the local villages, Jacobsen was determinedly at work on a new novel. "My new book—may the Gods expedite it—will probably be called *Niels Lyhne*," he wrote to Edvard Brandes.[15] He had written the first few pages several years before, in 1874, though the idea for the novel had occurred to him as far back as 1867.

Writing to Georg Brandes from Montreux in February 1878, Jacobsen explained the novel would follow a group of "poor freethinkers"—idealistic youths who had come of age in the middle of the nineteenth century, a generation or so before Jacobsen. He aimed to show "how difficult it is to be a freethinker, with the siren voices of childhood memories and tradition on the one hand and the condemnation of society on the other."[16] Though he didn't say so outright, his choice of subject matter was deeply personal. The fact that tuberculosis kept bringing him back into the care of his family and childhood home meant that he never entirely broke away from it. The conflict between his own freethinking ideas and the comforting allure of a childhood home was palpable to him; he saw repeatedly the existential strength his parents and the local community drew from their quiet, day-to-day belief. Though he could never bring himself to share in it, he may have developed a distant admiration for it.

This conflict was, to some degree, very much of its time. As early as 1857 Hans Christian Andersen had written a novel,

To Be or Not to Be?, directly addressing many of the tensions between traditional religious belief and the rise of the materialist worldview. Niels Bryde, the novel's central character, reads Strauss and Feuerbach and begins to doubt the pious faith of his childhood home. His relationship to a Jewish girl and his experiences as a doctor during the First Schleswig-Holstein War, however, bring him back into the bosom of his childhood faith. "There is a peculiar power in the sacred sanctuary where home-recollections linger, in the well-remembered, old melodies, which exalt us over, and carry us away from the scenes of every-day life," Niels thinks to himself toward the end of the novel.[17]

Though Jacobsen didn't mention the novel in any of his letters, he was an avid reader of Andersen and no doubt would have come across *To Be or Not to Be?*, especially given its thematic similarities to his own novel-in-progress (not to mention the shared first name of the main characters, Niels Bryde and Niels Lyhne). To his friends, however, he pointed at sources of inspiration beyond Denmark's borders. In his correspondence with Georg and Edvard Brandes he hinted that his new novel would be a kind of Danish *Sentimental Education*, a novel Edvard said he and Jacobsen often discussed, while to Vilhelm Møller Jacobsen suggested it would have much in common with *Fathers and Sons*. (Turgenev's novel, which Møller had translated, was published in Denmark in 1876.)

Jacobsen never wrote at any length about Turgenev, but what must have struck him when he read *Fathers and Sons* is the profound devotion of the young nihilist Bazarov's pious parents to their radical son. At the end of the novel, Bazarov contracts typhus from cutting his finger while attending a patient. As a trained physician, he knows what's in store for him, and he stoically encourages his distraught parents to find strength in their religion ("There's an opportunity to put it to the test," he caustically remarks). On his deathbed, Bazarov quietly rebuffs his father's wish for a priest to give him communion. When his son breathes his last sigh, Bazarov's father, movingly, is "seized by a sudden fury. 'I said I would cry out in defiance,' he shouted hoarsely, his face twisted and aflame, shaking his fist in the air as if threatening someone, 'and I will cry out, I will cry out!'" A servant later says that Bazarov's parents eventually "laid down their heads like lambs at noon."[18]

We can imagine Jacobsen thinking of his own parents as he read of the desperate grief of Bazarov's father, his anger and disillusionment with the God he had served patiently his entire life. Perhaps Jacobsen saw his own situation reflected in Bazarov's, a man who like himself lay dying in the home of his parents in a provincial town far from the intellectual society he had once frequented and whose passion was for the natural sciences rather than religion. Or maybe he was moved by the humanism of Turgenev, his ability to "unself himself," to use V. S. Pritchett's great phrase,[19] and to allow his characters to stand on their own feet without any irritable prodding from the author.

In *Fathers and Sons*, nature is shown to be indifferent to ideological conflicts between the generations. Bazarov dies with a resigned dignity—a difficult death—not as a martyr or a saint. No doubt Jacobsen, like many other writers at the time, was inspired by what Georg Brandes identified as

Turgenev's special brand of melancholy: "the melancholy of a thinker who has understood that all the ideals of the human race—justice, reason, supreme goodness, happiness—are a matter of indifference to nature."[20]

With the exception of Zola and Flaubert, no other foreign writer matched Turgenev's influence in Scandinavia at the time. Between 1872 and 1879, Vilhelm Møller translated more than ten books by Turgenev, including *Rudin, Smoke, Spring Torrents,* and *The Sportsman's Sketches.* "We all worshipped Turgenev," the writer Karl Larsen later remarked.[21] Jacobsen simply thought of Turgenev as "one of the greatest living masters," and was struck in particular by the gentle lyricism of his style.[22] When Jacobsen died, his brother found a collection of Turgenev's short stories on his bedside table.

Jacobsen returned to Thisted from Montreux in late May 1878 by way of Bern, Frankfurt, and Strasbourg, where he saw *Hamlet* performed while drinking beer at a café across from the cathedral. He was in good spirits; his new novel and vastly improved health encouraged him. His letters were unusually chipper, filled with anecdotes and wordplay and light-hearted accounts of his traveling difficulties. On his return to "Siberia" (Thisted), he joked to Georg Brandes, all that greeted him was a toothache and a sore back. How he despised traveling by rail!

But in late June Jacobsen suffered a very sudden and very severe pulmonary hemorrhage. For two weeks he was confined to his bed, watched over by his anxious family and the local doctor. It was a crushing blow. All the progress he felt he'd made in Switzerland vanished in an instant. "I'm weak but fine otherwise," he assured Edvard Brandes a few weeks later, "though I'm in such a mood that if this goes on for much longer, I'll end up quitting this life. Maybe a quinine mixture can cheer my thoughts."[23]

Jacobsen was so alarmed by his relapse that he immediately set about making arrangements to head south again. Earlier in the year he'd received a travel grant that he had intended to use toward a trip to Italy. Thus in late September 1878, once he'd recovered sufficiently, he embarked on his third, and final, trip abroad—to Rome.

It took him almost three weeks to reach the Italian capital; train after endless train brought him through Cologne, Lyons, Avignon, and Genoa. (In Genoa, Jacobsen was impressed with the ornate cemetery—an impression shared by Anton Chekhov on his visit to the city sixteen years later.) Jacobsen had come to despise these journeys. "I shudder at the thought of all those hours on a train," he wrote to Georg Brandes. "To think that in 1879 one still has to rattle along like that! I'd like to know what the inventors are really up to these days."[24]

Jacobsen installed himself on Via dei Due Macelli 124, where he rented two well-lit rooms in a building owned by a German watchmaker. It was an ideal location—within walking distance of Piazza del Popolo and the Villa Borghese, not to mention cafés, restaurants, a bakery, a wine merchant, a pharmacy, and a bookstore. Jacobsen drank cocoa at the café in the morning and ate eggs or beef for lunch and meat and soup for dinner. The local pharmacist supplied him with the arsenic he occasionally used to treat his symptoms. Jacobsen even managed to find a "smokeable" cigar.[25]

Rome, meanwhile, offered its whirl of excitement. Following the attempted assassination of King Umberto I in Naples in mid-November, the capital erupted with pro-monarchist demonstrations. "Naturally Rome lit up at once, drawing a train of cheering crowds and torch bearers through the streets," Jacobsen laconically reported to Edvard Brandes.[26] He had also, he declared, resigned himself to Italian food and weather; he now ate pasta and never went anywhere without an umbrella, the month of November being marred by excessive rainfall that completely inundated the city. The Tiber overflowed its banks, flooding parts of Rome and leaving the Via del Corso under water for several days.

Jacobsen's life in Rome proved to be quite sociable. On Saturdays he attended the weekly salon of the Scandinavian Foundation, an organization of expats that had formed around the celebrated sculptor Thorvaldsen earlier in the century.[27] The salons, held at the foundation's home in the Palazzo Correa (later demolished by Mussolini), usually included about thirty or forty people and consisted of dinner, card games, singing, dancing, and lively conversation.

Though usually quite jovial, these gatherings could on occasion become a sort of offshore battleground of Scandinavian social and political tensions. Jacobsen experienced this firsthand when Henrik Ibsen arrived in Rome in late October. Ibsen had recently completed *A Doll's House* and was more than usually combative. The following January he proposed that the foundation allow women a more authoritative role within its ranks, suggesting it hire a female librarian. His recommendation did not sit well with the foundation's members. One of them even entertained the idea of challenging the

Norwegian agitator to a duel, though nothing came of it. For the duration of the controversy Jacobsen stood by Ibsen "through thick and thin"—greatly amused by the "terrific insolence" with which the mutton-chopped playwright quelled his opponents. When he read *A Doll's House* a year or so later, Jacobsen told Edvard Brandes that it helped to explain Ibsen's behavior in Rome. He also considered it the most "significant and flawless" of Ibsen's plays.[28]

Ibsen and Jacobsen spent several evenings together in Rome, often dining or drinking at a local *osteria* with the Norwegian poet Gunnar Heiberg. Ibsen eagerly picked Jacobsen's brains about Darwin's theory of evolution, which he didn't really understand and couldn't be bothered to study on his own. Whenever Ibsen ventured to speak on scientific matters, Jacobsen smiled knowingly and calmly shook his head. He later told Heiberg that he knew "many little boys with more knowledge of botany than the old pharmacist" (Ibsen had been an apprentice to a pharmacist in his youth).[29]

Among other artists Jacobsen befriended were P. S. Krøyer, Theodor Philipsen, and Axel Helsted. Helsted in particular would remain a close friend in Jacobsen's final years, visiting him in Thisted and etching a famous deathbed portrait of the emaciated author. The religiously inclined Helsted, who would plunge into a crisis of faith following the death of his wife in 1886, likely felt that in Jacobsen he had found a sympathetic listener more understanding than most when it came to matters of belief. The extent of their intimacy became evident in 1952, when a previously unknown painting showing the two friends seated next to each other turned up at an auction in Odense. It was painted by Peter Syrak Hansen in Copenhagen in 1882.

The fresh-faced Helsted is seated upright with his legs crossed and playing the guitar, while next to him a visibly pale Jacobsen stares thoughtfully into the distance with a cigar dangling from his mouth and a flute of champagne in front of him. He looks like a ghost.

While still in Rome, Jacobsen was also portrayed in a slightly livelier, though hardly more cheerful, fashion by the Swedish artist Ernst Josephson. His iconic painting shows the author leaning his head, heavy with melancholy, on a half-clenched fist while in the foreground a pink rose rests limply on a leather-bound book. Jacobsen intended the portrait as a present for his mother.

Josephson's saturnine portrayal of his subject seems an accurate reflection of Jacobsen's demeanor in the last few months of his Italian sojourn. Though his health benefited from the change in climate—as his social life did from the proximity to the Scandinavian Foundation—his appetite for exploration and sightseeing, so ravenous on his first trip to Italy in 1873, had significantly dampened. "Do you recall," he asked Edvard Brandes, "how voracious my appetite for galleries was, how afraid I was that a painting in some obscure corner should go unnoticed, and now here I am on my tenth day and I still haven't seen the Sistine Chapel."[30] He wrote similarly to Georg Brandes: "It's awful how old we're getting, terrible how rarely anything makes an impression on us. I've now seen St. Peter's Basilica, the Roman Forum, Colosseum, and the skeletons in Santa Maria della Concezione, and yet the only thing that has really affected me down here are a couple of portraits in the Doria Pamphili. I don't know what it is that dies away inside us."[31]

In April Jacobsen was briefly visited by Edvard Brandes, who wrote to his older brother to report on their mutual friend: "Same old J. P. J. Naturally we spent a lot of time together in the three days I was down there. I had expected him to be very European and worldly, but he was just as strange and introverted as usual. He didn't look too bad, though he coughed a lot and couldn't walk too fast. Whenever I forgot he became very short-winded. He was in a good mood."[32]

The good mood didn't last. Shortly after Edvard's visit, Jacobsen made an ill-fated excursion to Naples and Capri, only to encounter the most insufferable weather: torrents of rain, storm-like winds, and freezing temperatures. The rooms he rented were cold and damp, and he quickly began to endure a stubborn toothache. Before long, he had a terrible cold to boot. Worse still, his carriage was overturned by a startled horse during a trip to Sorrento, scattering his belongings across the road and into the bushes. He was relieved when he finally returned to Rome. "It's lovely here," he wrote to Georg Brandes, "especially when you've just had to spend a month in filthy Naples and steep, breathtaking Capri with its stupid lemon trees and beggar children."[33]

Jacobsen was more forthcoming in his letters to his brother. "I can't say that my time here in Italy has done me any good," he confessed from Capri. "A lack of appetite has emaciated me somewhat, though my aforementioned headache has abated a little." William suspected his brother of withholding the truth about his condition so as not to cause any undue alarm, but Jacobsen denied the charge: "I always tell truth as I see it and conceal nothing. I am, as I wrote before, quite emaciated and fragile, my legs especially feel quite weak, but there is no danger—or, rather, on the whole I'm not much different from what I usually am."[34]

More denial. While staying at a hotel in Leipzig on his long journey home, Jacobsen alarmed the maid with his increasingly severe night sweats. When she came to clean the room in the morning, she was convinced he'd spilled water all over the bed.

The short story Jacobsen wrote on his return to Denmark that summer gives us a glimpse into the state of his mind at the time. Though just a handful of pages long, "Two Worlds" is saturated with a world-weariness new to Jacobsen's writing. "The Salzach is not a cheerful river," it begins, "and there is a little village on its eastern bank that is quite dismal, quite poor, and singularly silent." The houses of this village, we're told, "stare with a scowl of malignant anguish at the happier houses across the river." They are surrounded by "brooding darkness" and the sounds of the river "murmuring to itself on its way, so weary of life, so strangely oblivious."[35]

In this village lives a woman who has spent years suffering from a mysterious and painful illness no doctor or holy spring can cure. One day she encounters a one-eyed man who tells her to gather a bundle of "edelweiss and withered rue, of corn and smut and cemetery ferns, a lock of her hair and a splinter from a coffin" and to throw that bundle at a healthy young woman, to whom the illness will be transferred. The woman waits impatiently by the river as a boat approaches. There are a handful of people on board, and snatches of conversation are overheard: "Happiness . . . is a perfectly heathen notion," a passenger exclaims. "You won't find the word anywhere in the New Testament." As the boat draws nearer, the woman spies a happy young couple at the tiller. She waits for them to get close before she throws the bundle. The story then abruptly jumps a year ahead. The woman, now cured of her disease, has grown sick with remorse. The image of the healthy young woman haunts her, whispers to her in the night, and gives her no peace. At the exact spot on the river-bank where she cast her bundle she kneels and prays by a little cross. Then she drowns herself. Just as the woman sinks be-neath the surface, a boat passes by. It's the same boat from before, with the same couple—now happily married—at the tiller. The young woman, seemingly healthy, sings a song that ends, "A toast to happiness ere it came, / A toast to the pov-erty of hope. / A toast to dreams!"[36]

"Two Worlds," perhaps a little too obviously, pits a sickly, Christian worldview against a healthier, earthbound paganism. Jacobsen wants to disparage the Christian notions of fatalism and guilt and the woman's inability to bear life as it is. Yet the story is also a confession of Jacobsen's own inability to escape a Christian eschatology. The pagan worldview remains distant; it merely glides by somewhere beyond us, just as the "happier" houses across the river are seen "far off in the misty golden distance."[37] Jacobsen's once jubilant atheism is shipwrecked amid the detritus of an inescapably religious sensibility.

As we read "Two Worlds," it is difficult not to think of Jacobsen's own incurable disease. His description of the wom-an's face has the tenor of a self-portrait: "A curiously wan smile lay on her weary mouth, but the vertical furrows on her prominent curved brow spread a shadow across her whole face of the certainty of despair."[38] Moreover, the story's unreal melancholy, its heavy blanket of despair, is surely rooted in Jacobsen's growing sense of isolation and dejection. He confessed to Vilhelm Møller while writing "Two Worlds": "It's as if it's getting quieter and quieter around me, in ever-widening circles."[39]

Death, indeed, appeared to be all around him. In 1878 his childhood friend, the painter Viggo Wørmer, passed away, possibly as a result of tuberculosis, and that summer he received word that Edvard Brandes's wife Harriet had taken her own life. Edvard had discovered that Harriet was having an affair with his cousin and threatened to divorce her. On the evening of July 23 the couple dined at home with their two little daughters as usual, when Harriet suddenly retreated to her room, drank a vial of hydrogen cyanide, and then reemerged to declare that she had just consumed poison. She died almost instantly. Edvard was sunk with guilt, anger, and grief—he looked like he'd aged thirty years, Georg Brandes wrote. Jacobsen may not have known the precise details of Harriet's death, but he nevertheless sent a brief letter that Edvard later said touched him greatly: "I wish words existed that might numb and soothe, but they don't, so the only thing I find I am able to tell to you is that you and your sorrow are constantly in my thoughts, my dear friend."[40]

By 1879 the literary scene in Copenhagen had changed significantly; the left was now too numerous to be ignored, and Georg Brandes had cause to feel a little triumphant. That year alone saw the premiere of Ibsen's *A Doll's House* and the publication of Strindberg's novel *The Red Room*, as well as the emergence of a new generation of writers, among them Erik

Skram, whose novel *Gertrude Colbjørnson* was almost a text-book fulfillment of Brandesian aesthetics, and the young Karl Gjellerup, who would go on to win the Nobel Prize for Literature with Henrik Pontoppidan in 1917. Gjellerup's *Det unge Danmark* (The young Denmark), an overtly polemical novel about a steadfast atheist whose proposal of marriage to a merchant's daughter is rejected, was viewed by some as an inferior piece of writing yet tolerated by the Brandes brothers because of its author's liberal ideas and unwavering dedication to the cause.

More broadly, 1879 was the zenith of Zolismus, the craze for Émile Zola,[41] and the rise of anti-idealism in the novel. Jacobsen had, in his own way, played a significant part in bringing literary realism to Scandinavia. *Marie Grubbe*'s reception as a Danish counterpart to the novels of Flaubert, Zola, Mérimée, Turgenev, and the Goncourts was central to its notoriety and success, helping to pave the way for like-minded writers whose objective and naturalist styles, whose impartiality and shrinking from moral judgment, whose perceived focus on all that was considered obscene, immoral, and depraved by bourgeois society was met with hostility by the conservative cultural elites who continued to dominate Copenhagen until the turn of the century. Even from abroad there came a distinguished wrinkling of the nose: the Nobel Prize–winning German author Paul Heyse wrote to Georg Brandes accusing the young Danish authors of having established a "veritable clinic in which all the wounds and boils of society are exposed."[42]

From the trial of *Madame Bovary* in 1857 to the complete outlawing of Zola's novels in England in 1888, it was obvious that literary realism was a dangerous occupation. Scandinavia was not exempt from such moralizing vigilance. In 1875 the Danish translator of Claude Prosper Jolyot de Crébillon's novel *The Sofa: A Moral Tale* was imprisoned for a month. In 1891, the translator of Guy de Maupassant's *Bel Ami* was fined 200 kroner. In Sweden, Strindberg was tried (and acquitted) for blasphemy when he published his story collection *Getting Married* (1884). Other writers, including Edvard Brandes, Herman Bang, and Hans Jæger, similarly ran afoul of the authorities. While writing *Marie Grubbe*, Jacobsen worried that he might also be prosecuted for obscenity. His publisher, the genteel but squeamish Hegel, voiced similar concerns. He even wrote to Jacobsen advising him to be careful; a book critic at *Dagstelegrafen* had reportedly complained of a slew of recent "bordello novels," among which he included *Marie Grubbe*.[43]

Debates about the influence of literary realism on the moral fabric of society were legion. In response to one such debate, the twenty-two-year-old journalist Herman Bang wrote "Thoughts on Danish Realism," which appeared in *Dagbladet* in April 1879. Bang defended realism on the grounds that it was not an ideology but an art form that allowed for a multiplicity of points of view. In a remarkable passage that anticipates Knut Hamsun, he wrote the following:

> The portrait of the individual life of the soul will always fracture into several portraits. The multiplicity of what is perceived is too overwhelming, and the author is taken aback by his own power to fuse the many disparate and contradictory parts contained in a single life. I therefore know of no realist novel that is not also a collection of portraits, loose pages torn from the great book of the human soul, a book no one has read all the way through, and whose conclusion therefore remains a mys-

tery. Writers in this sense are like scientists: their progress discourages them by showing them all the things they don't know, since they cannot vouch for something they have not observed. Unfortunately, it must be added, they have observed very little. But the good thing is that they don't attempt to show us any more than they are capable of. The same goes for writers.[44]

The article was expanded into a book, *Realism and Realists*, published later that summer, and it included essays on, among others, Balzac, Zola, and J. P. Jacobsen. Bang was a friend of Vilhelm Møller and even dedicated the book to him; when it eventually reached Jacobsen, sequestered in Thisted, he only remarked that H. P. Hansen's illustration of him, included in the book, made his mustache resemble the head of a baleen whale—"That's how toothbrushy it is."[45]

Bang's essay on Jacobsen was perhaps the most perceptive of the contemporary reviews of *Marie Grubbe*. He rightly saw that Marie's journey to the ferry transport did not constitute a fall and certainly did not warrant any condemnation from the novel's author. Bang, in fact, lamented that Jacobsen had not been *more* objective, *more* ruthless. "Zola would have understood to let this woman, who begins by searching for a man, slowly but surely end up searching for a body, for Zola knows no mercy," he wrote.[46]

Edvard Brandes repeatedly tried to convince Jacobsen to intervene in the realist polemics—without any luck. Despite being repeatedly invoked as a champion of naturalism, Jacobsen was steadily distancing himself from the prevailing literary fashion he had helped to inaugurate. He told Edvard that he admired Zola but considered him an inferior craftsman. "Zola is not detailed enough psychologically, and he hands me his details in a bundle; but I don't want them in a bundle, I want them in a properly arranged bouquet," he complained. "Very well, he has the courage to be truthful, but that's not enough."[47]

Nothing could have been further from the gluttony of Zola than the bleak visions of "Two Worlds"—or, indeed, the deepening interiority of Jacobsen's novel-in-progress *Niels Lyhne.* Perhaps Edvard Brandes tried to goad Jacobsen into public debates because he knew what a remarkably discerning reader he was. To his friends he had already gained a reputation for being a quite ruthless critic. He said of Skram's *Gertrude Colbjørnson* that it was "one of those novels that walks on all fours," and he dismissed Holger Drachmann's *Poul og Virginie under nordlig bredde* (1879), claiming, "There is absolutely nothing to the book. Nothing." He reserved particular venom for Karl Gjellerup, whom he accused of wearing his freethinking lightly and casually: "He's like a child playing with razors; when he cuts his fingers, he just wipes the blood all over the adults' dinner jackets."[48]

It's fair to assume that Jacobsen was also slightly envious of the productivity of his peers, even if he didn't always care for what they wrote. In the almost four years since *Marie Grubbe*'s publication, Drachmann alone had written five novels, a travelogue, four books of poetry, and a short story collection. Georg Brandes, meanwhile, had written a book on Danish poets and a biography of Søren Kierkegaard, as well as studies of Esaias Tegner and Benjamin Disraeli. In *Niels Lyhne,* Jacobsen would leave it to a minor character to describe the fate of being an artist who cannot create:

> I sit here and mope and don't get anything done, can't get anything done, and then I start to notice how time is slipping

away from me, hours, weeks, months! With nothing in them they rush past me, and I can't nail them to the spot with work. I don't know if you can understand what I mean, it's just a kind of feeling I have, but I want to take hold of time with something that I've created. You see: when I paint a picture, the time it takes will always be mine, or I get something out of it; time doesn't end because it has passed. I feel sick when I think about the days that are passing—interminably. And I don't have anything, or I can't get at it. It's torture; I can get so furious that I have to pace the floor at something idiotic so that I won't start crying with rage, and then I almost go crazy when I stop again and realize that meanwhile time has been passing, and is passing while I'm thinking, and keeps on passing and passing. There is nothing so wretched as being an artist.[49]

Jacobsen's slow, gradualist approach to writing has often been upheld as a testament to his purity and Flaubertian reverence for *le mot juste*. Edmund Gosse wrote in Jacobsen's obituary that his books were "built up sentence by sentence, phrase by phrase. He would linger for days over a single page, until his ear was satisfied with the cadence and his eye with the color of every clause,"[50] while Edvard Brandes similarly wrote that for Jacobsen there was no higher truth than the perfect word: "He worshipped *the word*. For him it was the beginning and the end of all things. His pious disdain for any profanation or poor execution of the highest and most significant, the essential and beautiful holy Word, meant that he wrote himself and his entire personality into even the most mundane and light-hearted communication."[51]

The reality was probably less romantic. Jacobsen himself confessed that he was lazy, that he had a knack for daydreaming, and that he was capable of spending many hours a day doing absolutely nothing. In a letter to Axel Helsted he compared being an artist to being like Sisyphus, sentenced to roll a rock up a mountain over and over again. Perhaps being both a discerning, careful writer and a dawdling gradualist were, in Jacobsen's case, two sides of the same coin: writing was the only meaningful thing he could wrest from the untold hours he spent living horizontally, but by its very nature this writing would have to be incremental and slowly, even languidly, observed. Perhaps, then, the circumstances under which he wrote helped to shape his aesthetics. In the endless and uneventful days, the even longer nights, the darkness, the blankness, the emptiness yawning open, the longing and the sorrow, day upon day—"like the slow continual fall of snow, one flake after another"[52]—Jacobsen wrote with a sensitivity to the external world and the passing of time that other, more active, engaged authors might not have shared or even noticed.

Jacobsen's long-awaited second novel was beginning to seem a distant prospect. In Rome he'd read a few pages to Edvard Brandes, who delivered his earnest verdict to Georg: "It made a poor impression on me. I suspect the book will fall apart into little pieces."[53] To Georg's impatient inquiries Jacobsen responded, "My book has become very sad but good, especially as far as the internal composition goes."[54]

"Sad" is putting it mildly. Something more fundamental had changed since Jacobsen had first described his novel as being about "poor freethinkers," and "Two Worlds" is an obvious clue. Critics have argued the story marks a crucial change not only in Jacobsen's style, but also in his outlook on life. The scholar Aage Knudsen argues that Jacobsen, motivated by the thought of the few years he had left in life, developed a tendency to make a strong distinction between different kinds of lived experience: "His faith in Darwinism, the gospel of nature, and the fellowship of belonging to the army of progress did not alter the fact that when it came to his tragic fate he was utterly alone."[55]

"Two Worlds," Knudsen argues, sprang from Jacobsen's acute sense of isolation—an isolation that was physical as much as it was intellectual. Jacobsen's impatience with his contemporaries, even his friends, is a testament to both his hard-won independence and his artistic integrity. "As soon as you don't believe what you're supposed to believe," he wrote to Emanuel Fraenkel, "proponents become just as formidable as opponents."[56]

But his isolation was also emotionally felt. The cavalier attitude of the many so-called atheists running around the cafés in Copenhagen, with their cursory familiarity with Darwin and Strauss and Feuerbach, was a sign that they had not thought seriously about godlessness. To someone quite literally wasting away from a mortal illness, however, such issues were not merely the stuff of literary salons and opinion pages, but also matters of life and death. No doubt the sight of these writers casually tossing around ideas so dear and hard earned to Jacobsen was grueling. He felt he had twice their talent but none of their energy. "Speech is poor silver but silence golden," he wrote to Edvard Brandes, "and all the gold I've accumulated over the past four years will enshrine me and my forgotten person when I reemerge once again."[57]

CHAPTER SIX

The Atheist

He could not stand the indifference of life any longer, of
being released at every turn and always thrown back on
himself. No home on earth, no God in heaven, no goal out
there in the future!

—Jacobsen, *Niels Lyhne*

Two gifts perforce he has given us yet,
Though sad things stay and glad things fly;
Two gifts he has given us, to forget
All glad and sad things that go by,
And then to die.

—Charles Algernon Swinburne, "Félise" (1866)

IN late November 1880, the young Herman Bang was sent to
Thisted to cover a recent shipwreck near Klitmøller. The
Copenhagen-bound *Sleipner* had set sail from Grimsby in the
United Kingdom on November 12, carrying 480 tons of coal.
Just a few days later a severe leak prompted the captain to
divert to Klitmøller, but the ship banked on a reef just half a
mile off shore and was pummeled with waves during a storm.

All fourteen crew members drowned before rescue boats were able to reach them.

Bang went to see the remains of the ship that had washed up on the beach and interviewed locals who had witnessed the tragedy. Then he crossed the thin strip of land separating Klitmøller from the Limfjord and arrived at Thisted, where he decided to seek out the small harbor town's most famous living resident. Yet when he asked locals where he might find Jacobsen, people assumed he was referring to Christen, Jacobsen's father. "Oh, his son," they said, perhaps privately wondering why anyone would want to speak to that consumptive blasphemer. For Bang, however, it was a momentous occasion. He had greetings to convey from mutual friends in Copenhagen, and was surely curious to meet the famous and elusive author in the flesh. "I wasn't very old back then," he later recalled, "and I was very excited and nervous as I stood there in the little foyer or hallway or whatever it was, waiting to meet the author of *Marie Grubbe* for the first time." But when Jacobsen entered, Bang was startled. "I hadn't expected him to look like *that*—not *that* sick. His tall figure was almost doubled over. I, who had seen so much lurking disease, did not expect him to be so marked by death already."[1]

Death had long preoccupied Jacobsen. In a letter to Edvard Brandes he wrote that "there is really no other resolution possible than death," adding, "I would go so far as to say that any modern work of literature that ends is no good (a death ending excepted, and all conditions synonymous with it)."[2] Indeed *Niels Lyhne*, the last pages of which Jacobsen dispatched just a few days after Herman Bang's visit, is perhaps the most death-haunted novel in European literature. Compressed into fewer than two hundred pages are the deaths of no fewer than seven characters—including, famously, the hero himself. If in *Marie Grubbe* the emphasis was on the individual death we carry within us, death in *Niels Lyhne* is a metaphysical problem that asks questions of life—especially as the answers of religion have ceased to offer assurance. Tellingly, when Jacobsen first conceived of the novel, he called it *The Atheist*. Undoubtedly it is the fullest and most nuanced account of atheism in European literature—atheism not simply as an idea but as a living, fluctuating belief. In this respect it has been called a Kierkegaardian novel, haunted perhaps by *The Sickness unto Death* not only in its final words, but also in its dramatization of "the agonizing self-contradiction of not being able to do without a confidant and not being able to have one."[3]

For anyone still under the impression that Jacobsen had been writing a novel about Danish intellectuals in the mid-nineteenth century, *Niels Lyhne* must have seemed a curious failure. Georg Brandes, for one, complained that it wasn't historical enough. The intellectuals to which Niels Lyhne supposedly belongs (judging from Jacobsen's letters and notes) are those of the generation of 1848—"the strongest political generation in Danish history," according to the historian Henrik Gade Jensen.[4] These intellectuals oversaw the transition of Denmark from an absolute monarchy to something resembling a constitutional democracy, watching excitedly as liberal ideas blossomed across the European continent. They wrote poems about the November Uprising in Poland, distributed Paine-like leaflets advocating for the freedom of the press, and learned Arabic and exoticized the Orient.

None of this figures in Jacobsen's novel. The intellectual circles Niels travels in are "filled with what was new at the time, intoxicated with the theories of the New, wild with the power of the New," yet what the "gospel of the New" is remains unclear.⁵ The setting, too, is often thinly sketched. "All the concrete and everyday is left out of the novel," as one scholar puts it.⁶ Far from being a Zola-style plunge into the sights and sounds and smells of a teeming metropolis, *Niels Lyhne* is a seaside stroll at dusk. The novel's tragic events are compressed into unreality, into metaphor, and the prose seems at times to almost detach itself from the narrative—

> And now came a joyous time for Niels—that joyous time when the mighty swing of development sends you cheering beyond dead points in your nature, when everything in you grows and is filled so that, with the excess of your strength, you press your shoulder against mountains if required and bravely build up that Tower of Babel which is supposed to reach to heaven but which only becomes a pitiful stump of a colossus you build onto for your whole life with abject spires and curious orels.⁷

—and at other times, it seems to appeal directly to the reader's experience:

> Who among us—positioned by a kind fate in such a way that we could tend to the development of our own spirit—has not stared out over the mighty sea of knowledge with an enthusiastic gaze, and who has not been pulled down toward its clear, cool waters, to begin scooping it up in the hollow of our hands with the gullible arrogance of youth, just like the child in St. Augustine's legend?⁸

At such moments it seems as though Jacobsen had tried to dispense with inherited novelistic furniture altogether—some plot here, a little character there—in order to stretch the novel into one long and unbroken metaphor. In this way *Niels Lyhne* sometimes pinballs awkwardly between pure imagery and detached, observed detail. Alas, "It is not easy to free yourself from the ancestral bookcase," as Jacobsen writes,[9] and perhaps *Niels Lyhne*, like its hero, suffers from having been born half a century too late or half a century too early. Certainly it is a novel in which the strands of both realism and modernism are greedily imbricated. Much of what was so radical about *Niels Lyhne* was later streamlined into form by the likes of Hamsun, Rilke, Joyce, and Mann.

But as each of those writers acknowledged, it really was Jacobsen, who, with remarkable clarity and foresight, first gave expression to an entire *Weltanschauung*, one that would have a profound influence on European art, literature, and philosophy for decades to come. *Niels Lyhne* is one of the earliest evocations of the feeling of absurdity that Albert Camus canonized in *The Myth of Sisyphus*, a feeling brought on by a universe devoid of meaning, a universe in whose godless twilight man has become a stranger to himself—"deprived of the memory of a lost home or the hope of a promised land." Jacobsen's novel is a measured lament, an elegy for a life that is never fully lived. Niels Lyhne walks around with "the great coins of life jingling in his pocket" and longs to be seized and overwhelmed by life, *defined* by it. Instead, he finds himself "living in still waters with the coast in sight," a vessel without a crew. Later he tells his friend Erik Refstrup, "Generally, people don't really live. Most of the time people just exist."[10]

Niels Lyhne's conflicted nature is emphasized from the start. Born on the estate of Lønborggaard to a romantic mother and a prosaic father, he is the divided product of both; he inherits from his mother a dreamy nature that yearns for lyricism and imagination and from his father a down-to-earth pragmatism, a willingness to look on as life idly passes him by. This ambivalent double inheritance is emphasized by Jacobsen, who observes that Niels's parents, "without knowing it, were fighting a battle for his young soul from the moment a glimmer of intelligence appeared for them to seize hold of."[11]

When Niels is twelve, his glamorous aunt, Edele Lyhne, comes to live at Lønborggaard. A beautiful and much-envied socialite from Copenhagen, Edele suffers from consumption, and her doctor has advised her to pursue a more sedentary life in the country. But nothing at the provincial Lønborggaard is to her liking. The people there speak of Copenhagen "as if it were a city in the heart of Africa," the mealtimes are regulated by the sun, and "[all the] furniture crowded up against the walls, as though it were afraid of people."[12] She pines for Copenhagen:

> It was not only the amusements themselves that she missed so much; it was feeling her life resound audibly in the sound-filled air of the great city, and here in the country there was a silence in thoughts, in words, in eyes, in everything, so that you perpetually heard yourself with the same inescapable certitude with which you hear the ticking of the clock on a sleepless night. And knowing that back there people were living as they had lived before—it was like being dead and hearing the notes from a ballroom dying out over your grave in the still night air.[13]

One afternoon Niels encounters his aunt dozing on a sunlit chaise longue in one of the parlor rooms of the estate. Jacobsen's description is beautifully evocative: "She was stretched out on the sea-green satin of the chaise longue, dressed in a fantastic gypsy costume. She lay there on her back, her chin in the air, her throat extended, her forehead tilted back, and her long, loose hair flowing over the end of the chaise longue and onto the carpet. An artificial pome-granate flower had washed ashore on the island formed by a bronze-colored leather shoe in the middle of the dull-gold stream."[14] Niels is dumbstruck by the beauty and sensuality of Edele's figure. Handing her some flowers she'd asked him to pick, he bends over her "matte-white, gently curving legs and those long, narrow feet that had something of a hand's intel-ligence in their finely cradled contours."[15] On the verge of fainting, he runs off to his room and throws himself on his bed, hot with adolescent desire. Henceforth Niels vows to look on Edele as a "wonderfully exalted creature, made divine through a strange mystery and beauty."[16]

But soon Edele's illness takes a turn for the worse, and it is clear to all that she will shortly die. Niels is inconsolable. He prays tearfully, desperately to God, begging him not to take her away. "You can't see that she's dying, you can't see that she's dying, listen to me, take your hand away, take it away, I can't lose her, God, I can't."[17] Edele, meanwhile, thinks fondly of Copenhagen on her deathbed, lying pale and still while, below her window, "white flowers blushed like roses in the glow of the setting sun."[18] Her final, inaudible words are, "Send my greetings to . . . Copenhagen!" Surrounded by her family, she dies at twilight: "The shadows grew—the shadows of evening and death."[19]

God's silence, his refusal to spare young Edele's life, pro-pels Niels into decisive, blasphemous rebellion: "If God had no ears, then Niels would have no voice; if God had no mercy, then Niels would have no adoration, and he defied God and turned Him out of his heart." Jacobsen adds: "His faith had flung itself in blind flight against the gates of heaven, and now it lay on Edele's grave with broken wings. For he had believed, he had had that straightforward, dazzling, fairy-tale faith that a child so often has."[20]

It's a familiar sort of rebellion, recognizably adolescent in its stubborn resolve and wounded bitterness. We know it from John Stuart Mill's *Autobiography* and Edmund Gosse's *Father and Son* and from contemporary accounts by Richard Dawkins (in *The God Delusion*) and Ayaan Hirsi Ali (in *Infidel*). But Jacobsen is much more explicit about the paradoxes of Niels's rebellion: "He took sides, as completely as he could, against God, but like a vassal who takes up arms against his rightful master because he still believed he could not banish his faith."[21] Niels longs to pray, longs to call out to God, but he adamantly refuses to act on this desire. In other words, he merely shuts the door on God as one might an angry parent. He cannot quit the house of faith altogether.

Niels grows up to become an aspiring writer and embarks on the provincial's familiar march to the metropolis, where, like another Frederic Moreau, he moves in a circle of young, freethinking artists clustered around a slightly older woman, the charming, bohemian Fru Boye, with whom he falls in love. Yet their relationship, if we can call it that, is cut short when Niels receives a letter from home telling him his father is dying. By the time he arrives, his father has already died, and soon his mother too is taken ill. Niels remains at Løn-borggaard to take care of her. There is a moving exchange in which she chastises herself for having filled her son's head with nonsense and useless dreams. "Mother," Niels tells her, "I am a poet—truly—in my very soul. Don't think these are childish dreams or dreams of vanity. . . . I *will* join in the fight for Greatness, and I promise you that I will never falter, always be faithful to myself and what I possess; only the best will be good enough for me and nothing more; no compromises, Mother."[22]

Niels takes his mother abroad—to Clarens, in Switzerland, the setting of her beloved Rousseau's famous novel *Julie, ou la nouvelle Héloïse*. She dies there, and Niels buries her in the "pleasant cemetery . . . where the brown mulch of the vineyards protects the children of so many lands and where the broken pillars and veil-shrouded urns repeat the same words of sorrow in so many languages."[23]

On his return to Copenhagen, Niels is devastated by the news that Fru Boye is engaged. He is bitter and indignant, contemptuous that she of all people should have "thrown herself into the arms of the society she had so often ridiculed."[24] Heartbroken, he isolates himself to focus on his writing. Dining alone in a restaurant on Christmas Eve, he runs into Dr. Hjerrild, a family acquaintance known for his religious freethinking and political conservatism. Walking through the streets of Copenhagen together, they begin to discuss religion. Dr. Hjerrild challenges Niels's atheism, reminding him of the power Christianity still holds. "There is no God, and the human being is His prophet!" is Niels's bitter reply. Dr. Hjerrild agrees but cautions Niels that depriving people of the illusion of religion will not make them any happier. Far from it. Atheism, he argues, "is so boundlessly pedestrian, and its goal, in the long run, is nothing less than a disillusioned humanity."[25] Niels responds with an exalted vision of utopian atheism:

> "But don't you see," exclaimed Niels, "that the day humanity can freely cry, 'There is no God,' on that day a new heaven and a new earth will be created as if by magic. Only then will heaven become free, infinite space instead of a threatening, watchful eye. Only then will the earth belong to us and we to the earth, when the dim world of salvation and damnation out there has burst like a bubble. The earth will be our proper fatherland, the home of our heart where we do not dwell as foreign guests for a paltry time but for all our days. And what intensity it will give life when everything must be contained in life and nothing is placed outside of it. That enormous stream of love, which now rises up toward that God who is believed in, will bend back over the earth when heaven is empty, with loving steps toward all the beautiful, human traits and talents with which we have empowered and adorned God in order to make God worthy of our love."[26]

Dr. Hjerrild is impressed by Niels's faith in humanity but not convinced: "Atheism will make greater demands on people than Christianity does," he suggests.[27] Niels agrees but insists that the struggle for enlightenment and progress will gradually win over its share of followers—little by little, generation by generation—until one fine day the few have become the many.

One summer Niels and his childhood friend Erik Refstrup, a painter recently back from Rome, visit Niels's Aunt Rosalie in Fjordby. During their stay they both fall in love with Niels's cousin Fennimore, who in turn falls in love with Erik. Then, in characteristic Jacobsen fashion, the narrative jumps ahead three years: Fennimore and Erik are married and living in Mariagerfjord in Jutland. Niels, meanwhile, has sunk into a listless tedium. He drifts about in Copenhagen, neither writing nor wanting to, disillusioned and alone: "Niels Lyhne was tired; those perpetual attempts at a leap that was never leaped had exhausted him; everything was empty and worthless for him, distorted and confused, and so trivial as well. It seemed most natural to him to close his ears and shut his mouth and then sink down into studies that had nothing to do with the nausea of the world."[28]

Erik and Fennimore's marriage, meanwhile, has begun to disintegrate. Niels is summoned by his troubled friend, whose dissatisfaction with his life in the country, a wasteland of inspiration, has driven him into the company of a dissolute group of local farmers and landowners who spend their nights and weekends drinking and playing cards. But while Erik indulges his newfound vices, Niels and Fennimore grow intimate and eventually engage in an affair. Niels moves in across the fjord, and for several months the deception continues—until one night when Erik is thrown from his horse in Aalborg and killed. Fennimore immediately concludes that God is punishing her: "She looked around her with a frightened gaze, then fell to her knees and prayed for a long time. She repented and confessed, wildly and recklessly with ever-increasing passion, with exactly the same fanatical hatred toward herself that makes a nun flagellate her naked body."[29]

Stricken with grief, pale with remorse, Niels travels abroad. He is entirely alone in the world, with no family or friends or even a home to speak of. He resides briefly in Riva del Garda in northern Italy, where he befriends the singer Madame Odero, but after two years of aimless wandering he returns resignedly to his childhood home, Lønborggaard. There he takes up farming and finds a certain comfort in the unreflective labor it involves: "There was no stone of Sisyphus in agriculture."[30] He also—at last—finds love: he marries Gerda, the young daughter of a neighbor, and together they have a son.

Though Niels has no desire to take Gerda's faith away from her, his young wife nevertheless insists that he instruct her in his atheism. Niels obliges her, careful to make "his beliefs as beautiful and beneficent as he could, but he also did not hide from her how oppressively heavy and inconsolable the truth of atheism could be to bear during hours of sorrow, in comparison with that bright, joyous dream of a heavenly father who guides and rules."[31]

Three years into their marriage, Gerda suddenly falls deathly ill. In the deeply moving scene of her death, she recoils from her husband's atheism, falling back fearfully on the bosom of her childhood faith: "It's impossible, Niels, for everything to be over at death. You can't feel it, you who are healthy. You think it must kill us completely because we grow so listless and everything disappears, but that is only true outwardly."[32] She is visited by the local pastor, who reads to her from the Gospels and the Psalms, and Gerda's reconciliation with the God she had rejected out of love for her husband is like a homecoming: "Then the right won out in her heart— the deep submission before the almighty, judging God; the bitter tears of remorse before the forsaken, blasphemed, and tortured God; and the humble, bold yearning for the new pact of bread and wine with the inscrutable God."[33]

Niels has barely recovered from the loss of his wife when his son, too, becomes sick. One day he returns from the fields to find his little boy in bed with a fever. The sight of his suffering is, finally, too much even for Niels to endure:

> Niels raised his clenched fist threateningly toward heaven; he seized hold of his child with the insane thought of fleeing, and then he threw himself to his knees on the floor and prayed to the Lord who is in heaven, who keeps the kingdom of earth in fear with trials and admonitions, who sends poverty and sickness, suffering and death, who wants everyone's knees to bend with trembling, and from whom no escape is possible, not to the farthest ocean nor down into the abyss—He, God, who if He pleases will trample on the one you love most here in the world and torture your loved ones underfoot, back into the dust from which He Himself has created them.
>
> With thoughts like this, Niels prayed to God and threw himself down helplessly before the throne of heaven, recognizing that His was the power, His alone.[34]

But as with Niels's prayers for God to save Edele, so his admonition for God to spare the life of his little boy is likewise met with cruel silence.

Niels is a broken man. Not only has he lost his wife and son, but he has also lost his "faith in the power of humanity to bear the life it must live." Jacobsen mischievously turns the religious categories on their head, paradoxically describing Niels's temptation into prayer as "a fall from grace, a fall away from himself and from the Idea."[35] Disillusioned with his lapsed atheism yet contemptuous as ever of the Christian God, Niels enlists in the army and is mortally wounded in the war of 1864. At the field hospital he is visited by Dr. Hjerrild, who asks him if he would like to see a pastor. "I have no more use for pastors than you do," Niels rebuffs him, even as he thinks to himself that it would have been "so good to have a god to whom he could complain and pray." In his final hours he begins to hallucinate, says he wants to die on his feet, and then slowly succumbs: "And finally he died the death—the difficult death."[36]

Niels Lyhne is an astonishingly candid and full-blooded account of the ambiguities of atheism. For Jacobsen atheism was not simply an idea, a radical posture; it was a difficult moral commitment. Despite protestations to the contrary, he took atheism far more seriously than any of his contemporaries. Like the new atheists of today, the café society atheism so common among liberal intellectuals at the time was by and large "a protest against a God others believed in."[37] These atheists railed against religion as a system of belief, as a moral and political influence on society, not as an existential injustice. Jacobsen's quarrel with God, on the other hand, was a metaphysical rebellion. It was, indeed, almost a kind of God-hatred—what the literary scholar Bernard Schweizer calls misotheism: "a response to suffering, injustice, and disorder in a troubled world. Misotheists feel that humanity is the subject of divine carelessness or sadism, and they question God's love for humanity."[38]

Claudio Magris has rightly described *Niels Lyhne* as a "critique of positivistic atheism."[39] Contrary to most nineteenth-century atheists, Magris argues, Jacobsen's narrative of godlessness is not a deliverance from dark superstition into rational light; *Niels Lyhne* is often quite explicit about the consequences the loss of faith entails. Jacobsen in this regard is close to Nietzsche, who around the same time *Niels Lyhne* was published wrote, "God is dead. God remains dead. And we have killed him. How shall we, the murderers of all murderers, comfort ourselves?"[40] *Niels Lyhne* raises similar questions. We can see the development of Niels's atheism from a Feuerbachian humanism into a sink of exhaustion. The man who triumphantly declares, "The day that humanity can freely cry, 'There is no God,' on that day a new heaven and a new earth will be created as if by magic,"[41] is not the same man who, at the end of the novel, wearily asks: "Atheism, the New, truth's holy cause—what purpose do they all serve? What were they but names of tinsel for the one simple idea: to endure life as it was!"[42]

Niels resigns himself to the fact that atheism can offer no more answers to our suffering than theology can; his proud non-belief has contracted into despair and disillusion. What is so deeply haunting about the novel's ending is its bleak uncertainty, its Hardyan remorselessness. The warring ideas of religion and atheism have been quashed by mere life; the novel has chipped away at everything that might bring comfort to human existence, leaving Niels alone in an existential no-man's-land. He has no home, no friends, and no spouse; he has no direction, no ambition; he has neither belief nor unbelief to take comfort in. His death is "difficult" because it poses a metaphysical problem for life. The fact that we die, and that we live to see even our loved ones die, is an existential cruelty, demanding of answers about the purpose of our existence—a demand that is essentially religious, as James Wood has argued: "For life to have meaning life must in some way be *extended*."[43] But since he vehemently rejects the idea of eternal life, Niels dies his uneasy, rebellious death without resolve, his illusions shattered. "It's a beautiful death, to die for our poor country," Dr. Hjerrild consoles him on his deathbed.

"Yes," Niels responds, "but that's not the way we dreamed about doing our utmost, that time long, long ago."[44]

Niels Lyhne appeared in bookstores on December 9, 1880. Once again Jacobsen was reduced to simply looking on from Thisted as Copenhagen's baffled literati argued over whether or not *Marie Grubbe*'s young author was living up to his promise. "His whole outlook has undoubtedly been strongly affected by his isolation," *Dagbladet* wrote; "it is a depressing book one ought not to read for pleasure."[45] *Berlingske Tidende* likewise lamented the novel's lack of "a healthy foundation,"[46] while *Fædrelandet* strongly emphasized that though undoubtedly a work of extraordinary polish, it was "far from a masterpiece."[47]

Reviews were mixed, to say the least. Once again, no one knew quite what to make of Jacobsen's prose. It was very evocative, but what did it mean? To a slightly younger generation of new literary voices, like Henrik Pontoppidan and Jakob Knudsen, it bordered on pure affect. Even Georg Brandes thought the novel had "500 adjectives too many."[48] Few had the patience, or the inclination, to pause over Jacobsen's prose and notice its ringing precision, its nimble lyricism—the way, for instance, Lyngby's red church is seen "on its pedestal of graves,"[49] or "the gentle, sleepy, steady tapping of the venetian blinds" heard in a Copenhagen apartment,[50] or the "slow now-again now-again dropping of a parlor clock into the bowl of the day, full of meaningless seconds."[51]

Too often, *Niels Lyhne*'s prose was seen as beautiful but incoherent, a necklace of glittering details but never a totality. In his *Theory of the Novel* (1914), Lukács echoes much of this ambivalence: "The hero's life which was meant to become a work of literature and is instead only a poor fragment, is actually transformed into a pile of debris by the form-giving process; the cruelty of disillusionment devalues the lyricism of the moods, but it cannot endow the characters and events with substance or with the gravity of existence. The novel remains a beautiful yet unreal mixture of voluptuousness and bitterness, sorrow and scorn, but not a unity; a series of images and aspects, but not a life totality."[52]

Of course Lukács, not unlike Brandes, is a poor reader of modernist prose (he wrote elsewhere that the tragedy of the post-Flaubertian writer was that he "did not actively participate in society"),[53] so *Niels Lyhne* remains for him a socially and politically useless novel. Lukács wants totality, wholeness, unity; for Jacobsen such grandeur would be dishonest. The modern individual stands alone in an absurd world, subject to thoughts and impressions and impulses he cannot fathom, let alone control. He is a stranger to himself and others and knows that joy and sorrow are but fleeting convulsions of feeling, waves lapping at his being but never guiding it.

Lukács's reading of *Niels Lyhne*, like many of the novel's contemporary reviews, seems based on a frustration with Jacobsen's perceived *lack* of realism: the absence of the naturalistic impulse for social, political, and material detail. Naturally there are flashes of intense, Flaubertian visuality, but the careful accumulation of detail—what the critic Peter Brooks calls "thing-ism"[54]—is less pronounced in *Niels Lyhne* than in *Marie Grubbe*. Hence the complaints about the novel being vague and plotless. Even Robert Musil had to confess the following to his diary in 1936: "It is at least the third time in my life that I have read this novel but I have no idea what happens in it."[55]

But these perceived failures or limitations, the cause of so much consternation and head scratching among Jacobsen's friends, turn out to be prescient intimations of modernism. Jacobsen does not dispense with Niels Lyhne's childhood and background the way Hamsun does with the narrators of *Hunger* and *Mysteries*, but he gives less weight to them than many of his contemporaries might have. Similarly, the fact that Rilke felt he could recognize Copenhagen from *Niels Lyhne* is ironic given that the physical setting of the novel is only ever thinly sketched. Jacobsen's Copenhagen is hardly Zola's Paris or Gissing's London.

In fact, Jacobsen almost entirely jettisons the referential babble often associated with the late nineteenth-century realist novel—the same babble Virginia Woolf later took up arms against in her literary essays of the early 1920s. Street names, physical objects, articles of clothing, material goods, food, and furniture are mentioned only sparingly in *Niels Lyhne*. What we get instead is an emphasis on interior states, atmosphere, and impressions. It's interesting that the foremost literary Darwinist of his time had no interest in the prevailing fashion of literary Darwinism; Zola's claim, set forth in *Le Roman expérimentale* (1880), that the scientific method could be applied to the creation of fictional character (what Peter Brooks wittily calls "the Bronx Zoo principle"),[56] is deeply contrary to Jacobsen's art, as he explained at length in a letter to Edvard Brandes: "It has lately become fashionable in the natural sciences to say that too much has been made of the theory of evolution. Such an accusation could not reasonably be leveled at *works of fiction*. Here we almost always encounter fully evolved characters. Even in those cases where an attempt has been made at development, there's never any real evolution, just a fixed nature embellished and refined and repeated, page after page. The fact that they aren't capable of doing all sorts of things naturally strengthens their consistency, but it robs them of life."[57]

Against these fixed and static characters, Jacobsen emphasized the fluidity and incongruousness of human nature—a cause Hamsun would take up in his essays and lectures of the late 1880s and 1890s, when he began his assault on literary establishment figures like Henrik Ibsen and Bjørnstjerne Bjørnson. In this regard, *Niels Lyhne* represents a break with literary tradition. It marks the point at which the novel turned inward, anticipating the more resolute disruptions of Hamsun, Rilke, and Joyce, among others. Adorno was right to say of Proust that his work belonged to a tradition that began with *Niels Lyhne*; few, if any, novels before it have represented the sensations of contingency, randomness, and disintegration so fully and so poignantly. No wonder Freud loved it.

In the Norwegian press *Niels Lyhne* provoked a fierce debate between Amalie Skram and the poet and theater critic Kristofer Randers. In an essay titled "Modern Pessimism," Randers claimed that reading *Niels Lyhne* was like strolling through a burial chamber.[58] He deplored its perceived nihilism and accused Jacobsen of upholding Niels as an ideal to be emulated. Skram accused him of willful misreading. In her response she defended Niels Lyhne as a type, a necessary literary product of his time. Jacobsen's novel, she wrote,

shows us that life in the late nineteenth century "makes greater demands of human beings than their constitutions can
deliver."[59]

The exchange caught the attention of Bjørnstjerne Bjørnson, newly returned from America, who deplored Skram's
admiration of "this sensual monk, who sits in his cell painting
lustful pictures on his canvas." If *Marie Grubbe* had left
Bjørnson cold, *Niels Lyhne* set his temper ablaze. He accused
Danish literature of "art for art's sake," of being politically
toothless, and he simply couldn't fathom Georg Brandes's
admiration for that "consumptive" and his yearning, colorful
prose. Amalie Skram, aghast, was having none of it. "I admire
Jacobsen so much that I would happily kiss him right on his
lips for the sake of this book," she exclaimed.[60] Her comment
must have sent Bjørnson reeling.

Brandes intervened in the Norwegian debate, rising to
his friend's defense, but privately he was not particularly en-
amored of *Niels Lyhne* either. Few of Jacobsen's friends were.
"What a strange talent Jacobsen is," Sophus Schandorph
wrote to Brandes; "he both excites and discourages me at
once. I experience the strangest vacillations on every page of
this book!"[61] Georg Brandes agreed: "Your objections to *Niels
Lyhne* are absolutely right. It is (1) a purely subjective, grandly
stylized book, (2) the work of a sick man. But I feel so sorry for
J. P. J., who is forced to live up there in Thisted and doesn't
have any money."[62] Even Edvard was displeased: "The entire
book is so strangely empty; all its emphasis is on style, and at
times it's so damned affected."[63]

Their reservations were not lost on Jacobsen, who, when
he read Georg Brandes's review of *Niels Lyhne*, published in

Morgenbladet in February 1881, confessed to Edvard that "the article gives me the impression that Georg largely, perhaps even unconsciously, wrote it as a favor to me." He rightly suspected this was true of most of his friends. "I entertain dark suspicions that you all think I've been unfortunate and regressed, and yet none of you want to be the first to tell me," he wrote.[64]

Brandes's review was indeed dutiful and workmanlike—a gesture of reluctant diplomacy. He praised Jacobsen's style and talent and his ear for unusual expressions and exquisite imagery, but the novel's ambiguities were altogether lost on him. Instead, he kept trying to tease out what wasn't there: a material diagnosis of contemporary Danish society. Jørgen Knudsen, Brandes's biographer, argues that Jacobsen's portrayal of a weak freethinker, his "paralyzed levelheadedness" and slow disillusionment, was poison to Brandes's demand for robust intellectual strength. Knudsen even goes so far as to say that his review of *Niels Lyhne* was among the most pedestrian things Brandes ever wrote.[65] In a letter to his brother, Georg was more open about his criticisms: "He makes a big deal out of all this God stuff, don't you think? The masses will probably view it as an admission of the despairing condition of the unbelievers."[66] In other words, *Niels Lyhne* was fodder for the enemy.

In a no less dutiful letter thanking Brandes for his review, Jacobsen wrote of his disappointment with the novel's overall reception and of the focus on its perceived pessimism in particular:

> Isn't it odd that everyone, not just *Dagbladet*, but absolutely everyone, complains that the story is sad, discouraging, hopeless,

sick! Everyone breathes a sigh of longing for something life-affirming, delightful, healthy, hopeful. It's almost as if the author had exposed a secret doubt in everyone, and yet he is pounced on with anger and accusations of pessimism. But the author isn't a pessimist; it's the readers who are afraid of becoming one.[67]

Yet *Niels Lyhne* was not without its champions. One of the earliest reviews, published in *Illustreret tidende*, came from the pen of H. S. Vodskov, Jacobsen's old friend from Studiestræde. "There's no longer any doubt that J. P. Jacobsen is among our most independent authors," he cheekily wrote, no doubt with the Brandes brothers in mind.[68] Vodskov rightly intuited Jacobsen's breakthrough in his representation of "all that is unconscious and semi-conscious in our inner lives" and even anticipated criticisms about the novel's plotlessness: "The wave-like motion of our feelings, the thousands of tiny impressions we don't know about but whose many nuances determine our being, are often more dear to him than the words or actions they result in."[69] The review thrilled Jacobsen. He wrote at once to Vodskov, expressing his deepest gratitude. Even Frederik V. Hegel thought it an exceptional piece of writing and told Jacobsen that it was "considerably better" than Georg Brandes's.[70]

Two noteworthy voices that likewise joined *Niels Lyhne*'s small but passionate group of admirers came from Norway. One was the novelist Alexander Kielland, who wrote to Edvard Brandes that Jacobsen "really is, between you and me, the only novelist writing in our language today whom I bow deeply for."[71] The other was Henrik Ibsen. In a letter to Hegel he called *Niels Lyhne* "a fine work in every respect; I venture to say that it is one of the very best of its kind which has been written in our day."[72] Jacobsen couldn't help gushing in a letter to Edvard Brandes: "Through Hegel, who heard it from John Paulsen, I'm told that Ibsen is very preoccupied with *Niels Lyhne*, that he spent four weeks reading it, talks about it every day, and reads from it to his dinner party guests."[73]

Even so, *Niels Lyhne*'s lukewarm reception, compounded by the fact that the first edition did not sell out the way *Marie Grubbe* did, weighed heavily on Jacobsen. He himself regarded it as the finest thing he'd ever written and certainly the most personal. Scattered throughout the novel and among its characters were observations, impressions, and sentiments he felt he'd paid a steep price to experience. In some respects the novel was a confession of his anxieties, fears, and uncertainties—things he knew many of his friends would not necessarily understand or sympathize with.

Rather than despair over his novel's immediate reception, however, Jacobsen cautioned himself to be patient. "I may yet be a sought-after author one day," he wrote to Hegel, "if only I can keep myself alive long enough."[74]

CHAPTER SEVEN

The Sickness unto Death

I rarely let go an opportunity to behold something magnificent; it's so healthy in this grey world to fill one's eyes with
color every once in a while.
—Jacobsen, letter to Emanuel Fraenkel, November 24, 1878

ON May 29, 1881, after an absence of more than four years, J.
P. Jacobsen finally returned to his beloved Copenhagen. He'd
spent months making arrangements—writing letters, looking
for apartments, and checking in with friends and acquaintanc-
es, many of whom he had not seen in years. ("Five years is a
long time," he wrote to Vilhelm Møller, "but I'm sure we'll
recognize each other. I am, for my part, almost entirely unchanged.")[1] On his arrival he wrote at once to his brother that
he'd only thrown up three times during the crossing of Kattegat and that he would spend the first few days at a hotel
before moving into what was intended to be a temporary
lodging on the third floor of Ny Adelgade 5 but which turned
out to be Jacobsen's last home in Copenhagen.

The Norwegian writer Alexander Kielland and Jens Peter Jacobsen
(right), photographed in 1881. Courtesy of Thisted Museum.

This small but spacious two-bedroom apartment, described by one visitor as downright "ghastly,"[2] was hardly
ideal (even Jacobsen admitted it was extremely shabby), but it
was located just a stone's throw from Kongens Nytorv, the
city's largest public square, surrounded by the Hotel
d'Angleterre, the Hotel du Nord and its expanding depart-
ment store, the Thott Palace, the Royal Danish Theater, and
Charlottenborg Palace, where Denmark's youngest painters
were on display (including Carl Ludvig Tilson Locher, God-
fred Christensen, Wenzel Tornøe, and Jacobsen's friend from
Rome, Axel Helsted). One of Helsted's paintings, in fact,
would eventually grace the otherwise naked walls of Jacobsen's apartment, which would remain as drab and uninspiring

as when he first moved into it. Only a maroon chaise longue, donated by anonymous female admirers, added a little color to the wanting surroundings.

In spite of *Niels Lyhne*'s lukewarm reception and perhaps because the mere sight of the pale and wasted author aroused sympathy in anyone who laid eyes on him, Jacobsen was eagerly fêted by Copenhagen's literati. He dined at the estate of Frederik V. Hegel in Ordrup, visited the homes of prominent politicians on the left, and was invited to attend a dinner in honor of the French actor Benoît-Constant Coquelin. In letters to his brother Jacobsen boasted of all the people who stopped to chat with him in the street—critics, painters, editors, ladies—some of whom he'd never even met before. He also noted all the changes since he'd last been in the city. It was filled with Englishmen, a fact that surprised him, and everything had become very expensive.

In letters home Jacobsen repeatedly had to placate his family's concern about his health. "No cough worth mentioning," he'd say parenthetically, though it was almost certainly a lie.[3] His family had every reason to be worried: shortly before leaving for Copenhagen, Jacobsen had written to his old friend Fraenkel, asking his medical advice. For almost a week he'd suffered severe stomach cramps and bouts of diarrhea, despite having consumed only boiled milk and oatmeal. He went on in great detail to list a number of physical symptoms—a sign, perhaps, of his confidence in Fraenkel's medical expertise and his own alarm about his condition. Fraenkel, with almost equal alarm, immediately dispatched a number of pills to Thisted, which Jacobsen assured him had taken immediate effect.

For anyone concerned with what "a repository of human frailty" Jacobsen had become, as he put it in a letter to Agnes Møller, there was comfort to be taken from the fact that "when I'm at rest, it still looks as though the old machine is functional."[4] Resuming his old nocturnal habits, however, was out of the question, and Jacobsen's social life quickly contracted to the company of a few select friends. Even walking for too long could easily leave him gasping to catch his breath. Mostly he kept to himself, lying on his chaise longue in his gloomy apartment.

The sheer volume of letters Jacobsen exchanged with William reveals not only his ambivalence about being so far away from home in such precarious health, but also the deepening affection between the two brothers. While Jacobsen lived in Thisted, they had grown especially close, as Holger Drachmann noticed when he visited them during a trip to to Skagen in 1880. Being apart was difficult; Jacobsen regretted not being able to attend William's wedding to Elise Nielsen, sending instead a heartfelt letter wishing them a life of love and happiness. "I dearly would have liked to celebrate your wedding day with you, but given the impossibility of doing so I will drink a toast to you here, all by myself."[5]

But the difficulty of their separation was most keenly felt when Elise tragically passed away on September 8, 1881, just three days after giving birth to a baby daughter. Imagining his brother's sorrow made Jacobsen forget about his own illness: "I don't need to tell you, dear brother, that my heart is with you and that if you feel I can be of any use or comfort I will come home to you for a couple days. Just let me know."[6] He wrote to William several times in the days following Elise's death, doubtless eager to return the comfort and support William had shown him in his time of need. But he also knew his condition precluded him from being able to merely visit his remote and unreachable hometown. "I know you don't have time to write at any length," he wrote to William; "just send a few words here and there so that I can follow you in your grief. Just as this is only intended to be a handshake, a greeting. For I have no other comfort to offer you except the solemn fact that death is the eternal peace, the great silence, where no suffering exists and no sorrows, no worries, no disappointments—nothing at all."[7]

Jacobsen was already writing as if only half-present in this life—as if the ashen decade he'd already spent suffering from tuberculosis had been just a foretaste of the silence yet to come. The deaths of others were now like dress rehearsals. It is not a stretch to imagine that Jacobsen intended his words of comfort to be applicable not only to William's loss of his wife, but also to the inevitable loss of his older brother.

The Copenhagen Jacobsen returned to was a scene of great political turmoil. During the 1870s the growing influence of the Danish liberal party Venstre (Left), the advent of the socialist movement in Copenhagen, and not least the assault on religion and morality wrought by Georg Brandes had only strengthened the conservative grip on Danish political and cultural life. Internal conflict prevented Venstre from mounting a serious challenge to the political status quo; Louis Pio, leader of the Socialist International in Denmark, had been bribed by the Danish police to emigrate to America; Georg Brandes remained in exile in Berlin.

By the early 1880s, however, the conservative grip appeared to be loosening. In 1880, Edvard Brandes even managed to get himself elected to public office. A parliamentary seat on behalf of the electoral district on the island of Langeland had become vacant, and in September a constituency of 1,100 traditionally conservative Christian farmers elected a notoriously freethinking Jew to represent them in parliament for the Danish liberal party. Edvard, who scarcely knew that a Denmark existed beyond the streets of Copenhagen, was as surprised as anyone: "There was a rumor on the island that I was some sort of a monster who wouldn't dare to appear in public on Election Day," he wrote to Georg Brandes in Berlin. "On the contrary, the locals found that I was a *nice young man.*"[8]

Though in Georg's absence Edvard had managed to nourish some much-needed political allegiances, the issue of obtaining a professorship for Georg at the University of Copenhagen remained a thorny subject. Even the liberal party couldn't reconcile itself to the enmity Brandes continued to display toward religion. Nor did Edvard help matters when, during his election to parliament, he was asked to clarify his stance on religion. "He openly declared that he didn't believe in the god of the Christians or the Jews," a local newspaper in Langeland reported.[9]

Georg Brandes's status as a persona non grata in Danish political life was temporarily resolved in 1882, when a group of anonymous donors, forty-eight in total, raised enough money to compensate for a professor's salary if Brandes would only return to Copenhagen. The donors included friends, artists, schoolteachers, journalists, merchants, and academics.

The announcement of his return was emblazoned with equal parts triumph and dread in the Danish newspapers on July 14, 1882—Bastille Day, of all days.

Though as usual he remained interested but uninvolved, these political conflicts directly affected Jacobsen. Before returning to Copenhagen, he had been trying to qualify for a government stipend, desperately enlisting the services of Edvard Brandes and Frederik V. Hegel. His first two applications to the Ministry of Culture had gone unanswered; his third was rejected. Having earned a total of only 2,500 kroner in the last four years, Jacobsen imagined himself ideally qualified. And as he coolly wrote to Edvard, "It seems to me that it would be quite inexpensive to support a writer who, to the benefit of his writing but to the detriment of his wallet, always completes his projects before publishing them; who is by no means beneath his country's literary standards; who doesn't have an occupation or any fortune; and who in all probability would not be able to present the required life certificate to the ministry for more than a few years at most."[10]

Jacobsen was given a temporary grant of 1,000 kroner. A successful application for the regular stipend would take another two years for him to finally qualify for. Apparently the conservative minister of culture himself, Jacob Scavenius, was quite opposed to granting Jacobsen anything, just as he had been instrumental in preventing Georg Brandes from receiving a stipend a few years earlier. In Copenhagen, freethinking still had its consequences.

During these final years in Copenhagen Jacobsen formed a close attachment to the Norwegian writer Alexander Kielland, one of *Niels Lyhne*'s greatest admirers. Kielland was so smitten with Jacobsen's prose that he arranged to meet him when he found out he was living in Copenhagen again. Edvard Brandes helped facilitate the meeting, just as he had helped Kielland publish his first book, *Novelletter* (Novellas), with Gyldendal in May 1879. The book was a great success; Kielland and his family moved to Copenhagen two years later and spent the next few years on the outskirts of Østerbro, near Nordhavn.

At first glance, the two writers had precious little in common: Jacobsen—tall, pale, rail thin—was a sorry sight next to the portly, dandified Kielland. "He's so quiet and withholding," the Norwegian told Georg Brandes; "when I see this feeble creature I think to myself: he must find you so unbearable with all your vulgar good health. I could sit down and cry when he coughs and all his bones rattle inside him like an empty sack. There's something unfair about being a bull like me. There's enough strength and health in me for two people, and then one has to stare helplessly while someone like Jacobsen is consumed and extinguished and takes his leave of us. And then to sit here drinking burgundy, bursting with health."[11]

What Kielland possessed in flesh and health, however, Jacobsen made up for in critical severity. "I've tried my best, but much as I'd like to, I simply can't find anything significant or what you might call promising in it," Jacobsen wrote to Edvard Brandes of Kielland's *Noveletter*.[12] Kielland's second book, *Nye Novelletter* (New novellas, 1880), didn't make an impression either, but his novel *Garman and Worse* (1880) was "much improved" and seemed to Jacobsen reminiscent of the contemporary German novel, especially the works of "Spiel-hagen, Heyse, Gutzkow and those guys."[13] Little wonder Kielland called him a strict judge.

Despite their differences, Jacobsen and Kielland warmed immediately to one another. "I don't know that I've ever come to care for another human being as quickly as I have for Jacobsen," the Norwegian author confessed.[14] (In 1882 he dedicated *Else: A Christmas Story* to him.) Jacobsen quickly established himself as a regular fixture in Kielland's home, particularly on Sunday evenings, which were reserved especially for him. He dined there with Erik and Amalie Skram, never more at ease than when he could assume his customary seat on the sofa beneath a palm tree, sipping cognac and smoking a strong cigar. It was then that Jacobsen became known among his friends as "His Excellency"—so-named for his delicate bearing, polite conduct, and the top hat he had recently taken to wearing. His soft-spoken manners endeared him to the Kiellands' children, who eagerly gathered around him to hear the latest installment of *Robinson Crusoe* or *Thousand and One Nights*, which Jacobsen knew by heart.

Jacobsen even spent Christmas on Østerbro and on one occasion remained there for several weeks. Apparentlly Kielland's sister, the landscape painter Kitty, was quite taken with the mysterious house guest, a matter Jacobsen dismissed as being "quite unnecessary."[15] Edvard Brandes reported that Jacobsen occupied Kielland's study in those weeks, prevent-ing his host from beginning work on his new novel. Jacobsen himself, meanwhile, had with unusual haste written a new story, "The Plague in Bergamo," which first appeared in the collection of his short fiction published by Gyldendal in 1882, *Mogens and Other Stories.*

If people thought *Niels Lyhne* was pesimisstic, "The Plague in Bergamo" must have seemed downright misanthropic. Jacobsen's astonishing little fable, among the finest things he ever wrote, describes the effects of an outbreak of the plague on the inhabitants of Bergamo in northern Italy. At first, the citizens do everything in their power to contain the threat and preserve law and order. Victims are buried properly, medicine is distributed to the poor, and the church is filled with humble prayers and desperate laments. Before long, however, it becomes clear that no amount of divine entreaties will save the town. The citizens angrily reject God and throw themselves into sin: "The air was full of blasphemy and ungodliness, of the moans of gluttons and the howls of drunkards, and their wildest night was no blacker with iniquity than were their days."[16]

One day a procession of cross-bearing monks approaches the city. Hollow-cheeked and robe-clad, they solemnly enter Bergamo to the scorn and ridicule of its now debauched citizens. Once inside the church, the monks proceed to lash themselves with knots of rope in a frenzy, blood spraying from their shoulders and backs. The citizens are silenced by the spectacle. A young monk steps forth to the crowd and begins to preach at length about hell, about the severity of the law, and about the crucifixion of Christ. He tells the citizens that when Jesus looked down from the cross and saw the masses beneath him, he decided they were not worth saving:

He ripped his feet off the head of the nail, and he clenched his hands around the nail heads and yanked them out so that the arms of the nail cross curved like a bow, and he leapt down to earth and snatched up his robe so the dice rattled down the slope of Golgotha, and he slung it around him with the fury of a king and rose up to Heaven. And the cross stood there empty and the great work of atonement was never completed. There is no mediator between God and ourselves; there is no Jesus dead on the cross for us; there is no Jesus dead on the cross for us; *there is no Jesus dead on the cross for us.*[17]

The citizens of Bergamo are terrified by the sermon. One of them, a butcher, asks the monk if he wants them to crucify Jesus again. The desperate crowd agrees, shouting in unison: "Yes, yes, crucify him, crucify him!"[18] But the monk, gazing out over the crowd with its outstretched hands and contorted faces, simply raises his arms toward heaven and laughs. Then he picks up his cross and rejoins his procession as it walks silently into the vanishing light.

Again, Jacobsen uses the idea of unanswered prayer as a theological theme. To the citizens of Bergamo, God's silence means that everything is permitted; indeed, His absence is almost a kind of release. Yet when the monks begin to lash themselves, the citizens suddenly feel "something cold [tightening] around their scalps." They are seized by what they are witnessing: "There was a tiny spot of insanity in their brains that understood this madness."[19]

The story is savagely ironic: the people who abandon themselves to sin when their prayers go unanswered are the same people willing to crucify Jesus all over again if it means saving their souls. The monk's laughter is also, perhaps, Jacobsen's; as a darkly ironic parable of human nature, the story recalls the writings of Kierkegaard and anticipates both Kafka and Camus.

"The Plague in Bergamo" is unique in Jacobsen's work for its clipped precision, the detached and clinical manner of its prose. Kielland told Georg Brandes that it was "the most exceptional thing I've ever read in Danish. . . . There is nothing of the vagueness and imprecision I occasionally come across in [Jacobsen's] work—everything is incomparably brilliant and polished."[20]

Kielland was not alone in his opinion. At a meeting of the literary club Bogstaveligheden, established in 1880, Jacobsen read from the story to a small audience of enthralled admirers. The artist Erik Henningsen memorialized the occasion in his drawing *A Meeting at Bogstaveligheden on 1 March 1882* from 1910; in it Jacobsen is seated with his gaunt legs crossed at a round table surrounded by attentive friends. Georg Brandes is seated directly across from Jacobsen, astride a chair with his arms hooked over its back. Also portrayed are Erik Skram, Edvard Brandes, Sophus Schandorph, Karl Gjellerup, Holger Drachmann (arms crossed, a pipe dripping from his lips), and Harald Høffding, among others—in short, a who's-who of the Copenhagen literati. Henningsen recalled in his memoir that although Jacobsen read in a frail voice, his story made an overwhelming impression on everyone present.[21]

Since they had first united around Georg Brandes back in 1872, these "Men of the Modern Breakthrough" (as Brandes called them) were an alliance in disarray. Brandes's decisive return from his German exile in 1883, intended to reinvigorate the movement, only served to expose its weaknesses and shortcomings. Edvard had escaped briefly to Paris in pursuit of another man's wife; Holger Drachmann had practically embraced conservatism; Bjørnson refused to collaborate with Edvard on a proposed newspaper; the new political allegiances with the liberal party were already crumbling.

Bjørnson's 1883 play *En hanske* (The gauntlet), which bombed in the theater, eventually ignited the so-called Morality Feud (Sædelighedsfejden), a protracted public debate lasting several years that once more compromised Georg Brandes in the eyes of the Copenhagen bourgeoisie. At its peak, the debate was so sweeping that it touched not only on sexual morality in literature, but even encompassed sexually transmitted diseases, marital equality, the use of contraceptives, and prostitution. Brandes had already revealed his opposition to prevailing standards of sexual morality when he translated John Stuart Mill's *The Subjection of Women* back in 1869. "We treat our women's spirits the same way the Chinese treat their women's feet," he wrote in his foreword, "and like the Chinese, we perform this operation in the name of beauty and femininity."[22] During the Morality Feud he reiterated this argument. The suppression of female sexuality, he thundered, was both hypocritical and unhealthy.

The debate reached all corners of Scandinavia, galvanizing an already insurgent generation of young female authors, including Amalie Skram, Adda Ravnkilde, and Victoria Benedictsson (all of whom, perhaps revealingly, died by their own hand). In Norway, the writer Hans Jæger was jailed for two months in 1885 when he published *Fra Kristiania-Bohêmen* (From the Kristiania Bohemians), in which sexual acts were described with raw, Zola-like detail. In Sweden, August

Strindberg routinely employed a kind of scorched-earth tactic on all issues related to sex and women, provoking condemnation from all angles. "Love between the sexes is a battle," a character says in *The Father* (1887),[23] and Strindberg was a bloodthirsty warrior.

Though Jacobsen was too sick to involve himself in these or any other public debates, in his own quiet way he'd already done much to challenge prevailing moral standards about the sexes. *Marie Grubbe* shocked many readers with its frank portrayal of female sexuality, while *Niels Lyhne*'s Fru Boye directly addresses the double standards of male-female relations in an early scene in the novel:

> We are forced to fit into the man's ideal. Like Cinderella, chop off a heel and snip off a toe! Whatever in us does not match up with his ideal image has to be banished, if not by subjugation then by indifference, by systematic neglect, by denying all development; and whatever is lacking in us or is not part of our nature must be driven to the wildest flowering by praising it to the skies, by always assuming that we possess it to the highest degree, and by making it the cornerstone upon which the man's love is built. I call that violence against our nature. I call that conditioning.[24]

Jacobsen was also outraged to hear of the fate of his younger admirer Herman Bang, whose first novel, *Hopeless Generations* (1880), was deemed "immoral" and swiftly banned by the government. (It remained unpublished in its original form until 1965.) When Jacobsen heard of the decision, he was incensed. "Wouldn't it be neat if realist literature was censored by the police and we all had to write books suitable for confirmation gifts?" he wrote to Georg Brandes.[25] It was Bang's portrayal of his main character's love affair with an older woman that scandalized the reading public, though no doubt Bang's sexuality (he was openly gay and something of a dandyish socialite—à la Proust—to boot) singled him out as an obvious target. In years to come Bang would see his reputation constantly tarnished by the Danish press, driving him into a state of constant homelessness. In 1912 he died in a Mormon hospital in Ogden, Utah, of all places. He was on his way to San Francisco.

Maurice Blanchot writes in *The Space of Literature* (1955) of the authentic and the inauthentic death: the possibility that we can die either on good terms with death or that we can die badly—falsely, inessentially, even inadvertently. By way of Rilke he writes, "To die an individual death, still oneself to the very last, to be an individual right up to the end, unique and undivided: this is the hard, central kernel which does not want to let itself be broken. One wants to die, but in one's own time and one's own way. One doesn't want to die just anybody's undistinguished death."[26]

It is noble to die but not to decease, Blanchot continues. He acknowledges that Rilke was inspired in his thinking about death by Jacobsen, particularly by the final pages of *Marie Grubbe*, in which the elderly heroine tells Ludvig Holberg that she believes "everyone dies their own death."[27] In opposition to this individual death is the anonymous death, as Blanchot calls it. He quotes Nietzsche: "There is nothing more banal than death"[28]—a sentiment Rilke backed away from. In Rilke's *Malte Laurids Brigge* the narrator's grandfather's death is described in lofty, edifying terms: "It was not the death of some wretch dying of a dropsy; it was the evil, regal death the Chamberlain had borne with him his whole life long, nurturing it from within himself. All those vast resources of pride and will and mastery that he had been unable to use up himself in his calmer days over now into his death."[29]

Jacobsen's notion of a "difficult death" is probably located between these two interpretations—between the banality of dying, on the one hand, and the desire to die individually, *authentically*, on the other. Niels Lyhne doesn't die authentically in Blanchot's sense (his atheism falters at a critical moment and never quite regains its equilibrium), but neither does he die *inauthentically:* he refuses the consolation of a priest right until the very end, despite thinking it might be good to have something to believe in. His death is difficult because it is ambiguous; Jacobsen's novel movingly abandons itself to uncertainty. Death is banal because it happens to us all and difficult because we die alone: "It was a great sadness that a soul is always alone," Niels Lyhne thinks to himself.[30]

By the early 1880s Jacobsen had been living in the shadow of his own mortality for a decade. His later works—"Two Worlds"; *Niels Lyhne;* "The Plague in Bergamo"—demonstrate the extent of his artistic occupation with death and dying. In fact, all of Jacobsen's works are to some degree inquiries into the ability of human beings to bear life as it is—without any irritable reaching after religious consolation. Among his posthumous papers was the fragment of a novella, written in the spring of 1884 and later published as "Doctor Faust," in which Jacobsen envisions Death and Amor arriving at the home of the forty-year-old Faust. They ride on horseback through a barren forest landscape—so quiet that the hoofbeats of Death's horse "were like the only sound in the world."[31] The horses come to a halt outside Doctor Faust's window, where they find him reflecting on his own mortality and yearning for his lost youth: "Now I am forty! . . . 10, 20, 30 more years and then everything will be over!"[32]

Edvard Brandes, who oversaw the publication of the fragment in the magazine *Juleroser* in 1885, outlined Jacobsen's idea for the remainder of the story. Amor would persuade Death not to take Faust yet but to grant him instead another forty years of life. Death acquiesces. When the two return forty years later, they find that the now eighty-year-old Faust has spent his extended lease on life mourning over his youth. The forty years were a waste—"a dead life," as Brandes phrased it.[33]

Jacobsen knew all too well the sound of death's galloping hoofbeats. With every passing day they were getting closer, as anyone who paid a visit to Ny Adelgade saw clearly. When Emanuel Fraenkel visited him in the spring of 1882, he was deeply alarmed by his friend's emaciated condition. In his capacity as a doctor he implored Jacobsen to get out of Copenhagen and into the countryside; if he was just going to lie around, he might as well do it in a quiet place with fresh air and more appealing surroundings. Though he didn't say so to Jacobsen, he was astonished that he'd even made it this far. In a letter to Vodskov he wrote that the only reason Jacobsen had survived as long as he had was because he lived like a convalescent. "What has so far prevented a disaster for Jacobsen," Fraenkel wrote, "is the completely vegetative life he is somehow capable of leading. Only very few people could stand living that way, but it seems to suit him. He can't write, and it seems he's given up hope of ever doing so again."[34]

Jacobsen reluctantly spent the summer of 1883 in Vallø, a small community south of Køge built up around Vallø Castle. At the inn where he stayed, he strung a hammock between two apple trees in the garden, where he read or dozed off in peace. His appetite was improving, he assured William; he enjoyed plenty of local meat and fish and lots of fresh strawberries and cucumber salad. A local library offered a decent supply of English literature, and the locals were all nice enough. But a visit from one of the country's most famous writers did not go unnoticed, and soon Jacobsen noticed heads turning wherever he went. "Since Køge's local newspaper has reported that I'm staying out here, church ladies, small deer, and visitors pause to stare at me," he wrote to Agnes Møller.[35] Happily, he was visited in August by both Kielland and Georg Brandes. "I saw a lot of Jacobsen during those weeks," Brandes later recalled; "[he] was as loveable and remarkable as always but coughed miserably and was dreadfully weak."[36]

Despite entertaining his friends with plans for a play, a historical novel, and a book on Danish plant life, Jacobsen had almost entirely ceased writing. The physical act of putting pen to paper had become an excruciating ordeal. When he returned to Copenhagen, his appetite once again disappeared. He had trouble sleeping and suffered the most wretched coughing fits and splintering headaches. Edvard Brandes said he was so pale that one could look into his soul. One day he suffered a blood spitting at a café and decided then and there to retreat entirely from what little social life he had left. The occasional trip out to Vilhelm Møller in Humlebæk was all he could permit himself.

Later in the summer of 1883 Jacobsen's parents and younger sister visited him in Copenhagen for the first time, staying in the apartment in Ny Adelgade for three long weeks. It was a trip Jacobsen and William had been planning for months. Jacobsen took his family to all the city's museums, hired a carriage to take them out to Vilhelm and Agnes Møller in Humlebæk, and joined them as they visited friends throughout the city. The trip was a huge success, and loneliness laid heavily on Jacobsen once his parents and sister had left for Thisted again. "Please tell father that I've bought a proper razor blade," he wrote to William, "and tell him I shave every other day now with increasing success, though not without leaving a few cuts here and there."[37]

Eventually William himself came to visit as well. On April 7, 1884, Vilhelm Møller had secretly arranged for him to arrive in Copenhagen and surprise his older brother on his thirty-seventh birthday. Jacobsen was overjoyed. That night the two brothers dined at the Møllers' home with several of Jacobsen's friends, including Edvard Brandes. Jacobsen later said that introducing his entire family to Møller had made the bond of their friendship stronger than ever.

But of course the time came, as everyone had been expecting and preparing themselves for, when Jacobsen and his family decided it would be best for him if he returned to Thisted, where he could be looked after regularly and where the robust ocean breeze, as the thinking went back then, might do his lungs some good. Jacobsen was under no illusion about what the move suggested about his medical prospects. "When you hear that I've once more returned to Thisted," he told a friend, "it means you won't see me again."[38]

Saying goodbye was not easy. When after his final visit to Ny Adelgade Georg Brandes began to descend the stairs, he looked back and saw Jacobsen standing on the landing—"with straight and exemplary posture"—listening to Brandes's footsteps fade. Jacobsen probably kept such emotional goodbyes to a minimum, preferring not to make a fuss and to simply withdraw from his life in Copenhagen as quietly and unobtrusively as he had taken to living it. Word traveled fast, however. Alexander Kielland, who had already moved back to Norway, wrote with grief from Stavanger: "Even if I never see you again, you will live on, for as long as I live, as the man I have loved most."[39]

In late July 1884 a long and arduous trip by train and boat finally brought Jacobsen back home to Thisted, where a small arbor with a hammock had been constructed for him in the garden of his parents' property. (It is all that remains of the house today.) There he could rest and read English novels or simply look on as life quietly passed him by. "I still hope to undertake something immortal here at my desk," he wrote to a friend, "though I do nothing except lie in my hammock out in the garden."[40]

Jacobsen soon regained his old taste for gallows humor. When William began to arrange for new furniture for the apartment they shared in their father's house, Jacobsen looked him in the eyes and said, "Do you really think it's worth it?"[41] He struck a similar tone in letters to friends, repeatedly making light of his condition and joking about his nonexistent appetite. "I feel alright," he wrote to Agnes Møller, "though my five-fried-fish appetite from last year is not especially prominent."[42]

A recurring subject in letters to friends was the kindness and devotion of his brother. William almost never left Jacobsen's side; at night, the door separating their bedrooms was left ajar in case Jacobsen should suffer one of his death-rattling coughing fits. "I now live in Thisted with my brother, who never blinks," Jacobsen wrote to Kielland, "except on Saturday night at 1 a.m., whereupon he sits up straight, blinks twenty-one times, and then goes back to sleep and doesn't blink again until next Saturday at 1 a.m."[43] William made it easy to live and hope, Jacobsen later wrote.

The months passed in quiet tedium, one day indistinguishable from the next. Jacobsen read his English novels, played solitaire with his parents, and otherwise lay out in his hammock and dreamt up new ideas for novels and stories. Hegel kept him stocked with the latest fiction, including new books by Ibsen, Georg Brandes, and Kielland, while Vilhelm Møller sent him a copy of his latest translation of Turgenev.

Jacobsen never grumbled about his rather ominous return to Thisted, nor did he complain about his symptoms even as they grew in severity. Only once did he allow a lament to pass his lips; standing at the window, he suddenly noticed a man shoveling coal with a pipe in his mouth. "Oh, what a chest that man must have, to be able to shovel coal and smoke a pipe at the same time!" he exclaimed.

In the spring Jacobsen's condition worsened significantly. He could no longer sleep lying down and resorted instead to sit bent over a tray with his forehead resting on his hands. His legs swelled up, and at times he felt he could barely breathe. A doctor gravely informed him that even the lung he thought was healthy was now seriously infected.

Still he soldiered on. He wrote to Frederik V. Hegel and told him he was working on a new novel but begged him to keep it a secret. If anyone found out, they'd just ask for contributions to magazines or journals, and he couldn't stand to turn them down. "All is well here," Jacobsen closed his letter; "my health relatively satisfying, and since I never get outside anymore, the weather doesn't matter much to me."[44]

On April 30 Jacobsen awoke to find himself in even greater pain than usual. With the aid of his mother he slowly got dressed and tried to find some comfort in the living room. When that didn't work, he climbed the steps to his room and reclined on his chaise lounge, only to discover that he couldn't find his own pulse. The doctor promptly arrived and pronounced a heart rate of eighty-four, then told the patient to drink a glass of port. He promised to look in again in the afternoon.

Jacobsen's mother and William set a lunch table for Jacobsen in his room, but he had no appetite and managed only to sip a little soda water. His voice had sunk to a raspy whisper. William spent most of the afternoon shuffling his brother back and forth between furniture. He finally got him settled in a plush armchair, where Jacobsen calmly flipped through a catalog of French paintings while his mother cooled his forehead with water. At one point he demanded that a window be opened; a light rain was softly falling.

At around 4:30 in the afternoon Jacobsen gave his mother a strange look, then dropped his head back against the seat and into her hands. William sat down next to him and placed Jacobsen's hand in his. The shadows grew—the shadows of evening and death.

That night, Vilhelm Møller received a telegram at his home in Copenhagen:

Editor Møller
  Peter Skramsgade 17, Copenhagen
  J. P. Jacobsen dead this afternoon at 5 p.m.
    Letter to follow.
    W. Jacobsen.[45]

Jacobsen's room in the home of his parents in Thisted, photographed after his death in April 1885. Courtesy of Thisted Museum.

CHAPTER EIGHT

The Jacobsen Fashion

Niels Lyhne—how fervently, how passionately we loved this
book in the first wakeful years of our youth; it was the *Werther*
of our generation.
—Stefan Zweig

Jacobsen has become a fashion here in Germany. I can't speak
to anyone without them mentioning that they're familiar
with one of my countrymen: J. P. J.
—Gudmund Hentze, Danish painter

Life no longer dwells in the whole. The word becomes sover-
eign and leaps out of the sentence, the sentence reaches out
and obscures the meaning of the page, the page gains life at
the expense of the whole—the whole is no longer a whole.
—Friedrich Nietzsche, *The Case of Wagner* (1888)

IN 1907 the Danish literary journal *Det ny aarhundrede* (The new
century) convened an "enquête" on *Niels Lyhne*. In the twenty-
odd years since its publication, the editors explained, Jacobsen's
book had grown to become one of the most influential and

Jacobsen's doodlings. Above them is an
outline for the short story "Mogens."
Courtesy of Thisted Museum.

talked about novels in all of Danish literature: "For many young
people this voice has penetrated so deeply that they have never
been able to wrest themselves from its faintly mournful and languidly resigned aura."[1] Contributors to the survey included Edvard Brandes, who admitted that although *Niels Lyhne*'s initial
impact was not quite as strong as *Marie Grubbe*'s, he now ranked
it first and foremost among Jacobsen's writing. The editors
asked him if he thought Jacobsen would be surprised by the

adoration and respect his writing had gained. "I don't think so," Edvard responded; "Jacobsen fully recognized his worth. He knew his time would come."[2]

And how that time came! If Jacobsen had lived only a decade longer, he would have seen himself ranked alongside Henrik Ibsen, August Strindberg, and Knut Hamsun as the most exciting and influential writer of northern Europe; he would have seen an entire generation of young poets recite him like they recited Baudelaire or Huysmans or Novalis; he would have heard his poems set to the music of Carl Nielsen and Emil Sjögren; he might even have been invited by the Literary-Historical Society in Bonn to speak on the issue that so perplexed it during a discussion of his work in 1907: "How has Jacobsen come to have such an enormous influence in Germany?"[3]

How indeed? Unlike other Scandinavian writers, such as Ibsen or Strindberg or Ola Hansson, Jacobsen never lived in Germany nor had any affiliation with its literary culture. (The time Jacobsen did spend there on his journeys to southern Europe was brief; he didn't like the food and complained that all the cafés closed early.) More important, the earliest translations of Jacobsen's writings into German, such as Adolf Strodtmann's 1878 version of *Marie Grubbe*, failed to make an impact. And yet by 1896 Reclam's inexpensive Universal-Bibliothek edition of *Niels Lyhne* had sold more than ten thousand copies. What had changed?

If we take a closer look, who do we see but Georg Brandes? Naturally he stalks this chapter of Jacobsen's biography too. There he is in the pages of the *Deutsche Rundschau*, the leading literary periodical of the German bourgeoisie, agitating tirelessly on behalf of his late friend. In 1888 he writes an angry letter to the journalist Theodor Wolff complaining about the Germans' poor literary judgment: "It would please me if you could succeed in awakening German minds to the strength and delicacy of Jacobsen's work. It is altogether ridiculous that Kielland, who is so monodimensional, is known everywhere, is famous, while the much greater Jacobsen, with whom Kielland has never compared himself, remains unknown and misunderstood."⁴ Brandes persuaded Wolff to write about *Niels Lyhne* in the *Berliner Tageblatt*, which in turn convinced Reclam to publish Jacobsen's novel. Whatever aesthetic reservations he held about Jacobsen in private, Brandes was unflinching in his admiration and support for his writing in public.

Georg Brandes was of course already a familiar figure in German literary circles, having made a name for himself as an impassioned advocate for European literature in the late 1870s and early 1880s, when he lived in Berlin. From his luxurious third-floor apartment on In den Zelten, with a view of the Tiergarten's Victory Column, he was ideally placed to assist the newly unified Germany in playing literary catch-up with the rest of Europe. Unlike in France, England, and Scandinavia (and to a lesser degree Portugal and Italy), naturalism had yet to penetrate the thickly conservative culture that had enveloped Germany after its unification. There were political reasons for this, of course. The resounding Prussian defeat of the Second French Empire in 1871 did not exactly facilitate a healthy Franco-German cultural exchange. As late as 1915 it was still thought to be in poor taste to champion French writers in Germany, as Heinrich Mann would learn when his own brother, Thomas Mann, publicly attacked him for his essays on Zola.⁵

As usual, then, Georg Brandes was fighting an uphill battle. His contributions to the *Deutsche Rundschau*, including essays on Zola, Flaubert, Ibsen, and Tolstoy, were instrumental in bringing modern European literature to Germany, but he had to cleave his way through thickets of reactionary politics and increasingly obvious anti-Semitism in order to be heard. Though Bismarck refused to sign a petition demanding that Jews be expelled from public office (a petition that gained nearly a quarter million votes), Berlin had become a hotbed of anti-Jewish tensions. To the likes of Adolf Stöcker, founder of the Christian Social Party, the Jewish foreigner Georg Brandes was an obvious target. "Denmark's defender of Judaism has no other recourse than to drag Christianity through the mud," Stöcker fumed.[6]

Despite these hurdles, Brandes succeeded in making the rapidly expanding Prussian capital, whose population trebled between 1870 and 1905, the center of a small but vocal Scandinavian-led counterculture, much of it clustered around Zum schwarzen Ferkel (The Black Piglet), a storied tavern on the corner of Unter den Linden and Neue Wilhelmstraße, where the likes of Strindberg, Edvard Munch, Christian Krogh, Ola Hansson, and the Polish novelist and dramatist Stanisław Feliks Przybyszewski gathered to drink, smoke, and debate well into the early morning hours.

The single most important aspect of Brandes's cultural mediation in Germany, however, came after he'd returned to Denmark. In 1886 a German publisher began sending him copies of the work of a former philologist at the University of Basel, now living in obscurity in Nice. His name was Friedrich Nietzsche. These books—*Beyond Good and Evil, Human,*

All Too Human, and *The Genealogy of Morals*—could not have reached the progress-weary Brandes at a more fortuitous time. "A new and original spirit breathes to me from your books," he wrote to Nietzsche in November 1887. "I do not fully understand what I have read; I cannot always see your intention. But I find much that harmonizes with my own ideas and sympathies—the deprecation of the ascetic ideals and the profound disgust with democratic mediocrity, your aristocratic radicalism."[7]

Brandes soon informed Nietzsche that he intended to begin a series of lectures on his work at the University of Copenhagen. "I suddenly felt a sort of vexation at the idea that nobody here in Scandinavia knew anything about you, and I soon determined to make you known at a stroke,"[8] Brandes wrote to his new friend. In April 1888 he thus delivered the first of five lectures on "The Aristocratic Radicalism of Friedrich Nietzsche." ("The expression *Aristocratic Radicalism*, which you employed, is very good," Nietzsche told Brandes. "It is, permit me to say, the cleverest thing I have yet read about myself.")[9] The first lecture was only modestly attended, but a write-up in the newspaper *Politiken* ensured that on the second occasion the lecture hall was filled beyond capacity. Among the faithful listeners was August Strindberg—the "mad Swede"—as Brandes called him in a letter to Nietzsche[10]—who was immediately smitten. When he read *Thus Spake Zarathustra*, he wrote at once to its author: "There is no doubt that you have bestowed upon humanity the deepest book that it possesses, and moreover, have had the courage and possibly also the urging to spit these magnificent words straight into the faces of this pack of rogues!"[11]

Brandes's lectures were published in book form the following year. In 1890, they appeared in the *Deustche Rundschau*, setting off "a veritable tidal wave of interest in the philosopher."[12] The wave swept through Europe with unexpected force. Paintings and photographs of the solemnly mustachioed Nietzsche adorned the walls of young artists and intellectuals everywhere; the German architect Peter Behrens designed a "Zarathustrian villa" in the Darmstadt artists' colony;[13] the cult of Nietzscheism was born. Prophetically, Nietzsche himself wrote to Brandes in his final letter to him before his death: "When once you had discovered me, it was easy enough to find me; the difficulty now is to get rid of me." He signed himself, "The Crucified."[14]

Nietzsche's overwhelming popularity was part of a general reaction against positivism, naturalism, and blind faith in progress. Suddenly the "broad general current which carries our age toward more science, more truth, and no doubt more happiness," as the Zola disciple Paul Alexis put it,[15] was eclipsed by a preoccupation with the irrational, the psychological, the mysterious and unconscious life of the soul. Decadence and symbolism displaced realism and naturalism, expressionism sidelined impressionism, and Nietzsche trumped pretty much everything else. Even Georg Brandes appeared to have lost faith in the very ideas he had first set forth back in 1871. "My principle reason for calling attention to [Nietzsche] is that Scandinavian literature appears to me to have been living quite long enough on the ideas that were put forward and discussed in the last decade," he wrote. "People are still busy with the same doctrines, certain theories of heredity, a little

Darwinism, a little emancipation of woman, a little morality of happiness, a little free thought, a little worship of democracy, etc."[16]

Against this background, it's no coincidence that Jacobsen's star shined brightest in the Germany and Austria of the 1890s. Many of the young artists then bingeing on Nietzsche found in *Niels Lyhne*'s creator a scintillating example of the author as refined aesthete whose withdrawal from life was a sign of creative genius, of his ability to see deeply beneath a surface that others could only scratch—in short, a kind of literary aristocrat. This notion (not at all uncommon in the Nervous Nineties) was essentially an updated version of the image of Jacobsen as Flaubertian monk, forever tinkering with a comma or adjective. The aforementioned Ola Hansson wrote a long and influential essay in the Berlin-based journal *Nord und Süd*, in which he celebrated Jacobsen as "the poet of longing," comparing his prose to "a strange plant that rightfully belongs in the tropics but that has been artificially grown in the humid heat of a luxurious Scandinavian greenhouse and whose flamboyant colors astonish the beholder."[17]

Hansson did his best to emphasize Jacobsen's symbolism and decadence, his sickness and morbidity—in short, all those aspects of his writing that so irritated Georg Brandes. Hansson did so knowingly, of course; he was a lapsed disciple of Brandes who now spoke ill of the venerable Dane whenever the opportunity presented itself. Since relocating to Germany in the late 1880s, he'd been competing with Brandes for the title of the leading Scandinavian champion of Nietzsche. His essay on the late German thinker, "Friedrich Nietzsche: An Outline of His Thought and Personality," narrowly beat

Brandes to the punch; it appeared in *Unsere Zeit* in 1889, while Brandes's essay was being held up by its translator, Laura Marholm—the *wife* of Ola Hansson. A calculated act of sabotage? Brandes seemed to think so. He called Hansson and Marholm "a literary gangster duo."[18]

Though Jacobsen's poetic achievement was recognized in Denmark only after his death, when Edvard Brandes and Vilhelm Møller arranged for the publication of his poems, it was central to his reception and popularity in Germany and Austria. The Viennese translator and critic Marie Herzfeld (1855–1940), probably the most significant German-language champion of Jacobsen, wrote in glowing terms of his poetry in a widely serialized essay first published in April 1897 in the *Wiener Rundschau*. "They are prototypical examples of what the symbolists attempt today," she observed.[19]

Jacobsen's poems turned up regularly in the most influential and important journals of the time, often alongside illustrations by the likes of Heinrich Vogeler. Translating them became a favorite pastime of those admirers who had taught themselves Danish, including Stefan George, Marie Herzfeld, and Rainer Marie Rilke. George, who spent 1890 in Copenhagen, translated Jacobsen's most celebrated poem, "Arabesque for a Sketch by Michelangelo," and published it in his prestigious *Blätter für die Kunst*. The poem, with its haunting images of the endless, wave-like recurrence of life and death, was also translated by Rilke and included in the annual *Insel Almanach* of 1914.[20]

By the turn of the century the Jacobsen fashion was at its peak. One could scarcely open a magazine or an arts journal in Berlin or Vienna without encountering his name. His poems and stories were published in places like *Ver Sacrum* and *Simplicissimus;* the German poet Hans Bethge wrote a book about him *(Jens Peter Jacobsen: Ein Versuch, 1904)* with an illustration by Friedrich Ahlers-Hestermann; the writer and painter Max von Dauthendey dedicated his first novel, *Josa Gerth* (1892), to Jacobsen and even modeled one of its characters after him;[21] Hermann Hesse and Gottfried Benn both read and discussed him, as did the procession of artists and intellectuals who frequented the Café Griensteidl in Vienna: Arthur Schnitzler, Hugo von Hofmannsthal, Stefan Zweig, Hermann Bahr, and many others.

It is perhaps at the Café Griensteidl that the composers Arnold Schoenberg and Alexander Zemlinsky first discussed Jacobsen's poetry together. Zemlinsky set a number of Jacobsen's poems to music, including the famous "Irmelin Rose," and in 1903 he gave Schoenberg a copy of R. F. Arnold's translation of Jacobsen's collected works as a Christmas present.[22]

In 1899 a competition for a cycle of songs with piano accompaniment was announced by the Wiener Tonkünstlerverein. Zemlinsky recalled that Schoenberg, who wanted to win the competition, composed a few songs after Jacobsen's poems. "The songs were wonderful and truly original," Zemlinsky said, "but we both had the impression that precisely on that account they would have little chance of winning the prize."[23] The cycle eventually metastasized into a much larger project and took over a decade for Schoenberg to complete. When he finished his *Gurre-Lieder*, as it was called, it had grown to be a massive cantata for six soloists, a reciter, four choirs (600 singers in total), and a 150-person orchestra.[24] Its premiere in

Vienna on February 23, 1913, in a performance conducted by Franz Schreker, was a tremendous success.

Rilke, of course, was Jacobsen's most passionately vocal admirer. It was while staying at an artists' colony in Worpswede, a small village in Lower Saxony, that he began reading him in earnest. There were good reasons for doing so: virtually all of the painters and sculptors Rilke befriended there—including Hans Vogeler, Paula Modersohn-Becker, and Rilke's future wife, Clara Westhoff—were eager admirers of the Danish writer. (Vogeler later illustrated the second volume of Jacobsen's collected works in the beautiful edition published by Eugen Diederich's Verlag in 1898–1899). On Sunday evenings they gathered in the "white hall" of Vogeler's residence-cum-atelier Barkenhoff and reveled in music, song, dance, and reading. "We all read Jacobsen," Rilke later recalled, "about whom it was said that *he writes as painters paint.*"[25]

The painterly aspects of Jacobsen's prose have been a topic of debate since "Mogens" was first published in 1872. Virtually every contemporary review of *Marie Grubbe* and *Niels Lyhne* credited their literary style with being highly visual, sometimes to a fault. Bjørnson, as we've seen, accused Jacobsen of imitating French decorative arts, while Georg Brandes and Herman Bang both extolled him for being a great colorist. An exhibit at the Faaborg Museum in Denmark in the summer of 2016 was dedicated entirely to Jacobsen's relationship to the visual arts, emphasizing his connection to Danish impressionists of the 1870s and detailing his own talent for satirical drawings and sketches, many of which he included in notes and letters.[26] The exhibit also emphasized the influence of Jacobsen on German and Austrian painters of the early twentieth century, particularly Otto Heinrich Engel and the Worspwede artists.

Of the Worspwede artists, Paula Modersohn-Becker was perhaps the most rapturous. She first encountered Jacobsen's novels on a trip through Norway in the summer of 1898. In a letter to her parents she vividly described the experience of reading *Marie Grubbe:* "I am completely spellbound by the images this book conjures up before me. I read it very, very slowly, in intoxicating little doses, partly beneath my buckthorn tree and partly on my little rock near the waterfall—another of my favorite little spots. I can sit there silently, surrounded by the roaring water and the passion of the elements, and still feel the book inside me."[27]

When Modersohn-Becker learned that Heinrich Vogeler had been commissioned to illustrate a new edition of Jacobsen's works, she was surprised. "Rarely has a writer had less need of illustration than Jacobsen," she wrote.[28] Yet as the exhibit at the Faaborg Museum showed, Jacobsen, despite his insatiable appetite for galleries and museums on his travels through Europe, had only a single painting in his possession: a "typical tourist painting" of the Castle of Chillon near Montreux.[29] His interest in the visual arts was manifested in words, not images. Despite his reputation as a "painter's writer," as Hermann Schlittgen called him, he was less purely visual than, for instance, Zola or Flaubert.[30] What appealed to so many poets and novelists and artists across Germany and Austria was not simply an aspect of style, but also a perceived worldview. Modersohn-Becker described reading Jacobsen as being emptied of herself only to be rediscovered again more fully: "I thought of nothing. But all my senses were alive, every fiber. I lay that way for a long time. And then I came back to myself again, to the wind and to the sun and to the happy buzzing of the insects all around me."[31] The poet-critic Eric Torgersen calls Modersohn-Becker's description a Jacobsen pastiche and compares it to a passage from *Niels Lyhne:*

> He closed his eyes but still could feel how the light seemed to seep into him, flickering through every nerve, while with every breath the cool, intoxicating air sent his oddly excited blood with wilder and wilder force through his veins, quivering with powerlessness, and a feeling came over him as though everything teeming, bursting, budding, multiplying in the springtime nature around him was mystically trying to gather inside him in one great big shout; and he thirsted for that shout, listened until his listening took the form of a vague, burgeoning longing.[32]

Torgersen is right: Jacobsen was cherished because he offered a unique combination of both nature-romanticism and a "deliciously modern" deflation of romantic ideals.[33] For this reason, Jacobsen's lush nature-lyricism probably contributed to various crackpot fashions and theories, such as Émile Gallé's belief that flowers had nerves or Rilke's love of walking barefoot through meadows and following a vegetarian diet. It's hardly surprising, for instance, that Jacobsen was beloved by the cultural vanguard in Vienna at a time when that city represented everything synonymous with the modern. In his famous essay "The Overcoming of Naturalism," the Austrian critic Hermann Bahr celebrated the new artists who "experience only with the nerves": "When nervousness becomes completely liberated and man, especially the artist, becomes entirely subordinate to the nerves, without regard for the rational and the sensuous, then the lost joy will return to art."[34] Here's Paula Modersohn-Becker again, on reading *Niels Lyhne:* "The fragrance is almost too much for me. . . . I can feel [Jacobsen] in all my nerves, in my wrists, the tips of my fingers, my lips. It envelops me. I read him physically."[35]

Like Nietzsche, Jacobsen became a cult figure to an entire generation of young men and women debating among themselves what it meant to be truly modern, to live a fully modern life without recourse to the ideals of past generations. "You are too steeped in the ideas of the previous generation," Paula Modersohn-Becker reprimanded her brother, Kurt Becker, in 1900. "It isn't yours. Your nervous system belongs to our generation. And if you have trouble keeping up, then you must learn to overcome your weakness and powerlessness. Remember Niels Lyhne. He didn't make it. But you can."[36]

The simultaneous cults of Nietzsche and Jacobsen were nowhere more perfectly entwined than in Rilke's early beginnings as a writer. In a famous essay in *The Disinherited Mind*, the great critic Erich Heller mapped out the influence of Nietzsche's thought on Rilke's poetry. In his conclusion, Heller makes the case that Nietzsche's claim that the purpose of art is to "*affirm, bless,* and *deify* existence" is in fact a perfect definition of Rilke's poetic project. Despite their differences, Heller argues, "in both Nietzsche and Rilke the human mind and imagination are engaged in the ultimate task of creating a world to take the place of the spiritually useless productions of God."[37]

It would be critical overkill to claim that Jacobsen was engaged in a similar task, yet the question of how to live meaningfully in the absence of God was clearly a question that preoccupied him for most of his short life. Jacobsen may not have set out to deify existence, but many came to the altar of his prose for its little bursts of sublimity—in the description of a blooming tree, say, or the delicately nuanced evocation of atmosphere. Robert Musil noted that he never forgot the detail about a maid polishing door handles in a scene from *Niels Lyhne* in which Niels and Fru Boye are in the midst of a row:

> It was so silent around them at first; then a maid could be heard out on the landing, humming and polishing the locks, and the creaking of the door handles brutally broke the silence and made it seem even greater when it suddenly returned. Then the noise stopped; now there was only the gentle, sleepy, steady tapping of the venetian blinds.
>
> It robbed them of words, this silence, almost of thoughts as well, and she remained sitting there as before, with her gaze toward the darkness of the foyer, and he remained standing there, leaning over her, staring down at the plaid of her silk lap, and unconsciously, seduced by the gentle silence, he began to rock her in the chair, very gently, very gently.[38]

It's a celebrated passage and rightly so; the prose is so wonderfully suggestive, so rhythmically precise, and the noticing absolutely first-rate. Here as elsewhere in Jacobsen, details are *things-in-themselves*—what James Wood calls "lifeness"[39] and Henry James, "the palpable present intimate."[40] It is the sort of attention to detail that seems to lift the trivial, the mundane, the insignificant, onto a higher plane. Fru Boye has just told Niels she has become engaged, he has reacted bitterly, the conversation has gone badly—and now they've fallen silent. The sound of the maid humming and polishing the door handles, like a lot of literary detail, is almost funny, a little reminder of insignificance in the midst of a confrontation that is anything but. What Rilke wrote about Rodin—that "his art was not built upon a great idea, but upon a minute, conscientious realization, upon the attainable, upon a craft"⁴¹—might equally be applied to Jacobsen's prose.

Jacobsen's art certainly was not built upon any great idea, however much his contemporaries and later generations strived to impart lessons or values or instructions from his writing. In his own time Jacobsen had tried to distance his writing from the polemical debates it was invariably caught up in, even if the issue was one in which he felt he had a stake. "I didn't write [*Niels Lyhne*] because I agreed with people—be they enemies or friends," he told Vilhelm Møller.⁴² It therefore seems reasonable to assume that he might have been perplexed to find himself the object of cult-like veneration to a generation of nervous aesthetes with an interest in religious mysticism.

One of the last times in his life that Rilke is known to have spoken at any length about Jacobsen was in 1925, a year or so before his death. To his French translator Maurice Betz, then at work on a French edition of *Malte Laurids Brigge*, he explained that there were essentially two Jacobsens. There was, on the one hand, the Jacobsen whose books plumed with scents and secrets and depths, a veritable forest of dreams in which everything trembles, quivers, and shimmers in a strangely unreal atmosphere. This was the Jacobsen who had showed Rilke the wellsprings of life, its immeasurable wealth and abundance, its energy and power. This Jacobsen was "an inspiration without equal," Rilke said. But behind him was another Jacobsen: a sick, embittered Jacobsen; a fundamentally unhappy man, inclined to doubt everything, and whose only means of struggle against death and disease were spite and mockery.

Rilke was more right than even he may have realized. Though his comments were framed as an explanation for why he had distanced himself from Jacobsen over the years, he unwittingly articulated a near-perfect description of the very distinction of his artistry. What were all the frustrations and disagreements and conflicts over the value of Jacobsen's writing during his lifetime but an unwillingness to acknowledge this central conflict, not just in his writing, but in life itself? And what does Jacobsen show us in his novels and stories and poems if not the fundamental incongruousness, the vexing doubleness of human nature?

What Jacobsen understood, what he fathomed—remarkably, for someone so young, someone whose experience of life was so cruelly limited—is best expressed by Ernest Becker in a passage on man's duality in his famous *Denial of Death* (1973):

> This is the paradox: he is out of nature and hopelessly in it; he is dual, up in the stars and yet housed in a heart-pumping, breath-gasping body that once belonged to a fish and still carries the gill-marks to prove it. His body is a material flesh casing that is alien to him in many ways—the strangest and most repugnant way being that it aches and bleeds and will decay and die. Man is literally split in two: he has an awareness of his own splendid uniqueness in that he sticks out of nature with a towering majesty, and yet he goes back into the ground a few feet in order blindly and dumbly to rot and disappear forever. It is a terrifying dilemma to be in and to have to live with.[43]

If the mark of a great artist is the ability to present multiple yet contradictory truths at the same time—the Darwinist grandeur of life, on the one hand, say, and the terrible loneliness, the awful futility, of human existence on the other—then Jacobsen is surely among the greatest.

Notes

Translations from Danish, Swedish, and Norwegian sources are my own unless otherwise specified.

PROLOGUE

1. Rainer Maria Rilke, *Letters of Rainer Maria Rilke 1892–1910*, trans. Jane Bannard Greene and M. D. Herter Norton (New York: W. W. Norton, 1945), p. 88.

2. Ibid., p. 86.

3. Ibid., p. 93.

4. Rainer Maria Rilke, *Letters to a Young Poet*, trans. M. D. Herter Norton (New York: W. W. Norton, 1954), pp. 24–25.

5. Rilke, *Letters of Rainer Maria Rilke*, p. 144.

6. Ibid., pp. 144–145.

7. Lydia Baer, "Rilke and Jens Peter Jacobsen," *PMLA* 54, no. 3 (September 1939): 909.

8. Quoted in Lydia Baer, "Rilke and Jens Peter Jacobsen," *PMLA* 54, no. 4 (December 1939): 1143.

9. Rainer Maria Rilke, *Rilke and Andreas-Salomé: A Love Story in Letters*, trans. Edward Snow and Michael Winkler (New York: W. W. Norton, 2006), p. 116.

10. Ibid., p. 125.

11. Ibid., p. 130.

12. Ibid., p. 129.

13. Ibid., p. 135.

14. Ibid., p. 135.

15. Ibid., p. 134.

16. Ralph Freedman, *Life of a Poet: Rainer Maria Rilke* (Evanston, IL: Northwestern University Press, 1996), p. 216.

17. F. J. Billeskov Jansen, ed. *J. P. Jacobsens spor i ord, billeder og toner* (Copenhagen: C. A. Reitzels Forlag, 1985), p. 111.

18. Thomas Mann, *A Sketch of My Life*, trans. H. T. Lowe-Porter (New York: Alfred A. Knopf, 1960), p. 13.

19. Quoted in Anthony Heilbut, *Thomas Mann: Eros and Literature* (New York: Alfred A. Knopf, 1995), p. 160.

20. Billeskov Jansen, *J. P. Jacobsens spor*, pp. 113, 122.

21. Quoted in ibid., p. 123.

22. *The Nation*, February 14, 1918, p. 185.

23. Sue Prideaux, *Strindberg* (New Haven: Yale University Press, 2012), p. 3.

24. Quoted in Niels Barfoed, *Omkring Niels Lyhne* (Copenhagen: Hans Reitzels Forlag, 1970), p. 232.

25. Kielland quoted in Wamberg, *Digterne og Gyldendal*, p. 161.

CHAPTER I. "SIMPLY TO BE REMEMBERED"

1. Quoted in Anna Linck, *J. P. Jacobsen: Et levnedsløb* (Copenhagen: Gyldendal, 1911), p. 124.

2. Quoted in Edvard Brandes, *Breve fra J. P. Jacobsen* (Copenhagen: Gyldendal, 1899), p. 132.

3. Quoted in Kristian Himmelstrup, *En sejlbåd for vindstille: En biografi om J. P. Jacobsen* (Copenhagen: Museum Tusculanums Forlag, 2014), p. 284.

4. Jens Peter Jacobsen, *Niels Lyhne*, trans, Tiina Nunnally (London: Penguin Classics, 2006), p. 170.

5. Vilhelm Møller, "Breve fra J. P. Jacobsen til Vilhelm Møller," in *Tilskueren: Maanedsskrift for litteratur*, ed. Valdemar Vedel (Copenhagen: Gyldendal, 1904), p. 955.

6. Himmelstrup, *En sejlbåd for vindstille*, p. 111.

7. Linck, *J. P. Jacobsen*, p. 29.

8. Quoted in Himmelstrup, *En sejlbåd for vindstille*, p. 111.

9. Quoted in Frederik Nielsen, *J. P. Jacobsen: Digteren og mennesket* (Copenhagen: G. E. C. Gads Forlag, 1953), p. 18.

10. Quoted in "Efter 1840," *Historisk årsbog for Thisted Amt 1924*, pp. 177–197.

11. Quoted in Anthon Larsen, "Minder fra barndoms- og ungdomsårene i min fødeby Thisted," *Historisk årsbog for Thisted Amt 1921*, pp. 258–269.

12. Quoted in Eric Torgersen, *Dear Friend: Rainer Maria Rilke and Paula Modersohn-Becker* (Evanston, IL: Northwestern University Press, 1998), pp. 74 and 18.

13. Quoted in E. Brandes, *Breve*, p. 136.

14. Quoted in Himmelstrup, *En sejlbåd for vindstille*, p. 288.

15. Jens Peter Jacobsen, *Mogens and Other Stories*, trans. Tiina Nunnally (Seattle: Fjord Press, 1994), p. 149.

16. E. Brandes, *Breve*, p. xliv.

17. Quoted in ibid., p. 291.

18. Quoted in Niels Birger Wamberg, *Digterne og Gyldendal* (Copenhagen: Gyldendal, 1970), p. 161.

19. Quoted in Billeskov Jansen, *J. P. Jacobsens spor*, p. 59.

20. August Strindberg, *Strindberg's Letters*, vol. 1: *1862–1892*, trans. and ed. Michael Robinson (Chicago: University of Chicago Press, 1992), p. 186.

21. Quoted in Svend Sørensen and Niels Nielsen, *At bære livet som det er: Om J. P. Jacobsen's liv og digtning* (Copenhagen: Sparekassen Thy's Forlag, 1997), p. 11.

22. Quoted in Kristian Hvidt, *Edvard Brandes: Portræt af en radikal blæksprutte* (Copenhagen: Gyldendal, 1987), p. 185.

23. Quoted in Sørensen and Nielsen, *At bære livet som det er*, p. 10.

24. Quoted in Jens Peter Jacobsen, *Samlede værker*, vol. 5 (Copenhagen: Rosenkilde og Bagger, 1973), p. 211.

25. Edvard Brandes, "Ligrøvere," *Politiken*, July 10, 1885.

26. Quoted in E. Brandes, *Breve*, p. 37.

27. Quoted in ibid., p. 25. Christoph Martin Wieland (1733–1813) was a prolific German poet and novelist, author of the epic *Oberon*.

CHAPTER 2. A SENTIMENTAL EDUCATION

1. Flemming Lundgreen-Nielsen, ed. *København læst og påskrevet* (Copenhagen: Museum Tusculanums Forlag, 1997), p. 109.

2. Jacobsen, *Samlede værker,* vol. 5, p. 15.

3. Quoted in Himmelstrup, *En sejlbåd for vindstille,* p. 26.

4. Quoted in F. Nielsen, *J. P. Jacobsen,* pp. 139–140.

5. Quoted in Sejer Kühle, "Fra J. P. Jacobsen's kreds," in *Fund og forskning,* vol. 4 (1957), p. 125.

6. Quoted in F. Nielsen, *J. P. Jacobsen,* p. 23.

7. Quoted in ibid., p. 137.

8. Quoted in ibid., p. 146.

9. Quoted in ibid., p. 129.

10. Quoted in Brita Tigerschiöld, *J. P. Jacobsen och hans roman Niels Lyhne* (Gothenburg: Gumperts Förlag, 1945), p. 21.

11. Elias Bredsdorff, *An Introduction to Scandinavian Literature* (Cambridge: Cambridge University Press, 1951), p. 145.

12. Herman Bang, *Tine* (Copenhagen: Gyldendal, 1889), p. 10.

13. Erik Skram, *Hinsides grænsen: Erindringer fra Sønderjylland* (Copenhagen: P. G. Philipsens Forlag, 1888), p. 20.

14. Quoted in Tigerschiöld, *J. P. Jacobsen,* p. 23.

15. Jacobsen, *Niels Lyhne* (Nunnally translation, 2006), pp. 39–40.

16. Quoted in Himmelstrup, *En sejlbåd for vindstille,* p. 79.

17. F. Nielsen, *J. P. Jacobsen,* p. 51; Jens Peter Jacobsen, *Lyrik og prosa* (Copenhagen: Borgen, 1993), pp. 40–41.

18. F. Nielsen, *J. P. Jacobsen,* p. 53.

19. Jacobsen, *Niels Lyhne* (Nunnally translation, 2006), p. 43.

20. Quoted in Robert Craft, *Moments of Existence: Music, Literature, and the Arts 1990–1995* (Nashville, TN: Vanderbilt University Press, 1996), p. 58.

21. Ibid., p. 80.

22. Quoted in Linck, *J. P. Jacobsen,* p. 40.

23. Quoted in Himmelstrup, *En sejlbåd for vindstille,* p. 85.

24. Quoted in Aage Knudsen, *J. P. Jacobsen i hans digtning* (Copenhagen: Gyldendal, 1950), p. 275.

25. Quoted in Linck, *J. P. Jacobsen,* p. 40.

26. Quoted in A. Knudsen, *J. P. Jacobsen i hans digtning,* p. 278.

27. Jacobsen, *Lyrik og prosa,* p. 9.

28. Quoted in A. Knudsen, *J. P. Jacobsen i hans digtning*, p. 273.

29. Quoted in Susanne V. Knudsen, "Kærlighedens kildevæld," *Thisted årsbog* (2000), p. 135.

30. Quoted in ibid., p. 135.

31. Quoted in Niels Haastrup, "J. P. Jacobsens kunsthistorie genfundet," *Magasin fra Det kongelige Bibliotek og Universitetsbiblioteket I* 1, no. 4 (1986): 3–22.

32. Jacobsen, *Lyrik og prosa*, p. 14.

33. Linck, *J. P. Jacobsen*, pp. 74–75.

34. Jacobsen, *Lyrik og prosa*, pp. 9–10.

35. E. Brandes, *Breve*, p. v.

36. Himmelstrup, *En sejlbåd for vindstille*, p. 48.

37. Quoted in Jon Stewart, ed., *Kierkegaard's Influence on Literature, Criticism and Art*, vol. 2: *Denmark* (London: Ashgate, 2013), p. 109.

38. Johannes Møllehave, *Til trøst* (Copenhagen: Lindhardt og Ringhof, 2012), p. 4.

39. Joakim Garff, *Søren Kierkegaard: A Biography*, trans. Bruce H. Kirmmse (Princeton, NJ: Princeton University Press, 2005), p. 809.

40. Quoted in Himmelstrup, *En sejlbåd for vindstille*, p. 48.

41. Jacobsen, *Samlede værker*, vol. 6, p. 12.

42. Jacobsen, *Niels Lyhne* (Nunnally translation, 2006), p. 106.

43. Quoted in Linck, *J. P. Jacobsen*, p. 45.

44. Quoted in Tigerschiöld, *J. P. Jacobsen*, p. 236.

45. Quoted in Himmelstrup, *En sejlbåd for vindstille*, p. 69.

46. H. S. Vodskov, *Spredte studier* (Copenhagen: Gyldendal, 1884), pp. i–ii.

47. Quoted in A. Knudsen, *J. P. Jacobsen i hans digtning*, p. 290.

48. Quoted in ibid., p. 9.

49. Quoted in F. Nielsen, *J. P. Jacobsen*, p. 147.

50. Quoted in ibid., p. 149.

51. Jacobsen, *Niels Lyhne* (Nunnally translation, 2006), pp. 84–85.

52. Jens Peter Jacobsen, *Marie Grubbe: Seventeenth Century Interiors*, trans. Mikka Haugaard (London: Dedalus Books, 2015), p. 14.

53. Quoted in Sørensen and Nielsen, *At bære livet som det er*, p. 40.

54. Quoted in Linck, *J. P. Jacobsen*, p. 61.

55. Quoted in ibid., p. 62.

56. Carsten Humlum, "Noter til J. P. Jacobsen's virke som botaniker," in *Historisk Årbog for Thy og Vester Hanherred* (1999), p. 46.

57. Quoted in Linck, *J. P. Jacobsen*, p. 46.

58. Charles Darwin, *On the Origin of Species*, ed. J. W. Burrow (London: Penguin Classics, 1985), p. 41.

59. Ibid., p. 14.

60. Nick Spencer, *Atheists: The Origin of the Species* (London: Bloomsbury, 2014), p. 180.

61. Quoted in Daniel C. Dennett, *Darwin's Dangerous Idea: Evolution and the Meanings of Life* (New York: Simon and Schuster, 1995), p. 62.

62. Darwin, *Origin of Species*, p. 45.

63. Jens Peter Jacobsen, *Darwin: Hans liv og lære*, ed. Vilhelm Møller (Copenhagen: Gyldendal, 1893), pp. 71–72.

64. Darwin, *Origin of Species*, pp. 459–460.

65. Jacobsen, *Darwin*, p. 142.

66. Ludwig Feuerbach, *The Essence of Christianity*, trans. George Eliot (Mineola, NY: Dover Classics, 2008), p. 15.

67. Jacobsen, *Darwin*, p. 241.

68. Quoted in ibid., p. 76.

69. Toril Moi, *Henrik Ibsen and the Birth of Modernism: Art, Theater, Philosophy* (Oxford: Oxford University Press, 2006), p. 43.

70. Quoted in L. C. Nielsen, *Frederik V. Hegel: Hans forgængere og hans slægt, et mindeskrift II* (Copenhagen: Fr. Bagges Kgl. Hofbogtrykkeri, 1909), p. 411.

CHAPTER 3. THE MODERN BREAKTHROUGH

1. Georg Brandes, *Essays* (Copenhagen: Gyldendal, 1963), p. 87.

2. Quoted in Georg Brandes, *An Essay on the Aristocratic Radicalism of Friedrich Nietzsche*, trans. A. G. Chater (London: Heinemann, 1915), p. 42.

3. G. Brandes, *Essays*, p. 88.

4. Quoted in Jørgen Knudsen, *GB: En Georg Brandes biografi* (Copenhagen: Gyldendal, 2008), p. 72.

5. Quoted in ibid., p. 73.

6. Quoted in Himmelstrup, *En sejlbåd for vindstille*, p. 158.

7. Georg Brandes, *Creative Spirits*, trans. Rasmus B. Anderson (New York: Books for Libraries Press, 1923), p. 195.

8. Ibid., p. v.

9. Quoted in Peter Madsen, "World Literature and World Thoughts: Brandes/Auerbach," in *Debating World Literature*, ed. Christopher Pendergast (New York: Verso Books, 2004).

10. Quoted in Jørgen Knudsen, *Georg Brandes: Frigørelsens vej 1842–77* (Copenhagen: Gyldendal, 1985), p. 267.

11. Quoted in ibid., p. 257.

12. Ibid., p. 259.

13. Herman Bang, *Københavnske skildringer* (Copenhagen: Gyldendal, 1954), p. 29.

14. E. Brandes, *Breve*, p. xx.

15. Quoted in ibid., p. 10.

16. Ibid., p. xxxix.

17. Quoted in Tigerschiöld, *J. P. Jacobsen*, p. 96.

18. Quoted in Julie K. Allen, *Icons of Danish Modernity: Georg Brandes and Asta Nielsen* (Seattle, WA: University of Washington Press, 2012), p. 78.

19. E. Brandes, *Breve*, p. xi–xii.

20. Linck, *J. P. Jacobsen*, p. 70.

21. E. Brandes, *Breve*, p. xvi.

22. Ibid., pp. xvi–xvii.

23. Erik Skram, "Nogle Meddelelser om J. P. Jacobsen," in *Tilskueren, Anden Aargang* (Copenhagen: P. G. Philipsens Forlag, 1885), p. 403.

24. Quoted in E. Brandes, *Breve*, p. 11.

25. Claudio Magris, "Nihilsme og melankoli: Jens Peter Jacobsens *Niels Lyhne*," trans. Peter Madsen, *Spring: Tidsskrift for moderne dansk litteratur*, no. 13 (1998): p. 27.

26. Charles Taylor, *A Secular Age* (Cambridge, MA: Belknap Press, 2007), p. 325.

27. Jens Peter Jacobsen, *Mogens and Other Stories* (Nunnally translation), p. 16.

28. Ibid., p. 19.

29. Ibid., pp. 31–32.

30. Ibid., p. 32.

31. Ibid., pp. 37–38.

32. Ibid., pp. 51–52.

33. Jacobsen, *Mogens and Other Stories* (Nunnally translation); Herman Bang, *Realisme og realister/kritiske studier og udkast* (Copenhagen: Borgen, 2001), p. 76.

34. Quoted in A. Knudsen, *J. P. Jacobsen i hans digtning*, p. 9.

35. Jacobsen, *Mogens and Other Stories* (Nunnally translation), pp. 10–11.

36. A. Knudsen, *J. P. Jacobsen i hans digtning*, p. 13.

37. Alrik Gustafson, "J. P. Jacobsen," in *Six Scandinavian Novelists*, ed. Alrik Gustafson (Minneapolis: University of Minnesota Press, 1940), p. 84.

38. Jacobsen, *Mogens and Other Stories* (Nunnally translation), p. 14.

39. Ibid., p. 59.

40. Ibid., p. 67.

41. Jørn Eslev Andersen, "J. P. Jacobsen and the Concept of Man," *Jacobseniana: Skrifter fra J. P. Jacobsen selskabet*, no. 1 (1999): xx.

42. Bang, *Realisme og realister*, p. 77; Donald C. Reichel, "Perfecting Failure: Musil on Hamsun, Jacobsen and D'Annunzio, and the Writing of *Der Mann ohne Eigenschaften*," *Modern Austrian Literature* 32, no. 1 (1999): 38.

43. Georg Brandes, *Main Currents in Nineteenth Century Literature*, vol. 1: *The Emigrant Literature* (London: Heinemann, 1906), p. 40.

44. Jacobsen, *Mogens and Other Stories* (Nunnally translation), p. 38; T. S. Eliot, *Collected Poems 1909–1962* (London: Faber and Faber, 2002), p. 3.

45. Quoted in E. Brandes, *Breve*, p. 61.

46. Quoted in Himmelstrup, *En sejlbåd for vindstille*, p. 170.

47. Jacobsen, *Samlede værker*, vol. 5, p. 69.

48. Quoted in Georg Brandes, "Breve fra J. P. Jacobsen," *Tilskueren: Fjerde aargang* (Copenhagen: P. G. Philipsens Forlag, 1887), p. 843.

49. Quoted in Linck, *J. P. Jacobsen*, p. 78.

50. Henrik Ibsen, *The Correspondence of Henrik Ibsen*, trans. Mary Morison (New York: Haskell House Publishers, 1905), p. 261; Fyodor Dostoevsky, *Writer's Diary*, vol. 1: *1873–1876*, trans. Kenneth Lantz (Evanston, IL: Northwestern University Press, 1994), p. 207.

51. Stefan Zweig, *The World of Yesterday* (Lincoln: University of Nebraska Press, 1964), p. 15.

52. Jacobsen, *Niels Lyhne* (Nunnally translation, 2006), pp. 168–169.

53. Quoted in Linck, *J. P. Jacobsen*, p. 78.

54. E. Brandes, *Breve*, p. xxix.

55. Quoted in Linck, *J. P. Jacobsen*, p. 79.

56. Quoted in ibid., pp. 79–80.

57. E. Brandes, *Breve*, p. xxxi.

58. Jacobsen, *Samlede værker*, vol. 5, p. 105.

59. Quoted in F. Nielsen, *J. P. Jacobsen*, pp. 104–105.

60. Helen Bynum, *Spitting Blood: The History of Tuberculosis* (Oxford: Oxford University Press, 2012), p. xiv.

61. Ibid., p. xix.

62. Den Store Danske: http://denstoredanske.dk/Krop,_psyke_og_sundhed/Sundhedsvidenskab/Infektions-_og_tropesygdomme/tuberkulose/tuberkulose_(Tuberkulosebekæmpelsens_historie_i_Danmark).

63. Susan Sontag, *Illness as Metaphor and AIDS and Its Metaphors* (New York: Anchor Books, 1989), pp. 30–34.

64. Bynum, *Spitting Blood*, p. 91.

65. Quoted in Aage Hansen and Erik Dal, eds., "Fire J. P. Jacobsen Breve" *Danske Studier 1970* (Copenhagen: Akademisk Forlag, 1970), p. 146.

66. Quoted in E. Brandes, *Breve*, p. 23.

67. Jacobsen, *Samlede værker*, vol. 5, p. 111.

68. Quoted in Víctor Farías, *Heidegger and Nazism* (Philadelphia: Temple University Press, 1989), p. 42.

69. Quoted in Bynum, *Spitting Blood*, p. xxii.

CHAPTER 4. A WOMAN WITHOUT QUALITIES

1. Edmund Gosse, *Two Visits to Denmark* (London: Smith, Elder, 1911), p. 324.

2. Quoted in ibid., p. 326.

3. Edmund Gosse, introduction to Jens Peter Jacobsen, *Siren Voices (Niels Lyhne)*, trans. Ethel F. L. Robertson (London: Heinemann, 1986), p. x.

4. Quoted in E. Brandes, *Breve*, p. 28.

5. Quoted in Møller, "Breve fra J. P. Jacobsen til Vilhelm Møller," p. 845.

6. Quoted in E. Brandes, *Breve*, p. 9.

7. Ludvig Holberg, "Epistel 89," *Jacobseniana* 7 (Copenhagen: J. P. Jacobsen Selskabet), pp. 47–48.

8. Quoted in Møller, "Breve fra J. P. Jacobsen til Vilhelm Møller," p. 843.

9. G. Brandes endnotes in Jens Peter Jacobsen, *Fru Marie Grubbe* (Copenhagen: Borgen, 2003), p. 209.

10. Jacobsen, *Marie Grubbe* (Haugaard translation), p. 54.

11. Wamberg, *Digterne og Gyldendal,* p. 118.

12. Quoted in E. Brandes, *Breve,* p. 33.

13. Mikka Haugaard, introduction to Jacobsen, *Marie Grubbe: Seventeenth Century Interiors,* p. 9.

14. Jacobsen, *Marie Grubbe* (Haugaard translation), p. 13.

15. Ibid., p. 16.

16. Ibid., p. 32.

17. Ibid., p. 34.

18. Ibid., p. 71.

19. Ibid., pp. 74–75.

20. Ibid., p. 84.

21. Ibid., pp. 84–85.

22. Ibid., p. 100.

23. Gustave Flaubert, *Madame Bovary,* trans. Eleanor Marx Arveling and Paul de Man (New York: W. W. Norton, 2005), pp. 54–57.

24. Jacobsen, *Marie Grubbe* (Haugaard translation), p. 140.

25. Ibid., pp. 140–141.

26. Ibid., pp. 147–148.

27. Ibid., p. 178.

28. Ibid., p. 195.

29. Ibid., p. 200.

30. Ibid., p. 167.

31. Ibid., p. 171.

32. Ibid., p. 210.

33. Ibid., p. 221.

34. Ibid., p. 227.

35. Georg Lukács, *The Historical Novel,* trans. Hannah and Stanley Mitchell (Boston: Beacon Press, 1962), p. 200.

36. Roger L. Williams, *The Horror of Life* (London: Weidenfeld and Nicholson, 1980), p. 111.

37. Jacobsen, *Marie Grubbe* (Haugaard translation), p. 235.

38. Ibid., p. 271.

39. Ibid., pp. 276–277.

40. Søren Matthiesen, *Rygtet om Guds død* (Aarhus: Hovedland, 2013), p. 26.

41. Robert Musil, *The Man without Qualities*, trans. Sophie Wilkins and Burton Pike (New York: Vintage Books, 1996), p. 1563.

42. Strindberg, *Strindberg's Letters*, p. 83.

43. August Strindberg, *Miss Julie*, trans. Edwin Björkman (Mineola, NY: Dover Thrift Editions, 1992), p. xii.

44. Quoted in E. Brandes, *Breve*, p. 102.

45. Quoted in Sverre Lyngstad, *Knut Hamsun, Novelist: A Critical Assessment* (New York: Peter Lang, 2005), p. 330.

46. Knut Hamsun, "Fra det ubevidste djæleliv," in *Artikler: 1889–1928* (Copenhagen: Gyldendals, 1966), p. 42.

47. Quoted in James Wood, *The Broken Estate: Essays on Literature and Belief* (New York: Random House, 1999), p. 81.

48. Knut Hamsun, *Hunger*, tran. Sverre Lyngstad (London: Penguin Classics, 1996), p. 110.

49. Quoted in Hvidt, *Edvard Brandes*, p. 270.

50. Quoted in ibid., p. 52.

51. Quoted in E. Brandes, *Breve*, p. 38.

52. Quoted in G. Brandes, "Breve fra J. P. Jacobsen," p. 850.

53. Quoted in E. Brandes, *Breve*, p. 42.

54. Quoted in Møller, "Breve fra J. P. Jacobsen til Vilhelm Møller," p. 847.

55. Quoted in ibid., p. 846.

56. Quoted in Jørgen Ottosen, ed., *Omkring Fru Marie Grubbe* (Copenhagen: Hans Reitzels Forlag, 1972), p. 28.

57. Quoted in ibid., p. 38.

58. Quoted in ibid., p. 24.

59. Quoted in ibid., p. 30.

60. Quoted in ibid., p. 25.

61. Jacobsen, *Marie Grubbe* (Haugaard translation), p. 173.

62. Quoted in Jacobsen, *Lyrik og prosa*, p. 245.

63. Jacobsen, *Marie Grubbe* (Haugaard translation), pp. 112, 41, 112, and 192.

64. Quoted in Ottosen, *Omkring Fru Marie Grubbe*, pp. 47–48.

65. Quoted in G. Brandes, "Breve fra J. P. Jacobsen," p. 856.

66. Quoted in Ottosen, *Omkring Fru Marie Grubbe*, p. 167.
67. Quoted in ibid., p. 165.

CHAPTER 5. "POOR FREETHINKERS"

1. Zweig, *The World of Yesterday*, p. 125.
2. Quoted in Ottosen, *Omkring Fru Marie Grubbe*, pp. 64–66.
3. Quoted in ibid., pp. 61–63.
4. Henrik Pontoppidan, *Lykke-Per* (Copenhagen: Gyldendal, 2006), p. 116.
5. Quoted in E. Brandes. *Breve*, pp. 105–106.
6. Quoted in G. Brandes, "Breve fra J. P. Jacobsen," p. 855.
7. Quoted in ibid., p. 857.
8. Quoted in ibid., p. 859.
9. Karl Baedeker, *Switzerland* (London: J. Murray, 1863), p. 238.
10. Quoted in G. Brandes, "Breve fra J. P. Jacobsen," 858.
11. Jacobsen, *Samlede værker*, vol. 6, p. 14.
12. F. Nielsen, *J. P. Jacobsen*, p. 117.
13. Jacobsen, *Niels Lyhne* (Nunnally translation, 2006), pp. 167–168.
14. Quoted in Linck, *J. P. Jacobsen*, p. 103.
15. Quoted in E. Brandes, *Breve*, p. 66.
16. Quoted in Barfoed, *Omkring Niels Lyhne*, p. 21.
17. Hans Christian Andersen, *To Be or Not to Be? A Novel*, trans. Mrs. Bushby (London: Richard Bentley, 1857), p. 364.
18. Ivan Turgenev, *Fathers and Sons*, trans. Peter Carson (London: Penguin Classics, 2009), p. 195.
19. V. S. Pritchett, *The Gentle Barbarian: The Life and Work of Turgenev* (New York: Random House, 1977), p. 146.
20. Georg Brandes, *Impressions of Russia*, trans. Samuel C. Eastman (New York: Thomas Y. Crowell, 1966), p. 215.
21. Quoted in Barfoed, *Omkring Niels Lyhne*, p. 146.
22. Quoted in Tigerschiöld, *J. P. Jacobsen*, p. 166.
23. Jacobsen, *Samlede værker*, vol. 6, p. 57.
24. Quoted in G. Brandes, "Breve fra J. P. Jacobsen," p. 865.
25. Quoted in E. Brandes, *Breve fra Jacobsen*, p. 81.
26. Quoted in ibid., p. 81.
27. The majority of the information about the Scandinavian Foundation, as well as Jacobsen's travels, comes from Steen Neergaard, "J. P.

Jacobsen og skandinavisk forening i Rom," in *Jacobseniana: Skrifter fra J. P. Jacobsen selskabet*, no. 4 (Thisted: J. P. Jacobsen Society).
28. Quoted in E. Brandes, *Breve*, p. 98.
29. Quoted in Billeskov Jansen, *J. P. Jacobsens spor*, p. 30.
30. Quoted in ibid., p. 80.
31. Quoted in G. Brandes, "Breve fra J. P. Jacobsen," p. 864.
32. Quoted in Barfoed, *Omkring Niels Lyhne*, p. 24.
33. Quoted in G. Brandes, "Breve fra J. P. Jacobsen," p. 865.
34. Jacobsen, *Samlede værker*, vol. 6, p. 84.
35. Jacobsen, *Mogens and Other Stories* (Nunnally translation), p. 91.
36. Ibid., p. 96.
37. Ibid., p. 91.
38. Ibid., p. 92.
39. Quoted in F. Nielsen, *J. P. Jacobsen*, p. 119.
40. Jacobsen, *Samlede værker*, vol. 6, pp. 89–90.
41. Moi, *Henrik Ibsen and the Birth of Modernism*, p. 90.
42. Quoted in ibid, p. 91.
43. Ottosen, *Omkring Fru Marie Grubbe*, p. 166.
44. Bang, *Realisme og realister*, p. 16.
45. Quoted in E. Brandes, *Breve*, p. 94.
46. Bang, *Realisme og realister*, p. 82.
47. Quoted in E. Brandes, *Breve*, pp. 61–62.
48. Quoted in ibid., p. 97.
49. Jacobsen, *Niels Lyhne* (Nunnally translation, 2006), pp. 134–135.
50. Edmund Gosse, "J. P. Jacobsen," *Athenæum*, no. 3002 (1885): 589.
51. E. Brandes, *Breve*, p. iii.
52. Jacobsen, *Marie Grubbe* (Haugaard translation), p. 140.
53. Quoted in Barfoed, *Omkring Niels Lyhne*, p. 24.
54. Jacobsen, *Samlede værker*, vol. 6, p. 84.
55. A. Knudsen, *J. P. Jacobsen i hans digtning*, p. 161.
56. Quoted in Tigerschiöld, *J. P. Jacobsen*, p. 157.
57. E. Brandes, *Breve*, p. 112.

CHAPTER 6. THE ATHEIST
Epigraph: Jacobsen, *Niels Lyhne* (Nunnally translation, 2006), p. 169.
1. Quoted in Barfoed, *Omkring Niels Lyhne*, p. 31.
2. Quoted in E. Brandes, *Breve*, p. 100.

3. Søren Kierkegaard, *The Sickness unto Death*, trans. Alastair Hannay (London: Penguin Classics, 1989), p. 98.

4. Henrik Gade Jensen, *Monrad: Vilje, tidsånd, og tro* (Copenhagen: Kristeligt Dagblads Forlag, 2015), p. 9.

5. Jacobsen, *Niels Lyhne* (Nunnally translation, 2006), p. 55.

6. Niels Lyhne Jensen, *Jens Peter Jacobsen* (Boston: Twayne Publishers, 1980), p. 95.

7. Jacobsen, *Niels Lyhne* (Nunnally translation, 2006), p. 73.

8. Ibid., p. 98.

9. Ibid., p. 97.

10. Ibid., p. 60.

11. Ibid., p. 10.

12. Ibid., p. 22.

13. Ibid., p. 21.

14. Ibid., p. 23.

15. Ibid., p. 24.

16. Ibid., p. 25.

17. Ibid., p. 34.

18. Ibid.

19. Ibid., p. 35.

20. Ibid., p. 37.

21. Ibid., p. 38.

22. Ibid., p. 80.

23. Ibid., p. 85.

24. Ibid., p. 96.

25. Ibid., p. 107.

26. Ibid., pp. 106–107.

27. Ibid., p. 107.

28. Ibid., p. 126.

29. Ibid., p. 159.

30. Ibid., p. 170.

31. Ibid., p. 176.

32. Ibid., p. 178.

33. Ibid., p. 180.

34. Ibid., pp. 181–182.

35. Ibid., p. 183.

36. Ibid., pp. 186–187.

37. Bernard Schweizer, *Hating God: The Untold Story of Misotheism* (Oxford: Oxford University Press, 2011), p. 10.

38. Ibid., p. 8.

39. Magris, "Nihilisme og Melankoli," p. 29.

40. Friedrich Nietzsche, *The Portable Nietzsche*, trans. and ed. Walter Kaufmann (London: Penguin Books, 1976), p. 95.

41. Jacobsen, *Niels Lyhne* (Nunnally translation, 2006), p. 106.

42. Ibid., p. 184.

43. James Wood, "The Sickness unto Life," *New Republic*, November 8, 1999, p. 93.

44. Jacobsen, *Niels Lyhne* (Nunnally translation, 2006), p. 186.

45. Quoted in Barfoed, *Omkring Niels Lyhne*, pp. 42–43.

46. Quoted in ibid., p. 52.

47. Quoted in ibid., p. 83.

48. Quoted in J. Knudsen, *GB*, p. 215.

49. Jacobsen, *Niels Lyhne* (Nunnally translation, 2006), p. 33.

50. Ibid., p. 91.

51. Ibid., p. 100.

52. Georg Lukács, *The Theory of the Novel*, trans. Anna Bostock (Cambridge, MA: MIT Press, 1971), pp. 119–120.

53. Georg Lukács, "Narrate or Describe?," in *Writer and Critic and Other Essays*, trans. Arthur Kahn (Sydney: Merlin Press, 1970), p. 118.

54. Peter Brooks, *Realist Vision* (New Haven: Yale University Press, 2005), p. 16.

55. Robert Musil, *Diaries 1899–1941*, trans. Philip Payne (New York: Basic Books, 1999), p. 387.

56. Brooks, *Realist Vision*, p. 17.

57. Quoted in E. Brandes, *Breve*, p. 102.

58. Billeskov Jansen, *J. P. Jacobsens spor*, p. 25.

59. Quoted in ibid., p. 26.

60. Quoted in ibid., p. 29.

61. Quoted in Barfoed, *Omkring Niels Lyhne*, p. 93.

62. Quoted in ibid., p. 104.

63. Quoted in ibid., p. 60.

64. Quoted in E. Brandes, *Breve*, p. 114.

65. J. Knudsen, *GB*, p. 215.

66. Quoted in ibid., p. 227.

67. Quoted in Barfoed, *Omkring Niels Lyhne*, p. 103.
68. Quoted in ibid., p. 35.
69. Quoted in ibid., pp. 37–38.
70. Quoted in ibid., p. 101.
71. Quoted in ibid., p. 65.
72. Henrik Ibsen, *The Correspondence of Henrik Ibsen*, trans. and ed. Mary Morison (London: Hodder and Stoughton, 1905), p. 336.
73. Quoted in E. Brandes, *Breve*, p. 120.
74. Quoted in Barfoed, *Omkring Niels Lyhne*, p. 102.

CHAPTER 7. THE SICKNESS UNTO DEATH

1. Jacobsen, *Samlede værker*, vol. 6, p. 155.
2. Quoted in Himmelstrup, *En sejlbåd for vindstille*, p. 265.
3. Jacobsen, *Samlede værker*, vol. 6, p. 159.
4. Quoted in Linck, *J. P. Jacobsen*, p. 112.
5. Jacobsen, *Samlede værker*, vol. 6, p. 163.
6. Ibid., p. 166.
7. Ibid., p. 167.
8. Quoted in Hvidt, *Edvard Brandes*, p. 141.
9. Quoted in ibid., p. 139.
10. Quoted in E. Brandes, *Breve*, p. 119.
11. Alexander Kielland, *Breve fra Alexander Kielland* (Copenhagen: Gyldendal, 1917), p. 125.
12. Quoted in E. Brandes, *Breve*, p. 92.
13. Quoted in ibid., p. 108.
14. Quoted in Billeskov Jansen, *J. P. Jacobsens spor*, p. 31.
15. Quoted in Hvidt, *Edvard Brandes*, p. 185.
16. Jacobsen, *Mogens and Other Stories* (Nunnally translation), p. 111.
17. Ibid., p. 121.
18. Ibid., pp. 121–122.
19. Ibid., p. 118.
20. Kielland, *Breve*, p. 143.
21. Henningsen in Himmelstrup, *En sejlbåd for vindstille*, p. 239.
22. Quoted in Bertil Nolin, *Georg Brandes* (Woodbridge, CT: Twayne Publishers, 1976), p. 116.
23. August Strindberg, *Three Plays*, trans. Peter Watts (London: Penguin Classics, 1958), p. 56.

24. Jacobsen, *Niels Lyhne* (Nunnally translation, 2006), p. 64.

25. Quoted in G. Brandes, "Breve fra J. P. Jacobsen," p. 869.

26. Maurice Blanchot, *The Space of Literature*, trans. Ann Smock (Lincoln: University of Nebraska Press, 1982), p. 122.

27. Jacobsen, *Marie Grubbe* (Haugaard translation), p. 277.

28. Blanchot, *The Space of Literature*, p. 123.

29. Rainer Maria Rilke, *The Notebooks of Malte Laurids Brigge*, trans. Michael Hulse (London: Penguin Classics, 2009), p. 11.

30. Jacobsen, *Niels Lyhne* (Nunnally translation, 2006), p. 185.

31. Jacobsen, *Lyrik og prosa*, p. 217.

32. Ibid., p. 219.

33. Quoted in ibid., p. 271.

34. Quoted in Himmelstrup, *En sejlbåd for vindstille*, p. 279.

35. Quoted in Hvidt, *Edvard Brandes*, p. 185.

36. Georg Brandes, *Levned: Snevringer og horizonter* (Copenhagen: Gyldendal, 1908), pp. 61–62.

37. Jacobsen, *Samlede værker*, vol. 6, p. 190.

38. Quoted in E. Brandes, *Breve*, p. xlv.

39. Quoted in Tigerschiöld, *J. P. Jacobsen*, p. 46.

40. Quoted in ibid., p. 131.

41. Quoted in Linck, *J. P. Jacobsen*, p. 123.

42. Quoted in ibid., p. 124.

43. Quoted in Himmelstrup, *En sejlbåd*, p. 285.

44. Jacobsen, *Samlede værker*, vol. 6, p. 203.

45. Quoted in ibid., p. 144.

CHAPTER 8. THE JACOBSEN FASHION

1. Quoted in Barfoed, *Omkring Niels Lyhne*, p. 136.

2. Quoted in ibid., p. 138.

3. Berthold Litzman, *Mitteilungen Der Literarhistorischen Gesellschaft Bonn* (Bonn: Gesellschaft Bonn), vol. 2, p. 158.

4. Quoted in Allen, *Icons of Danish Modernity*, p. 77.

5. Pericles Lewis, ed., *The Cambridge Companion to European Modernism* (Cambridge: Cambridge University Press, 2011), p. 34.

6. Quoted in J. Knudsen, *GB*, p. 169.

7. G. Brandes, *An Essay on the Aristocratic Radicalism of Friedrich Nietzsche*, p. 41.

8. Ibid., p. 53.

9. Quoted in ibid., p. 43.

10. Ibid., p. 66.

11. Quoted in Herman Scheffauer, "A Correspondence between Nietzsche and Strindberg," *North American Review* 198 (1913): 199.

12. Lewis, *Cambridge Companion to European Modernism*, p. 36.

13. Steven E. Aschheim, *The Nietzsche Legacy in Germany: 1890–1990* (Berkeley: University of California Press, 1992), p. 33.

14. Quoted in G. Brandes, *An Essay on the Aristocratic Radicalism of Friedrich Nietzsche*, p. 70.

15. Quoted in Malcolm Bradbury and James McFarlane, eds., *Modernism: A Guide to European Literature 1890–1930* (London: Penguin Books, 1991), p. 43.

16. G. Brandes, *An Essay on the Aristocratic Radicalism of Friedrich Nietzsche*, p. 34.

17. Quoted in Bengt Algot Sørensen, "Tyskland," in Billeskov Jansen, *J. P. Jacobsens spor*, p. 117.

18. Quoted in Petra Broomans, ed., *From Darwin to Weil: Women as Transmitters of Ideas* (Kooiweg, Netherlands: Barkhuis, 2009), p. 77.

19. Quoted in Kevin C. Karnes, *A Kingdom Not of This World: Wagner, the Arts, and Utopian Visions in Fin-de-siècle Vienna* (Oxford: Oxford University Press, 2013), p. 131.

20. Baer, "Rilke and Jens Peter Jacobsen," *PMLA* 54, no. 3: 901.

21. Billeskov Jensen, *Jens Peter Jacobsen spor*, p. 139.

22. Ibid., p. 291.

23. Quoted in Walter Frisch, *The Early Works of Arnold Schoenberg, 1893–1908* (Berkeley: University of California Press, 1993), p. 141.

24. Billeskov Jansen, *J. P. Jacobsens spor*, p. 295.

25. Quoted in Anders Ehlers Dam, "Berusede Sanser," *Jacobseniana: Skrifter fra J. P. Jacobsen selskabet*, no. 10 (2016): 16.

26. "J. P. Jacobsen and the Visual Arts," Faaborg Museum, May 14–September 18, 2016.

27. Quoted in ibid., p. 14.

28. Quoted in Anders Ehlers Dam and Gry Hedin, eds., *J. P. Jacobsen og kunsten* (Aarhus: Faaborg Museum/Aarhus Universitetsforlag, 2016), p. 101.

29. Ibid., p. 13.

30. Ibid., p. 86.

31. Quoted in Torgersen, *Dear Friend*, p. 33.

32. Jacobsen, *Niels Lyhne* (Nunnally translation, 2006), p. 59.

33. Torgersen, *Dear Friend*, p. 16.

34. Hermann Bahr, "The Overcoming of Naturalism," in *The Vienna Coffee House Wits 1890–1938*, trans. and ed. Harold B. Segel (Lafayette, IN: Purdue University Press, 1993), p. 51.

35. Quoted in Torgersen, *Dear Friend*, p. 46.

36. Quoted in Dam and Hedin, *J. P. Jacobsen og kunsten*, p. 83.

37. Erich Heller, *The Disinherited Mind: Essays in Modern German Literature and Thought* (New York: Farrar, Straus, and Cudahy, 1957), pp. 175–176.

38. Jacobsen, *Niels Lyhne* (Nunnally translation, 2006), p. 91.

39. James Wood, *The Nearest Thing to Life* (Waltham, MA: Brandeis University Press, 2015), p. 39.

40. Quoted in ibid., p. 39.

41. Rainer Maria Rilke, *Rodin*, trans. Jessie Lemont and Hans Trausil (London: Grey Walls Press, 1948), p. 10.

42. Jacobsen, *Samlede værker*, vol. 6, p. 115.

43. Ernest Becker, *The Denial of Death* (New York: Free Press, 1973), p. 26.

Selected Bibliography

SELECTION OF WORKS BY JACOBSEN IN DANISH

Fru Marie Grubbe. Copenhagen: Gyldendal, 1876.

Niels Lyhne. Copenhagen: Gyldendal, 1880.

Mogens og andre noveller. Copenhagen: Gyldendal, 1882.

Digte og udkast. Ed. Edvard Brandes and Vilhelm Møller. Copenhagen: Gyldendal, 1886.

Darwin: Hans liv og lære. Ed. Vilhelm Møller. Copenhagen: Gyldendal, 1893.

Samlede værker (volumes 1–6). Ed. Frederik Nielsen. Copenhagen: Rosenkilde og Bagger, 1973.

WORKS BY JACOBSEN IN ENGLISH TRANSLATION

Siren Voices (Niels Lyhne). Trans. Ethel F. L. Robertson, with an introduction by Edmund Gosse. London: Heinemann, 1896.

Marie Grubbe: A Lady of the Seventeenth Century. Trans. Hanna Astrup Larsen. New York: American-Scandinavian Foundation, 1917.

Niels Lyhne. Trans. Hanna Astrup Larsen. New York: American-Scandinavian Foundation, 1919.

Poems by J. P. Jacobsen. Trans. Paul Selver. Oxford: Oxford University Press, 1920.

Mogens and Other Stories. Trans. Anna Grabow. New York: Nicholas L. Brown, 1921.

BIBLIOGRAPHY

Niels Lyhne. Trans. Tiina Nunnally. Seattle: Fjord Press, 1990.

Mogens and Other Stories. Trans. Tiina Nunnally. Seattle: Fjord Press, 1994.

Niels Lyhne. Trans. Tiina Nunnally. London: Penguin Classics, 2006.

Marie Grubbe: Seventeenth Century Interiors. Trans. Mikka Haugaard. London: Dedalus Books, 2015.

WORKS ABOUT JACOBSEN

Andersen, Jørn Eslev. "J. P. Jacobsen and the Concept of Man." *Jacobseniana: Skrifter fra J. P. Jacobsen selskabet*, no. 1 (1999).

Baer, Lydia. "Rilke and Jens Peter Jacobsen." *PMLA* 54, no. 3 (September 1939).

———. "Rilke and Jens Peter Jacobsen." *PMLA* 54, no. 4 (December 1939).

Barfoed, Niels, ed. *Omkring Niels Lyhne.* Copenhagen: Hans Reitzels Forlag, 1970.

Billeskov Jansen, F. J., ed. *J. P. Jacobsens spor i ord, billeder og toner.* Copenhagen: C. A. Reitzels Forlag, 1985.

Brandes, Edvard. *Breve fra J. P. Jacobsen.* Copenhagen: Gyldendal, 1899.

———. "Ligrøvere." *Politiken*, July 10, 1885.

Brandes, Georg. "Breve fra J. P. Jacobsen." *Tilskueren: Fjerde Aargang.* Copenhagen: P. G. Philipsens Forlag, 1887.

Craft, Robert. *Moments of Existence: Music, Literature, and the Arts 1990–1995.* Nashville, TN: Vanderbilt University Press, 1996.

Dam, Anders Ehlers. "Berusede Sanser." *Jacobseniana: Skrifter fra J. P. Jacobsen selskabet*, no. 10 (2016).

Dam, Anders Ehlers, and Gry Hedin, eds. *J. P. Jacobsen og kunsten.* Aarhus: Faaborg Museum/Aarhus Universitetsforlag, 2016.

Gosse, Edmund. "J. P. Jacobsen." *Athenæum*, no. 3002 (1885).

Gustafson, Alrik. "J. P. Jacobsen." In *Six Scandinavian Novelists.* Ed. Alrik Gustafson. Minneapolis: University of Minnesota Press, 1940.

Himmelstrup, Kristian. *En sejlbåd for vindstille: En biografi om J. P. Jacobsen.* Copenhagen: Museum Tusculanums Forlag, 2014.

Humlum, Carsten. "Noter til J. P. Jacobsens virke som botaniker." In *Historisk årbog for Thy og Vester Hanherred.* 1999.

Knudsen, Aage. *J. P. Jacobsen i hans digtning. Copenhagen:* Gyldendal, 1950.

BIBLIOGRAPHY

Kühle, Sejer. "Fra J. P. Jacobsen's kreds." In *Fund og forskning*, vol. 4. Ed. John T. Lauridsen. Copenhagen: Royal Library–National Library of Denmark and Copenhagen University, 1957.

Linck, Anna. *J. P. Jacobsen: Et levnedsløb.* Copenhagen: Gyldendal, 1911.

Magris, Claudio. "Nihilsme og melankoli: Jens Peter Jacobsens *Niels Lyhne.*" Trans. Peter Madsen. *Spring: Tidsskrift for moderne dansk litteratur,* no. 13 (1998).

Møller, Vilhelm. "Breve fra J. P. Jacobsen til Vilhelm Møller." In *Tilskueren: Maanedsskrift for litteratur.* Ed. Valdemar Vedel. Copenhagen: Gyldendal, 1904.

Neergaard, Steen. "J. P. Jacobsen og skandinavisk forening i Rom." In *Jacobseniana: Skrifter fra J. P. Jacobsen selskabet,* no. 4. Thisted: J. P. Jacobsen Society.

Nielsen, Frederik. *J. P. Jacobsen: Digteren og mennesket.* Copenhagen: G. E. C. Gads Forlag, 1953.

Ottosen, Jørgen, ed. *Omkring Fru Marie Grubbe.* Copenhagen: Hans Reitzels Forlag, 1972.

Sørensen, Svend, and Niels Nielsen. *At bære livet som det er: Om J. P. Jacobsen's liv og digtning.* Copenhagen: Sparekassen Thy's Forlag, 1997.

Tigerschiöld, Brita. *J. P. Jacobsen och hans roman Niels Lyhne.* Gothenburg: Gumperts Förlag, 1945.

OTHER WORKS

Allen, Julie K. *Icons of Danish Modernity: Georg Brandes and Asta Nielsen.* Seattle: University of Washington Press, 2012.

Andersen, Hans Christian. *To Be or Not to Be? A Novel.* Trans. Mrs. Bushby. London: Richard Bentley, 1857.

Aschheim, Steven E. *The Nietzsche Legacy in Germany: 1890–1990.* Berkeley: University of California Press, 1992.

Baedeker, Karl. *Switzerland.* London: J. Murray, 1863.

Bahr, Hermann. "The Overcoming of Naturalism." In *The Vienna Coffee House Wits 1890–1938.* Trans. and ed. Harold B. Segel. West Lafayette, IN: Purdue University Press, 1993.

Bang, Herman. *Københavnske skildringer.* Copenhagen: Gyldendal, 1954.

———. *Realisme og realister/kritiske studier og udkast.* Copenhagen: Borgen, 2001.

———. *Tine.* Copenhagen: Gyldendal, 1889.

Becker, Ernest. *The Denial of Death.* New York: Free Press, 1973.

Blanchot, Maurice. *The Space of Literature.* Trans. Ann Smock. Lincoln: University of Nebraska Press, 1982.

Bradbury, Malcolm, and James McFarlane, eds. *Modernism: A Guide to European Literature 1890–1930.* London: Penguin Books, 1991.

Brandes, Georg. *Creative Spirits.* Trans. Rasmus B. Anderson. New York: Books for Libraries Press, 1923.

———. *An Essay on the Aristocratic Radicalism of Friedrich Nietzsche.* Trans. A. G. Chater. London: Heinemann, 1915.

———. *Essays.* Copenhagen: Gyldendal, 1963.

———. *Impressions of Russia.* Trans. Samuel C. Eastman. New York: Thomas Y. Crowell, 1966.

———. *Levned: Snevringer og horizonter.* Copenhagen: Gyldendal, 1908.

———. *Main Currents in Nineteenth Century Literature,* vol. 1: *The Emigrant Literature.* London: Heinemann, 1906.

Bredsdorff, Elias. *An Introduction to Scandinavian Literature.* Cambridge: Cambridge University Press, 1951.

Brooks, Peter. *Realist Vision.* New Haven: Yale University Press, 2005.

Broomans, Petra, ed. *From Darwin to Weil: Women as Transmitters of Ideas.* Kooiweg, Netherlands: Barkuis, 2009.

Bynum, Helen. *Spitting Blood: The History of Tuberculosis.* Oxford: Oxford University Press, 2012.

Feuerbach, Ludwig. *The Essence of Christianity.* Trans. George Eliot. Mineola, NY: Dover Classics, 2008.

Flaubert, Gustave. *Madame Bovary.* Trans. Eleanor Marx Arveling and Paul de Man. New York: W. W. Norton, 2005.

Freedman, Ralph. *Life of a Poet: Rainer Maria Rilke.* Evanston, IL: Northwestern University Press, 1996.

Frisch, Walter. *The Early Works of Arnold Schoenberg, 1893–1908.* Berkeley: University of California Press, 1993.

Garff, Joakim. *Søren Kierkegaard: A Biography.* Trans. Bruce H. Kirmmse. Princeton, NJ: Princeton University Press, 2005.

Gosse, Edmund. *Two Visits to Denmark.* London: Smith, Elder, 1911.

Hamsun, Knut. "Fra det ubevidste sjæleliv." In *Artikler: 1889–1928.* Copenhagen: Gyldendal, 1966.

———. *Hunger.* Trans. Sverre Lyngstad. London: Penguin Classics, 1996.

BIBLIOGRAPHY

Heilbut, Anthony. *Thomas Mann: Eros and Literature.* New York: Alfred A. Knopf, 1995.

Heller, Erich. *The Disinherited Mind: Essays in Modern German Literature and Thought.* New York: Farrar, Straus, and Cudahy, 1957.

Hvidt, Kristian. *Edvard Brandes: Portræt af en radikal blæksprutte.* Copenhagen: Gyldendal, 1987.

Ibsen, Henrik. *The Correspondence of Henrik Ibsen.* Trans. Mary Morison. London: Hodder and Stoughton, 1905.

Jensen, Henrik Gade. *Monrad: Vilje, tidsånd, og tro.* Copenhagen: Kristeligt Dagblads Forlag, 2015.

Jensen, Niels Lyhne. *Jens Peter Jacobsen.* Boston: Twayne Publishers, 1980.

Karnes, Kevin C. *A Kingdom Not of This World: Wagner, the Arts, and Utopian Visions in Fin-de-siècle Vienna.* Oxford: Oxford University Press, 2013.

Kielland, Alexander. *Breve fra Alexander Kielland.* Copenhagen: Gyldendal, 1917.

Kierkegaard, Søren. *The Sickness unto Death.* Trans. Alastair Hannay. London: Penguin Classics, 1989.

Knudsen, Jørgen. *GB: En Georg Brandes biografi.* Copenhagen: Gyldendal, 2008.

———. *Georg Brandes: Frigørelsens vej 1842–77.* Copenhagen: Gyldendal, 1985.

Larsen, Anthon. "Minder fra barndoms- og ungdomsårene i min fødeby Thisted." In *Historisk årsbog for Thisted Amt* (1921).

Lewis, Pericles, ed. *The Cambridge Companion to European Modernism.* Cambridge: Cambridge University Press, 2011.

Lukács, Georg. *The Historical Novel.* Trans. Hannah and Stanley Mitchell. Boston: Beacon Press, 1962.

———. "Narrate or Describe?" In Georg Lukács, *Writer and Critic and Other Essays.* Trans. Arthur Kahn. Sydney: Merlin Press, 1970.

———. *The Theory of the Novel.* Trans. Anna Bostock. Cambridge, MA: MIT Press, 1971.

Lundgreen-Nielsen, Flemming, ed. *København læst og påskrevet.* Copenhagen: Museum Tusculanums Forlag, 1997.

Lyngstad, Sverre. *Knut Hamsun, Novelist: A Critical Assessment.* New York: Peter Lang, 2005.

Madsen, Peter. "World Literature and World Thoughts: Brandes/Auerbach." In *Debating World Literature*. Ed. Christopher Pendergast. New York: Verso Books, 2004.

Mann, Thomas. *A Sketch of My Life*. Trans. H. T. Lowe-Porter. New York: Alfred A. Knopf, 1960.

Matthiesen, Søren. *Rygtet om Guds død*. Aarhus: Hovedland, 2013.

Moi, Toril. *Henrik Ibsen and the Birth of Modernism: Art, Theater, Philosophy*. Oxford: Oxford University Press, 2006.

Møllehave, Johannes. *Til trøst*. Copenhagen: Lindhardt og Ringhof, 2012.

Musil, Robert. *Diaries 1899–1941*. Trans. Philip Payne. New York: Basic Books, 1999.

———. *The Man without Qualities*. Trans. Sophie Wilkins and Burton Pike. New York: Vintage Books, 1996.

Nielsen, L. C. *Frederik V. Hegel: Hans forgængere og hans slægt, et mindeskrift II*. Copenhagen: Fr. Bagges Kgl. Hof-bogtrykkeri, 1909.

Nietzsche, Friedrich. *Basic Writings of Friedrich Nietzsche*. Trans. and ed. Walter Kaufmann. New York: Modern Library, 1992.

———. *The Portable Nietzsche*. Trans. Walter Kaufmann. London: Penguin Books, 1976.

Nolin, Bertil. *Georg Brandes*. Woodbridge, CT: Twayne Publishers, 1976.

Pontoppidan, Henrik. *Lykke-Per*. Copenhagen: Gyldendal, 2006.

Prideaux, Sue. *Strindberg*. New Haven: Yale University Press, 2012.

Pritchett, V. S. *The Gentle Barbarian: The Life and Work of Turgenev*. New York: Random House, 1977.

Reichel, Donald C. "Perfecting Failure: Musil on Hamsun, Jacobsen and D'Annunzio, and the Writing of *Der Mann ohne Eigenschaften*." *Modern Austrian Literature* 32, no. 1 (1999).

Rilke, Rainer Maria. *Letters of Rainer Maria Rilke 1892–1910*. Trans. Jane Bannard Greene and M. D. Herter Norton. New York: W. W. Norton, 1945.

———. *Letters to a Young Poet*. Trans. M. D. Herter Norton. New York: W. W. Norton, 1954.

———. *The Notebooks of Malte Laurids Brigge*. Trans. Michael Hulse. London: Penguin Classics, 2009.

——. *Rilke and Andreas-Salomé: A Love Story in Letters*. Trans. Edward Snow and Michael Winkler. New York: W. W. Norton, 2006.

——. *Rodin*. Trans. Jessie Lemont and Hans Trausil. London: Grey Walls Press, 1948.

Scheffauer, Herman. "A Correspondence between Nietzsche and Strindberg." *North American Review* 198 (1913).

Schweizer, Bernard. *Hating God: The Untold Story of Misotheism*. Oxford: Oxford University Press, 2011.

Skram, Erik. *Hinsides grænsen: Erindringer fra Sønderjylland*. Copenhagen: P. G. Philipsens Forlag, 1888.

——. "Nogle Meddelelser om J. P. Jacobsen." In *Tilskueren Anden Aargang*. Ed. Valdemar Vedel. Copenhagen: P. G. Philipsens Forlag, 1885.

Sontag, Susan. *Illness as Metaphor and AIDS and Its Metaphors*. New York: Anchor Books, 1989.

Spencer, Nick. *Atheists: The Origin of the Species*. London: Bloomsbury, 2014.

Stewart, Jon, ed. *Kierkegaard's Influence on Literature, Criticism and Art*, vol. 2: *Denmark*. London: Ashgate, 2013.

Strindberg, August. *Miss Julie*. Trans. Edwin Björkman. Mineola, NY: Dover Thrift Editions, 1992.

——. *Strindberg's Letters*, vol. 1: *1862–1892*. Selected, edited, and translated by Michael Robinson. Chicago: University of Chicago Press, 1992.

——. *Three Plays*. Trans. Peter Watts. London: Penguin Classics, 1958.

Taylor, Charles. *A Secular Age*. Cambridge, MA: Belknap Press, 2007.

Torgersen, Eric. *Dear Friend: Rainer Maria Rilke and Paula Modersohn-Becker*. Evanston, IL: Northwestern University Press, 1998.

Turgenev, Ivan. *Fathers and Sons*. Trans. Peter Carson. London: Penguin Classics, 2009.

Vodskov, H. S. *Spredte studier*. Copenhagen: Gyldendal, 1884.

Wamberg, Niels Birger. *Digterne og Gyldendal*. Copenhagen: Gyldendal, 1970.

Williams, Roger L. *The Horror of Life*. London: Weidenfeld and Nicholson, 1980.

Wood, James. *The Broken Estate: Essays on Literature and Belief*. New York: Random House, 1999.

———. *The Nearest Thing to Life*. Waltham, MA: Brandeis University Press, 2015.

———. "The Sickness unto Life." *New Republic*, November 8, 1999.

Zweig, Stefan. *The World of Yesterday*. Lincoln: University of Nebraska Press, 1964.

Index

Note: Page numbers in *italic type* indicate illustrations.

INDEX

bad death, 165
Bahr, Hermann, 183; "The
  Overcoming of Naturalism,"
  186–187
Balzac, Honoré de, 107
Bang, Herman, xxviii, xxix, 9, 55,
  106, 128–129; Jacobsen's style and,
  184; on Jacobsen's wasted physical
  condition, 129; on "Mogens," 64,
  67; Møller friendship with, 123;
  morality charges and, 164–165;
  works: Haabløse Slægter (Hopeless
  Generations), 104, 164–165; Realism
  and Realists, 123; "Thoughts
  on Danish Realism," 122–123;
  Tine, 21
Baudelaire, Charles, 68, 176
Becker, Ernest, The Denial of
  Death, 190
Becker, Kurt, 187
Behrens, Peter, 180
Bel Ami (de Maupassant), 122
Benedictsson, Victoria, 163
Benn, Gottfried, xxx, 183
Berlin: anti-Semitism in, 178; G.
  Brandes exile in, 103, 155, 156,
  177–178; literary group, 178
Berliner Tageblatt (publication), 177
Berlingske Tidende (publication), 146
Bertelsen, Johannes, 13, 14
Bethge, Hans, Jens Peter Jacobsen: Ein
  Versuch, 183
Betz, Maurice, 189
Beyle, Marie-Henri. See Stendhal
Beyond Good and Evil (Nietzsche), 178
biblical criticism, xi, 30
bisexuality, 25
Bismarck, Otto von, 20–21, 178
Bjørnson, Bjørnstjerne, 13, 45, 46,
  103, 146; dislike of Jacobsen's prose
  and, 101, 102, 147, 184; En hanske,
  163; Morality Feud inception
  and, 163
Black Piglet, The (Berlin tavern), 178
Blanchot, Maurice, The Space of
  Literature, 165
Blätter für die Kunst (publication), 182
Blicher, Steen Steensen, The Diary of
  a Parish Clerk, 81

Blüher, Hans, 25; "Niels Lyhne von
  J. P. Jacobsen und das Problem
  der Bisexualität," 25
Bogstaveligheden (literary club), 162
Bohème, La (Puccini), 75
Book of Hours, The (Rilke), xxv
"bordello novels," 122
Borgeby-gård (Malmö estate),
  xxvii–xxviii
Bornholm island, 36
botany, 1, 8, 19, 30, 36–40, 72, 79
Bovary, Emma. See Madame Bovary
  (Flaubert)
Brand (Ibsen), 46
Brandes, Edvard, 110, 121, 122, 124,
  163; critical political militancy of,
  34; as freethinking Jew, 51, 156;
  Hamsun's Hunger publication and,
  97; on historical Marie Grubbe,
  82; Jacobsen friendship with, xxxi,
  1, 3, 10, 34, 55, 56, 57, 58–60, 70,
  79, 80, 106, 114, 115, 116, 117, 127,
  145–146, 150, 157, 164; Jacobsen's
  atheism and, 13, 14, 129; Jacobsen's
  death and, 11, 12, 13; on Jacobsen's
  "Dr. Faust" novella fragment,
  167; on Jacobsen's physical
  deterioration, 3, 129, 168;
  Jacobsen's poetry and, 58–59,
  182; Jacobsen's tour of Europe
  with, 70, 71, 72, 73, 116; Kielland
  and, 158, 159; Marie Grubbe
  publication and, 83, 94–95, 98;
  Marie Grubbe review by, 99; Niels
  Lyhne review by, 147, 148, 149;
  Niels Lyhne revised assessment
  by, 175–176; parliamentary seat
  of, 156; personality of, 56; wife's
  suicide and, 120
Brandes, Emilie, 98
Brandes, Georg, 47–54, 71, 81, 106,
  171; anti-establishmentism of, 51,
  155; anti-Semitism and, 178; Berlin
  self-exile of, 103, 155, 156, 162,
  177–178; critical influence of, 34,
  104, 178–179; Freethinkers' Society
  founding by, 53–54; as freethinking
  Jew, 48–49, 51, 52, 178; Hamsun's
  Hunger and, 97; Jacobsen

220

Freie Bühne für modernes Leben (later
    Neue Rundschau), xxix–xxx
French literature. *See* Paris literary
    life; *specific writers*
French Revolution (1789), 50
Freud, Sigmund, xxx; on *Niels Lyhne*,
    26, 146
"Friedrich Nietzsche: An Outline of
    His Thought and Personality"
    (Hansson), 181–182
"From the Unconscious Life of the
    Soul" (Hamsun), 96
"Fru Fønss" (Jacobsen), 10–11
Fullerton, Lady Georgina, 82
fundamentalist religion, xix, 6–7

Gallé, Émile, 186
Garman and Worse (Kielland),
    158–159
Gautier, Théophile, 101, 107
gay men, 25–26, 165
gender roles. *See* women's rights
Genealogy of Morals, The (Nietzsche),
    179
generation of 1848, 130
Genie, Irssin und Ruhm (*The Problem
    of Genius*) (Lange-Eichbaum),
    25–26
Genoa (Italy), 113
George, Stefan, 182
Gérard, François, "Cupid and
    Psyche" (painting), 29
German painters, 185
German philosophy, 50
Germany: G. Brandes's cultural
    influence in, 177–178; Jacobsen's
    literary fame in, xxix–xxx, 174,
    176–177, 181–185; Jacobsen's travels
    in, 49; *Marie Grubbe* translation
    and, 105, 176; unification of, 177.
    See also Berlin; Prussia
Gertrude Colbjørnson (E. Skram),
    121, 124
Getting Married (Strindberg), 122
Gissing, George, xxx, 145
Gjellerup, Karl, 121, 124, 162; *Det
    unge Danmark*, 121
God: atheist reconciliation with, 139;
    creation by humans vs., 187; death

of, 93, 141–142; eternal life and, 93,
    142; as human projection, 33;
    metaphysical rebellion against,
    141–142; misotheists and, 141;
    mythology and, 61; question of
    existence of, 44; silence of,
    134–135, 139, 160–162
God Delusion, The (Dawkins), 135
Goethe, Johann Wolfgang von, 30,
    32; *The Sorrows of Young Werther*,
    xxx, 67
Goncourt brothers, 121
Goodbye to Berlin (Isherwood), 77
Gore, Catherine, 82
Gosse, Edmund, 77–78, 79, 125;
    Father and Son, 135; *Two Visits to
    Denmark*, 47
green algae, 38–40
Greenland, 21
Grubbe, Erik, 80
Grubbe, Marie (1643–1718), 80–82.
    See also *Marie Grubbe: Seventeenth
    Century Interiors*
Grundtvig, N.F.S, 6
"Gud, frels mig dog!" (Jacobsen), 24
Gurre-Lieder (Schoenberg), 71,
    183–184
Gustafson, Alrik, 65
guvernante romaner (governess
    novels), 82
Gyldendal (publisher), 24, 45, 46, 52,
    83, 105, 158, 160
Gyldendalske Boghandel. *See*
    Gyldendal (publisher)

Haabløse Slægter (Bang), 104, 164–165
Hamlet (Shakespeare), 32, 112
Hammershøi, Vilhelm, xxviii
Hamsun, Knut, xxix, xxxi, 94, 96–97,
    106, 132, 146; Jacobsen ranked
    with, 176; literary realism and,
    122–123; works: "From the
    Unconscious Life of the Soul,"
    96; *Hunger*, 54, 97, 104, 145;
    Mysteries, 145
Hansen, H. P., 123
Hansen, Peter Syrak, 115–116
Hansen, Theophilus, 71
Hanske, En (Bjørnson), 163

about sexuality of, 23–26; Turgenev
influence on, 112; turn-of-the-
twentieth century literary fashion
of, 182–183; vicarious lifestyle of,
79–80; visual literary imagery
of, 184–186; Vodskov friendship
and breakup with, 33–35; works:
"Arabesque for a Sketch by
Michelangelo," 182; *Collected
Works*, xxx, 184; "Darwin's
Theory," 42–43, 44, 45, 55;
"Doctor Faust" (novella fragment),
166–167; "Fru Fønss," 10–11; "Gud,
frels mig dog!," 24; *Hervert
Sperring*, 24; "Irmelin Rose," 183;
"Mogens," xxiv–xxv, 58, 59, 61–69,
81, 175, 184; *Mogens and Other
Stories*, 10, 160; "On Evolution in
the World of Plants," 40; "The
Plague in Bergamo," 159–162, 166;
Six Stories of J. P. Jacobsen, xxiv;
"Two Worlds," 118–120, 124,
126–127, 166. See also *Marie
Grubbe: Seventeenth Century
Interiors*; *Niels Lyhne*
Jacobsen, William (brother), 2, 4, 5,
6, 10, 27, 57, 151, 169; devotion to
JPJ of, 171; JPJ's death and, 11, 14,
170, 172–173; JPJ's last months and,
168; letter from Italy to, 117–118;
marriage and wife's death in
childbirth, 154–155
Jacobsen family, 4–6, 4; house and
warehouse of, 2, 5
Jæger, Hans, 122, 163; *Fra Kristiania-
Bohêmen*, 163
James, Henry, 188
Jensen, Henrik Gade, 130
Jensen, Johannes V., 100, 105
Jens Peter Jacobsen: Ein Versuch
(Bethge), 183
Jews, 48, 51, 156; anti-Semitism
and, 178
Josa Gerth (Dauthendey), 183
Josephson, Ernst, xxxi–xxxii, 116
Joyce, James, xxxi, 132, 146
J. P. Jacobsen: Digteren og mennesket
(Nielsen), 24–25
Juleroser (magazine), 167

Julie, ou la nouvelle Héloïse
(Rousseau), 67, 136
Juncker, Axel, xxviii
Jutland, Prussian occupation of, 21

Kafka, Franz, 25, 162
Kapital, Das (Marx), 42
Keats, John, 75, 101
Key, Ellen, xxiv, xxvi; *The Century of
the Child*, 9
Kielland, Alexander, 13, 69, 104, 177;
Jacobsen's close friendship with,
152, 157–159, 170, 171; on Jacobsen's
Niels Lyhne, 149, 158; on Jacobsen's
"Plague in Bergamo," 162; on
Jacobsen's reticence, xxxiii;
mourning for Jacobsen by, 11; visit
with Jacobsen of, 168; works: *Else:
A Christmas Story*, 159; *Garman and
Worse*, 158–159; *Novelletter*, 158
Kielland, Kitty, 159
Kierkegaard, Peter Christian, 31, 32
Kierkegaard, Poul, 31, 32–33, 53–54;
schizophrenia of, 32–33
Kierkegaard, Søren, xxvi, xxvii, xxviii,
29, 30, 31, 60, 124, 162; *The Sickness
unto Death*, 130
Kirk, Hans, *The Fishermen*, 7
Knudsen, Aage, 65, 126–127
Knudsen, Jakob, 143
Knudsen, Jørgen, 148
Koch, Robert, 74
Kollen, Ingar Sletten, 97
Kongens Nytorv (Copenhagen), 152
Krogh, Christian, 54, 105, 178
Krøyer, P. S., 105, 115

Læsø island, 38
Lange-Eichbaum, Wilhelm, *Genie,
Irssin und Ruhm (The Problem of
Genius)*, 25–26
Langeland island, 156
Langen, Albert, xxx
Larsen, Hanna Astrup, translation of
Marie Grubbe, xxxi
Larsen, Karl, 112
Larsen, Nella, xxxi
Larsson, Hanna, xxvii
Lawrence, T. E., xxx